Enemies of the Country

Enemies

Edited by John C. Inscoe
and Robert C. Kenzer

THE UNIVERSITY OF GEORGIA PRESS
Athens & London

of the Country

New Perspectives on Unionists in the Civil War South

© 2001 by the University of Georgia Press
Athens, Georgia 30602
All rights reserved
Designed by Walton Harris
Set in 10/14 New Caledonia
Printed and bound by Thomson-Shore, Inc.

The paper in this book meets the guidelines for
permanence and durability of the Committee on
Production Guidelines for Book Longevity of the
Council on Library Resources.

Printed in the United States of America
05 04 03 02 01   C   5 4 3 2 1

Library of Congress Cataloging-in-Publication Data

Enemies of the country : new perspectives on
Unionists in the Civil War South / edited by
John C. Inscoe and Robert C. Kenzer.
    p.   cm.
Largely papers presented at a conference held at the
University of Richmond in May 1998 on the topic "Families
at war: loyalty and conflict in the Civil War South."
Includes bibliographical references and index.
ISBN 0-8203-2288-1 (alk. paper)
1. Confederate States of America—Politics and government—
Congresses. 2. Confederate States of America—Social
conditions—Congresses. 3. Unionists (United States Civil
War)—Congresses. 4. United States—History—Civil War,
1861–1865—Social aspects—Congresses. 5. United States—
History—Civil War, 1861–1865—Public opinion—Congresses.
6. Public opinion—Confederate States of America—Congresses.
I. Inscoe, John C., 1951–   II. Kenzer, Robert C., 1955–

E487 .E56   2001
973.7'1—dc21   00-053653

British Library Cataloging-in-Publication Data available

Title page illustration: Unionists refugees moving from Georgia
into East Tennessee. *Harper's Weekly,* September 19, 1863.

Contents

Acknowledgments

*T*he editors are very grateful to Catherine Clinton, whose conference "Families at War: Loyalty and Conflict in the Civil War South," held at the University of Richmond in May 1998, served as the basis for this collection. Most of the essays in this collection were first presented as papers there. Catherine's initiative, energy, enthusiasm, and persuasive powers combined to make this an exceptional gathering of nearly forty scholars who presented a rich array of new work on the social impact of the Civil War on Southern home fronts and households. Catherine has compiled and edited her own collection of essays from the conference, and we much appreciate her gracious offer to let us compile ours as well, using the papers focusing on Southern Unionism as the basis for this volume. Her input and support since have much improved our efforts and made this a most pleasurable experience for us both, as has working with each of the authors whose work is included here.

We thank the history departments of the University of Richmond and the University of Georgia for the support and resources they have provided us during the editing and production of this volume. We, editors and authors, appreciate the insightful readers of the manuscript for the questions they raised and the suggestions they provided, which have strengthened both the whole and its individual pieces.

Finally, we are very grateful to Malcolm Call at the University of Georgia Press for his initial and sustained enthusiasm for this project and for his expeditious handling of the manuscript from the moment it landed on his doorstep. As always, it is a pleasure to be in the capable and caring hands of the press's editorial and production staff.

Enemies of the Country

Introduction

JOHN C. INSCOE

*T*oward the end of the much longer and far less remembered
address delivered at Gettysburg on November 19, 1863, Edward Everett
reminded his vast audience of just how vital the Unionist presence in the
South was. "The South is full of such men," Everett insisted. "I do not believe
there has been a day since the election of President Lincoln, when, if an ordinance of secession could have been fairly submitted . . . to the mass of the
people in any single Southern State, a majority of ballots would have been
given in its favor." He continued, "The heart of the people, North and South,
is for the Union. . . . The weary masses of the [Southern] people are yearning
to see the old flag again floating upon their capitols."[1]

Everett was not alone among Northerners in firmly believing that the
majority of Southerners did not at heart fully support secession and the
Confederacy. President Lincoln was among those who consistently overesti-
mated the strength of Unionist sentiment in the South and shaped much of
his policy regarding Southern civilians and their place in wartime occupation and postwar reconstruction around that assumption.[2] Yet, until quite

recently, the vast historiography of the Civil War has not given much attention to what Everett, Lincoln, and so many of their contemporaries saw as this key element in the struggle for the restoration of the Union. Given the variety of ways in which the social, economic, and political dimensions of the war have been and continue to be analyzed, the experiences of those Southerners who found themselves living in a new nation to which they chose not to give their allegiance remains relatively unexplored.

The topic is central to studies of the secession crisis, during which Unionist forces in most Southern states mounted significant resistance to leaving the Union. That resistance thus demands a central place in our historical analysis of the political events leading up to the war.[3] But with very few exceptions, historians have lost sight of those Unionists once the decision to secede was made and the war was under way. Most likely this is because the vast majority of those prewar dissenters whose states did secede from the Union were "conditional" rather than "unconditional" in their loyalty to the United States and thus capitulated to the Confederate cause and the war effort, at least temporarily and on the surface. A North Carolina Unionist who witnessed that capitulation bitterly denounced his erstwhile compatriots as those "who had not moral courage enough to *stick* to the Union."[4]

By no means were all Southerners swept up in that surge of Southern patriotism that so fueled the Confederacy's early war effort. Many of those who had opposed secession and the fight to defend it continued to do so. Yet, as Daniel Crofts demonstrates in his study of the sectional crisis in the upper South, once the secession process was completed and the war under way, the meaning of Unionism in the South changed as well.[5] The fluidity of the political debate as it had evolved in different ways in different states over the winter and spring of 1860–61 quickly gave way to the hard-and-fast allegiances demanded by two nations at war. Suddenly to be a Unionist made one part of a self-conscious minority viewed with suspicion and hostility, a minority whose very presence threatened the new regime and its cause. Once the die had been cast in the eleven states that seceded, those who clung to what had been merely one side of a vigorous political debate were suddenly perceived as subversive and even traitorous, as "enemies of the country."[6]

Although Unionists were scattered throughout the Confederacy, there were certain areas where their numbers were significant and their presence conspicuous. This was particularly true of highland areas, the Appalachians and the Ozarks; in frontier areas on the South's northern and western peripheries; and in Southern cities. Yet beyond locating those areas as points

JOHN C. INSCOE

of internal division and home-front tensions, we still have little sense of who remained loyal to the Union during the war, much less why and how they managed to do so and to survive in the hostile and often dangerous environment in which most suddenly found themselves.

We have yet to even firmly define what made one a Unionist. In his *One Nation Indivisible*, Paul Nagel has given us a remarkably full analysis of the complex factors that made allegiance to the Union so central to antebellum Americans' sense of patriotism and country.[7] Although he provided us with a firm foundation concerning the conceptual bases and ideological underpinnings that motivated Southern Unionists perhaps far more than we have thus far acknowledged, Nagel ended his study with the secession crisis, just before Southerners found themselves forced to think of those terms—patriotism and country—in new and often uncomfortable ways.

Given the various degrees of loyalty, of opportunism, of deception and role-playing, and of ever-changing circumstances over the course of four years of conflict, any concise portrait of a typical Unionist or Unionist experience remains beyond our grasp. Yet some observers at the time had no problem defining a wartime Unionist. For the Knoxville editor William G. "Parson" Brownlow, perhaps the most visible and vocal of all Southern Unionists, the litmus test he applied to his fellow loyalists was straightforward. Three features were essential for Brownlow: "uncompromising devotion" to the Union, "unmitigated hostility" to Confederates, and a willingness to risk life and property "in defense of the glorious Stars and Stripes."[8] Such absolutism in defining allegiance to the Union was by no means new in 1861. A decade earlier, William H. Seward provided an equally firm definition of a Unionist, although as a New Yorker he was never in a position to have his convictions put to the test. As if anticipating the strains and challenges Southern Unionists would later face, Seward stated in 1851: "We are in the Union for richer or poorer, for better or worse, whether in a majority or a minority, whether in power or powerless, without condition, reservation, qualification, or limitation, for ever and aye."[9]

If all Southern Unionists had demonstrated so unequivocal a stance throughout the course of the war, our efforts as historians to understand them would be somewhat simpler. But early on, scholars recognized a basic aspect of disloyalty to the Confederacy: that, as one historian has so succinctly put it, "as with all internecine conflicts, loyalties could be slippery as well as steadfast, a matter of expediency and circumstance even more than conviction."[10] For this reason historians have sought to draw distinctions among levels of commitment to the Union and to label them accordingly. Georgia Lee Tatum, in her landmark 1934 book, *Disloyalty in the Confederacy*, was the first to grapple seriously with such categorization and labeling. Acknowledging that the word *disloyal* can hardly be neutral, she used it as most wartime Southerners would have used it: to describe those within Confederate boundaries who refused to support the Confederate government and worked actively to undermine it. *Disaffection*, on the other hand, described those who resisted, in far more passive ways, efforts to draw them into wartime service or support. The term *Unionist* she reserved for those who "were from the first strong advocates of the Union." Because that implied a more active stance than was true of those who were merely disaffected, Tatum conceded that most Unionists would also fit her definition of *disloyal*.[11]

Nearly thirty years later, Carl Degler made a much more nuanced and rigorous attempt to characterize the various ways in which Southern Unionism manifested itself. Using prominent political figures as models, Degler demonstrated in *The Other South* just how vast and how complex the continuum of loyalties to the Union was. They ranged from the "conditional Unionists," like Georgians Howell Cobb and Alexander Stephens, who switched allegiances fairly early in the crisis and had few qualms about doing so, to the more persistent Unionism of North Carolina's Zebulon Vance and Tennessee's John Bell, who gave up their loyalist stance somewhat later (after mid-April 1861) and more reluctantly. Then there were those who remained committed to the United States throughout the war, though for different reasons and in various guises: the "Unionists for peace," such as Jonathan Worth of North Carolina, the "enduring Democratic Unionism" of Andrew Johnson, and the "enduring Whig Unionism" of Parson Brownlow.[12]

If Degler's focus was limited to the political dimensions of Southern Unionism and to the stances of prominent public figures whose opinions can be easily traced over the course of the war, Richard Current took a very different tack, examining closer to the grassroots level the contribution its proponents made militarily. In *Lincoln's Loyalists*, Current provided state-by-state analyses of white Southerners who enlisted in the Union army at some point during the war. Although such actions were certainly the surest indication of commitment to the Union cause, Current reminded us that other conditions were necessary for such enlistments: first, the courage and independence of those willing to make this ultimate demonstration of patriotism; and second, the opportunity to do so (meaning ready access to a standing Federal force).[13]

Current was also interested in the sheer numbers of Southern white men who served the Union cause militarily. He estimated that they, combined with those who served from border states and with black troops, amounted to over 200,000 men. Only if that figure is counted twice—as both deprivation for the South and gain for the North—can one appreciate the staggering losses of manpower the Confederacy suffered and understand why Abraham Lincoln referred to them as "the most valuable stake we have in the South."[14] Carl Degler too had considered the quantitative impact of Southern Unionists in Federal military service. Using more conservative bases (eight of the eleven Confederate states), he estimated that 54,000 white Southerners fought with Union armies. The vast majority of these men came from Tennessee, with Arkansas and Louisiana contributing the next largest numbers.[15]

If, as Degler has demonstrated, it is possible to categorize the political bases of certain Southern Unionists and, as both Degler and Current have done, to quantify, at least in general terms, Southern enlistments in the Union army, neither was able to answer that more elusive question of motive—why certain Southerners refused to shift their loyalties or sense of patriotic duty from the United States to the Confederacy. Current pinpoints only one common denominator, and that tentatively: "Whatever the feelings that impelled a white Southerner to enlist in the U.S. army, a strong sense of old-fashioned patriotism must have been one of them."[16]

A more promising approach to these questions, and thus more revealing treatments of Southern Unionism, have come through localized studies in which a finite group of Unionists found themselves oppressed, often in horrific ways, by the majority of Confederates in whose midst they lived. A growing number of Southern community studies set during the war years have moved beyond political and military contexts to explore the tensions wartime Unionism generated at the local level. Often such divisions are only minor parts of these multifaceted approaches to communities at war.[17] But in at least three such works, Unionists have been the central players—if only as minority victims of majority harassment, even mass execution.

In *Victims*, Philip S. Paludan provided an insightful analysis of a remote mountain community in North Carolina, where in January 1863 thirteen Unionist men and boys suspected of guerrilla activity were captured and summarily executed by Confederate troops, many of whom, including their commanders, were from elsewhere in the same county. Paludan used both the underlying causes and the controversial repercussions of the Shelton Laurel massacre, as this incident came to be known, to explore the tensions that split this and other Appalachian communities and the circumstances of both guerrilla warfare and more conventional commands that led to such atrocities.[18]

Richard McCaslin documented an equally infamous incident, the "great hanging" in Cooke County, Texas, in his book *Tainted Breeze*. Residents of a five-county frontier area fraught with instability and insecurities, the victims in that case were suspected Unionists. In October 1862 Confederate militia-men rounded up over two hundred such subversives and turned them over to local authorities in Gainesville, where they were tried by a "citizens' court" for treason and fomenting insurrection. At least forty-four of them were sen-tenced to death and hanged, all from the same tree, and others were lynched in surrounding counties over the same period of weeks.[19]

The third such local study, Thomas G. Dyer's *Secret Yankees*, is repre-sented in this collection. In his book-length examination of Atlanta's Unionist community, Dyer uses the experiences of a Vermont couple who had moved to Georgia's fastest growing city in the mid-1850s as the focal point from which he has meticulously reconstructed a vibrant and varied set of Union sympathizers—men and women, white and black, Northern- and Southern-born. He traces the dramatic shifts in the fortunes of and attitudes toward these subversive and beleaguered Atlantans from the secession crisis through Sherman's 1864 campaign and occupation of the city and on through the war's end and Reconstruction.[20]

What makes these three books such absorbing portraits of Southern Unionism is that each deals with Unionists and those who opposed them both as individuals and as groups; their authors portray the tensions gener-ated within very specific contexts of place and personality, as well as local politics and power struggles. The essays that make up this volume do like-wise. Here too are portraits of individuals and groups who chose not to support either the new government under which they suddenly found them-selves living or the military effort defending its existence. These men and women are portrayed in localized and personalized terms—as families, as neighborhoods and as communities, in households, in cities, and in counties.

The majority of those portrayed in these essays would have fit Parson Brownlow's litmus test of true Unionists. Most were uncompromising in their devotion to the Union, viewed the Confederacy and Confederates as enemies, and played active roles in thwarting the Southern nation and its war effort, often at great personal risk. These are the stories of men and women who not only endured as detested and feared minorities within Confederate communities, but also defied the oppression and harassment they faced in both covert and not so covert ways. Yet the circumstances in which they acted and the reasons they did so varied considerably. The very fact that they defy generalization in terms of their identities, their motives, and their experiences speaks to a central theme of this volume—the sheer diversity of the Unionist experience over the course of the war, and the importance of personal and local variables in providing a far more complex and colorful sense of who Southern Unionists were, what they did, and what was done to them.

With one exception, these men and women were all white, but otherwise they represent a wide spectrum of Southern citizenry.[21] They include natives to the region, foreign immigrants and northern transplants, affluent and poor, farmers and merchants, politicians and journalists, slaveholders and nonslaveholders. As residents of seven of the eleven Confederate states, some lived in cities, some in small towns, and some in rural settings ranging from the southern Appalachians to the Ozark foothills to the central Texas frontier. More often than not, they had been Whigs rather than Democrats if they were politically inclined during the antebellum period.[22] Most of the subjects treated here were very much minorities within pro-Confederate communities and regions, but few were so isolated in their loyalties toward the Union that they could not find support and group identity from others in their area. While their native origins or regional placement within the South provides part of the explanation for their allegiance to the Union, other determinants often remain elusive.

Carl Degler, Richard Current, and other scholars of Southern Unionists agree that opposition to slavery was not such a determinant in most cases. Abolitionist sentiments certainly played little part in shaping the allegiances of the Unionists portrayed here. One is struck by how many of these subjects were slaveholders themselves. Nearly all of the urban merchants and professionals who made up the Unionist circles in Atlanta, Montgomery, and Knoxville owned black property. This included many of those who had moved from the North, and even some who had opposed slavery when they moved South but found rationales for themselves and their families back home in making the transition.[23] The Faucettes of North Carolina and the Williamses in Arkansas, each the subject of an essay here, enjoyed slaveholding status as well.

Most of those who did not own slaves themselves were from highland or frontier regions in which slavery's presence was minimal. But even they recognized the legitimacy of the institution and resented any outside interference with it.[24] David Hunter Strother, for example, owned no slaves but was much offended by John Brown's raid on Harpers Ferry, not far from his home, and took great satisfaction in witnessing Brown's hanging. East Tennesseans, in particular, felt compelled to distinguish between their politics and their racial views. Parson Brownlow declared that "the Union men of the border states are loyal to their Government," but if they ever felt that the Lincoln administration "contemplated the subjugation of the South or the abolishing of slavery, there would not be a Union man among us in twenty-four hours." Once Lincoln did issue his Emancipation Proclamation, Thomas A. R. Nelson, a former congressman, expressed a strong sense of betrayal. He would have advocated secession, Nelson insisted in 1863, if he "had believed it was the object of the North to subjugate the South and emancipate our slaves. . . . The Union men of East Tennessee are not now and never were Abolitionists."[25]

Only the German community in Texas had long been opponents of slavery, and even they were not united in their abolitionist sentiments. As Anne Bailey points out in her essay, the greatest opposition came from a later, post-1848 wave of immigrants forced out of Europe by political oppression. Their antislavery stances were often linked to strong nationalistic feelings as well, which may have been an even more vital factor in their Unionism when the war broke out. Ironically, the most outspoken opposition to slavery voiced by a Unionist here was that of Nelly Kinzie Gordon, who had married into the family that owned more slaves, and thus had more at stake in the war, than any other represented in this volume.

Thus the sources of Unionism remain unclear in some of these cases, while fairly clear in others. Another factor that emerges as central in the cases of divided loyalties presented here is the dynamics of family. One is struck by the extent to which men often acted in concert with other family members in expressing their opposition to the Confederacy and to the war. The Williams clan of Arkansas enjoyed a particularly solid sense of loyalty not only to the United States but to one another as well, as Kenneth Barnes demonstrates. Scott Nelson documents the activities of the Faucettes of Alamance County, North Carolina, who also seem to have harbored no dissenters in their anti-Confederate sentiments during and after the war, an unusual case in that their kinship network included black members as fully in the forefront of that opposition as their white relatives. The Hennions, a couple in the mountains of north Georgia, represent family and marital loyalties that overrode different sectional backgrounds. In Keith Bohannon's portrayal of their wartime partnership, Margaret Hennion, a South Carolina native, never swayed in the loyalty to the Union she shared with her New

Jersey–born husband, despite the considerable risks and hardships that stance imposed on them both.

Although many families stood together in their loyalties, there are far more examples here of individuals who broke with other family members when forced to choose sides. David Hunter Strother's father was an important factor in his ultimate commitment to the Union, but, as Jonathan Berkey notes, other relatives and most neighbors in the lower Shenandoah Valley were Confederates. What makes Strother's story particularly interesting is the extent of his continued sympathies toward them; he even sought to use his position as a Union soldier in that very area to alleviate the hardships his fellow troops inflicted upon them as civilians in that war-torn region. Except for the Knoxville elite that so dominated East Tennessee's political and social leadership, few if any other Unionists portrayed here enjoyed the degree of influence and authority within their home region that Strother did.

As Gordon McKinney and I discovered for Southern highland households, husbands and wives, often separated by the war, made different choices as to which side they would support, with one spouse or the other resorting to deception in the subversive efforts he or she made to the cause they could only secretly embrace. In many cases it was blood kinship, rather than marital union, that dictated the allegiances spouses demonstrated once the war was under way. Many of the mountain women who aided escaped Union soldiers or subverted Confederate efforts in other ways while their husbands were away in Confederate service did so because of loyalties shared with their parents or other members of their own families.

Carolyn Stefanco describes a somewhat different sort of household division that the war imposed on spouses and provides a portrait of perhaps the most ambivalent and complex Unionist found in these pages. In Savannah a Chicago bride found herself the wife and daughter-in-law of staunch Confederates once the war broke out. Despite early attempts to maintain at least a surface loyalty to their cause, Nelly Gordon endured hostility and suspicion from those in the city and undue pressures from her husband and in-laws. She ultimately renounced any sympathy for the South, which only increased her problems at home and in the community.

Even in marriages in which both spouses declared their loyalties to the Union, there were often strains, as Tom Dyer and Keith Bohannon demonstrate in their portraits of two other Georgia couples. Amherst and Cyrena Stone remained staunch Unionists in Atlanta, although his opportunism and ambition involved him in schemes in which he played differing roles, particularly when he traveled north, where he spent much of the war separated from Cyrena. Particularly painful to her was the decision made by her younger brother, who had followed the Stones to Atlanta, to enlist in Southern service before 1861 was out.

Horatio and Margaret Hennion served as partners in a localized guerrilla warfare—she more inadvertently than he—to defend their home and family against the increasingly aggressive Confederate majority among whom they lived in the foothills of northeast Georgia. Her willingness to support her Northern-born husband's Unionism may not have demonstrated any independent spirit on her part, and yet she, like many women who found themselves caught up in areas wracked by guerrilla warfare, was forced to new levels of self-reliance in the waging of that war, and in her husband's frequent absences. "Disintegration, demoralization, and perverse adaptation engulfed women's behavior and self-conceptions as it assaulted the family and undermined male-female and female-female . . . relationships," Michael Fellman observed in his study of the war in Missouri. Women "were compelled to participate, which they did with varying degrees of enthusiasm, fear, and rage."[26] Margaret often took on the role of Horatio's protector and provider, as well as that of her children, as did many of the Unionist women in western North Carolina and East Tennessee. Civil War scholarship has now fully embraced the hardships that all Southern women endured during the war, but these essays document the added burdens and dangers that Unionist women's minority status as "enemies of the country" imposed on them.

One means by which Unionists, men and women, coped with their precarious state was by bonding with other Unionists. A few loyalists, both urban and rural, found themselves in communities where they were the beneficiaries of mutual support from like-minded residents; and it was often in communal ways that they responded, either defensively or offensively, to the precarious circumstances in which they found themselves. Although Texas Germans split in their allegiances, enough of them remained Unionists to allow them to organize to defend their interests and their homes. Yet, as Anne Bailey demonstrates, their very effectiveness in so doing made them more of a threat to Confederate Texans, who mobilized crushing offenses against them.

Warren Rogers provides a vivid group portrait of Unionists in Montgomery, Alabama, who, huddled in back rooms of stores to share war news and read Northern newspapers, drew considerable strength from these secret meetings. Cyrena Stone enjoyed a substantial network of support among like-minded men and women in Atlanta and found her morale bolstered by those with whom she interacted. Both groups, in Atlanta and Montgomery, used their connections to subvert Confederate war efforts however possible and to aid fellow Union sympathizers or wounded troops who found their way into their cities. One Montgomery Unionist even went so far as to provide military intelligence to nearby Federal forces, with indications of how they might attack and occupy Alabama's capital city.

Other networks of support were small, sometimes limited to family members or neighbors. Of all of the Unionists portrayed here, Nelly Gordon stands out as the most isolated, virtually devoid of any local kinship or neighborhood support in Savannah in her allegiance to the Union. Only a Northern cousin, with whom she spent a few months during the course of the war, provided any face-to-face contact with another Unionist, which is perhaps why that brief companionship proved so critical in Nellie's coming to terms with her own sense of loyalty.

Just as Unionists faced varying types and degrees of harassment and intimidation by the Confederate majorities in whose midst they lived, their responses to such persecution differed considerably. Many of the stories below are driven by the choices these Unionists made and the opportunities they took to defend themselves and their families and to combat the Confederacy. Some, such as those in Knoxville during the first half of the war, took a relatively passive approach. As an educated and more politically sophisticated elite, the Tennessee Unionists upon whom Tracy McKenzie focuses had more to lose than to gain by aggressive resistance to Confederate occupation. Because they saw it as temporary, they were willing to maintain "prudent silence" and "strict neutrality of conduct." So too did Montgomery's loyalists, without any such reason to feel that their minority status in that city would be short-lived.

But many of the Unionists portrayed here opted for a much more proactive role, often in the form of military or paramilitary activity. As Richard Current pointed out in his study of Southern Union enlistments, opportunity and access were necessary components for such service in regular Federal army units, and that was available to only a few of the subjects here. David Strother in the northern Shenandoah Valley had easy access to Northern troops and was among the earliest to cast his lot with them. In Arkansas, Jeff Williams and his brothers organized themselves into a company and marched off to join Union army forces stationed several counties away in the Ozark foothills. North Carolinian Wyatt Outlaw, the only nonwhite

Unionist portrayed here, probably joined the cavalry of the United States Colored Troops in Virginia when given the opportunity to do so in 1863. Buck Younce, a young Carolina highlander, was caught attempting to cross into East Tennessee to join the Union army there and was forced into a conscripted Confederate company instead. He soon deserted it and made good on his goal of serving militarily "under the flag of my country someday."[27] In Texas, German Unionists had served only as frontier patrols until the pressures of conscription forced them to take a more aggressive anti-Confederate defense of their families and communities.

The Confederate Conscription Act, passed in April 1862, proved particularly traumatic for Southern Unionists, and attempts to enforce it served as the catalyst for spurring Unionist communities and individuals into action. Not only did this new policy of enforced enlistments draw government attention to Unionists and intensify its harassment of them; it also, as Scott Nelson argues, violated more directly than any other aspect of wartime policy the traditional and highly valued boundaries between public and private. In piedmont North Carolina, resistance to the new act led to the formation of secret societies that became more and more subversive to the Confederacy, both politically and militarily, as the war dragged on. By often remaining part of Confederate companies or joining local home guard units, they undermined the Southern military effort from within.

The fact that so much Unionism was based in remote or frontier areas of the South had much to do with its linkage to guerrilla warfare.[28] Horatio Hennion in north Georgia, the Williams family in Arkansas, and many of the Southern highlanders of North Carolina and Tennessee formed small independent and informal bands of men who waged localized campaigns to defend their families and property from Confederate forces, often guerrilla bands themselves. As tensions escalated in the war's latter half, many of these same "Tory" bands resorted to more aggressive actions, often mounting brutal vendettas against Rebel neighbors, home guard units, or conscription officials.

For many of those for whom military engagement was not an option for resistance, survival depended on deception and role-playing. Those who failed to do so, in fact, often put themselves and their families in very real jeopardy. Montgomery's Unionist community came to acknowledge early on that their "safety lay in their silence"—a lesson driven home by the lynching of one of their number as a result of his carelessness in divulging his anti-Confederate opinions and activities too publicly. Horatio Hennion invited much of the hostility focused on him and his family in his north Georgia

JOHN C. INSCOE

community because he continued to make reckless public pronouncements in support of the Union well after the war was under way.

Others recognized much more quickly the necessity of concealing their sentiments, as the paranoia over "enemies in the country" grew in intensity. As escaped prisoners of war moved through the southern Appalachians, they were struck by how many highland Unionists, men and women, covertly aided their efforts, but without the knowledge of others in their household. Financial ambitions led Amherst Stone to play ambivalent roles in Atlanta and elsewhere; his wife was aware enough of the potential danger her diary posed that she changed all names, including her own and her husband's. Nelly Gordon certainly sent enough mixed signals about her commitment to the South or North—commitments confused by conflicting personal loyalties to her own Chicago-based family and her Savannah-based in-laws—that postwar accounts of her activity have often assumed that she capitulated fully to the side of the latter in her sentiments.

Finally, although many, if not most, of the people portrayed here remained staunch, even passionate, in their commitment to the United States throughout the war, one also comes to appreciate what Tracy McKenzie calls the "parameters of Unionism"—not only the varying degrees of that commitment, but the fluidity of feeling and action as well. The fact that deception and role-playing were so often a vital survival tactic for Southern Unionists can obscure our perceptions, in those cases just mentioned and others, of the genuineness and the intensity of their commitment to the Union throughout the war. Some of the subjects portrayed here wavered in their loyalties, either privately or publicly, in response to changes in their own fortunes and those of their communities and regions over the course of the conflict, as the dangers and pressures they faced intensified or subsided accordingly. But such fluctuations, confusions, and ambivalencies are what drive many of these stories, and what make the plights of those involved so compelling.

In introducing her study of divided loyalties in Charles County, Maryland, during the Revolutionary War, Jean B. Lee noted that "wars are flash points that provide unusual access to past communities. They throw into graphic relief the contours of the societies involved: their resilience and fragility, their capacity both to endure and to change."[29] So it was with the Civil War as well. These essays provide rich and varied examples of the Civil War as a flashpoint that ignited not only communities, but individuals and households within those communities. They remind us of just how differently Southerners of whatever loyalty or ideology experienced the war, and the range of ways in which, individually and in groups, Unionists saw their fragilities exposed and their resiliency tested. By juxtaposing these wartime stories of communities and families in terms of how they opposed the new Southern nation and its struggle to survive, we can come to appreciate again just what localized and personalized dynamics defined the war experience of Southerners, Unionist and Confederate alike.

NOTES

1. Edward Everett's speech at Gettysburg, November 19, 1863, is reproduced in full as Appendix III-A in Garry Wills, *Lincoln at Gettysburg: The Words That Remade America* (New York: Simon and Schuster, 1992), 213–47, passages quoted here, 240, 246.

2. William C. Harris, *With Charity for All: Lincoln and the Restoration of the Union* (Lexington: University Press of Kentucky, 1997), 7–9; Nina Silber, *The Romance of Reunion: Northerners and the South, 1865–1900* (Chapel Hill: University of North Carolina Press, 1993), 17, 26.

3. The broadest in scope and most comprehensive of these is Daniel W. Crofts, *Reluctant Confederates: Upper South Unionists in the Secession Crisis* (Chapel Hill: University of North Carolina Press, 1989). Other multistate studies of secession include William L. Barney, *The Road to Secession: A New Perspective on the Old South* (New York: Praeger, 1972), and *The Secessionist Impulse: Alabama and Mississippi in 1860* (Princeton, N.J.: Princeton University Press, 1974). State and regional studies include Michael P. Johnson, *Toward a Patriarchal Republic: The Secession of Georgia* (Baton Rouge: Louisiana State University Press, 1977); J. Mills Thornton III, *Power and Politics in a Slave Society: Alabama, 1800–1860* (Baton Rouge: Louisiana State University Press, 1978); James Woods, *Rebellion and Realignment: Arkansas's Road to Secession* (Fayetteville: University of Arkansas Press, 1987); Walter L. Buenger, *Secession and the Union in Texas* (Austin: University of Texas Press, 1984); James Marten, *Texas Divided: Loyalty and Dissent in the Lone Star State, 1856–1874* (Lexington: University Press of Kentucky, 1990); Richard O. Curry, *A House Divided: A Study in Statehood Politics and the Copperhead Movement in West Virginia* (Pittsburgh: University of Pittsburgh Press, 1964); John C. Inscoe, *Mountain Masters: Slavery and the Sectional Crisis in Western North Carolina* (Knoxville: University of Tennessee Press, 1989), chaps. 9 and 10; Kenneth W. Noe, *Southwest Virginia's Railroad: Modernization and the Sectional Crisis* (Urbana: University of Illinois Press, 1994); Robert Tracy McKenzie, *One South or Many? Plantation Belt and Upcountry in Civil War–Era Tennessee* (New York: Cambridge University Press, 1994); Jonathan

M. Atkins, *Parties, Politics, and the Sectional Crisis in Tennessee, 1832–1861* (Knoxville: University of Tennessee Press, 1997).

4. Alexander H. Jones, "Knocking at the Door: His Adventures and Escapes before the War, during the War, and after the War" (Washington, D.C.: McGill and Witherow, 1866), 4.

5. Crofts, *Reluctant Confederates*, chap. 13.

6. This term was used by William W. Gordon in a letter to his wife, Nelly Kinzie Gordon, July 29, 1862. The editors are grateful to Carolyn Stefanco for allowing them to appropriate this quote, the original title of her essay, as the title of this volume. See note 37 in her essay.

7. Paul C. Nagel, *One Nation Indivisible: The Union in American Thought, 1776–1861* (New York: Oxford University Press, 1964).

8. See first page of Robert Tracy McKenzie's essay in this volume.

9. Quoted in Nagel, *One Nation Indivisible*, 107.

10. William R. Trotter, *Bushwhackers! The Civil War in North Carolina*, vol. 2, *The Mountains* (Greensboro, N.C: Signal Research, 1988), 215.

11. Georgia Lee Tatum, *Disloyalty in the Confederacy* (Chapel Hill: University of North Carolina Press, 1934), viii. David Williams provides an insightful introduction to a new edition of Tatum's book, just published (1999) by the University of Nebraska Press.

12. Carl N. Degler, *The Other South: Southern Dissenters in the Nineteenth Century* (Boston: Northeastern University Press, 1982), chap. 4. A more recent contribution to the public face of political Unionism in the wartime South is Jon L. Wakelyn, ed., *Southern Unionist Pamphlets and the Civil War* (Columbia: University of Missouri Press, 1999), a collection of eighteen documents written by prominent state and local Unionists and circulated in the North and the border states, and smuggled behind Confederate lines. That book, and William C. Harris's *With Charity for All*, also delineate a range of variables—some subtle, some not so subtle—in the political views of Southern Unionists.

13. Richard N. Current, *Lincoln's Loyalists: Union Soldiers from the Confederacy* (Boston: Northeastern University Press, 1992), 146–47.

14. Ibid., 198, 3–5. See also Appendix, "The Question of Numbers," pp. 213–18.

15. Degler, *The Other South*, 174–75. According to Degler's figures, 31,092 Tennesseans served in Union armies, as did 8,289 Arkansans and 5,224 Louisianians. He doesn't include Virginians, Georgians, or South Carolinians, whose contributions were minimal or, in South Carolina's case, nonexistent.

16. Current, *Lincoln's Loyalists*, 146.

17. Besides the three discussed here, there are other Civil War community studies in which a Unionist presence is one of several issues explored, if not the central focus. These include Durwood Dunn, *Cades Cove: The Life and Death of a Southern Mountain Community, 1818–1937* (Knoxville: University of Tennessee

Press, 1988); Wayne K. Durrill, *War of Another Kind: A Southern Community in the Great Rebellion* [Washington County, N.C.] (New York: Oxford University Press, 1990); Daniel E. Sutherland, *Seasons of War: The Ordeal of a Confederate Community, 1861–1865* [Culpepper County, Va.] (New York: Simon and Schuster, 1995); Steven Tripp, *Yankee City, Southern Town: Race and Class Relations in Civil War Lynchburg* [Lynchburg, Va.] (New York: New York University Press, 1997); William Warren Rogers Jr., *Confederate Homefront: Montgomery during the Civil War* [Montgomery, Ala.](Tuscaloosa: University of Alabama Press, 1999); and at least three forthcoming books—Martin Crawford on Ashe County, N.C., Victoria Bynum on the "Free State of Jones" in Mississippi, and Ralph Mann on Burkes Garden, Virginia. Two unpublished dissertations in which Unionism is central to the multicounty areas under study are William T. Auman, "Neighbor against Neighbor: The Inner Civil War in the Central Counties of North Carolina" (Ph.D. dissertation, University of North Carolina, 1988); and Jonathan D. Sarris, "'Hellish Deeds in a Christian Land': Southern Mountain Communities at War, 1861–1865" (Ph.D. dissertation, University of Georgia, 1998), a study of Fannin and Lumpkin Counties in Georgia.

18. Phillip S. Paludan, *Victims: A True Story of the Civil War* (Knoxville: University of Tennessee Press, 1981). For another perspective of the Shelton Laurel massacre, see John C. Inscoe and Gordon B. McKinney, *The Heart of Confederate Appalachia: Western North Carolina in the Civil War* (Chapel Hill: University of North Carolina Press, 2000), 117–20.

19. Richard B. McCaslin, *Tainted Breeze: The Great Hanging at Gainesville, Texas, 1862* (Baton Rouge: Louisiana State University Press, 1994).

20. Thomas G. Dyer, *Secret Yankees: The Unionist Circle in Confederate Atlanta* (Baltimore: Johns Hopkins University Press, 1999).

21. One of the central figures in Scott Nelson's essay is Wyatt Outlaw, the illegitimate but openly acknowledged mulatto son of the white Unionist Chesley Faucette.

22. See Crofts, *Reluctant Confederates*, 130–34, on the strong links between Whigs and Unionists during the secession crisis.

23. See, for example, the rationales of Cyrena Stone in Thomas Dyer's essay and Horace Maynard in Robert Tracy McKenzie's essay.

24. Both Harris, *With Charity for All*, 54–57, 97–100, and several documents in Wakelyn, *Southern Unionist Pamphlets*, deal with the split among political Unionists over Lincoln's policies regarding slavery.

25. William G. Brownlow, *Sketches of the Rise, Progress, and Decline of Secession* (Philadelphia: George W. Childs, 1862), 109. For other proslavery pronouncements by Brownlow, see Robert Tracy McKenzie's essay in this volume. Nelson's quote from Current, *Lincoln's Loyalists*, 38. East Tennessee has long attracted, and continues to attract, more scholarly attention than any other part of the disaffected South during the war. Recent work includes Dunn, *Cades Cove*,

chap. 4; Noel C. Fisher, *War at Every Door: Partisan Politics and Guerrilla Violence in East Tennessee, 1860–1869* (Chapel Hill: University of North Carolina Press, 1997); W. Todd Groce, *Mountain Rebels: East Tennessee Confederates and the Civil War, 1860–1870* (Knoxville: University of Tennessee Press, 1999); and essays by Groce and Peter Wallenstein in *The Civil War in Appalachia: Collected Essays*, ed. Kenneth W. Noe and Shannon Wilson (Knoxville: University of Tennessee Press, 1997). For a broader sense of the relationship between Unionism and abolitionism in the Southern highlands, see John C. Inscoe, "Race and Racism in Nineteenth-Century Southern Appalachia: Myths, Realities, and Ambiguities," in *Appalachia in the Making: The Mountain South in the Nineteenth Century*, ed. Mary Beth Pudup, Dwight B. Billings, and Altina Waller (Chapel Hill: University of North Carolina Press, 1996), 103–31.

26. Michael Fellman, *Inside War: The Guerrilla Conflict in Missouri during the American Civil War* (New York: Oxford University Press, 1989), 193.

27. W. H. Younce, *The Adventures of a Conscript* (Cincinnati: Editor Publishing Co., 1901). Younce's story is told in Inscoe and McKinney's essay in this volume. See also Martin Crawford's study of the county in which Younce lived, *Ashe County's Civil War: Community and Society in the Mountain South* (Charlottesville: University Press of Virginia, 2001), and his essay on Unionism in that county, "The Dynamics of Mountain Unionism: Federal Volunteers of Ashe County, North Carolina," in *The Civil War in Appalachia*, ed. Noe and Wilson, 55–78.

28. For a multifaceted study of the relationship between Unionism and guerrilla warfare, see Daniel E. Sutherland, ed., *Guerrillas, Unionists, and Violence on the Confederate Home Front* (Fayetteville: University of Arkansas Press, 1999).

29. Jean B. Lee, *The Price of Nationhood: The American Revolution in Charles County* [Md.] (New York: W. W. Norton, 1994), 8.

Fighting the Devil with Fire

David Hunter Strother's Private Civil War

JONATHAN M. BERKEY

*I*n anticipation of Virginia's secession, a group of armed Confederate sympathizers marched on the Federal armory at Harpers Ferry in April 1861. The Federal government's failure to respond to this unlawful act caused one local Unionist, David Hunter Strother, to despair. Like Washington officials, he assumed a passive approach, vowing to let the government "go to the Devil in its own way." Soon, however, Strother had made the transition from a passive Unionist to a Union soldier waging war against his relatives and neighbors in Virginia's northern (or lower) Shenandoah Valley. "The audacious and unscrupulous spirit of revolution," he declared, "must be counteracted by a spirit as bold and remorseless as itself." Strother summarized his feelings with the earthy expression "One must fight the Devil with fire."[1]

President Abraham Lincoln's call for seventy-five thousand troops to put down the Southern rebellion in the aftermath of the attack on Fort Sumter sent shock waves through the upper South and caused most of the region's remaining Unionists to pledge their support to the Confederacy. Despite the rapid disintegration of Unionist feeling in most areas of the South, some Southerners remained loyal to the United States. These "absolute" Unionists formed one end of a spectrum of wartime Unionism that ranged from Southerners who actively worked for the Confederacy's destruction to more passive dissidents and then to those who embraced the Union cause out of war weariness as the conflict continued into its third and fourth year.[2]

David Hunter Strother's behavior placed him at the extreme or absolute end of the Unionist spectrum. He passed what Carl Degler has called "the severest test" of Southern Unionism by serving in the Union army. In his study of Southerners who joined Federal ranks, Richard N. Current has argued that "a strong sense of old fashioned patriotism," great courage, and opportunity were the key factors that motivated them. All of these factors were crucial in Strother's decision to enlist, but above all else, the example of his father inspired him to join the Union army. Indeed, much of Strother's wartime experience was entangled with issues and questions about family relations. Strother's private civil war reveals that although they often competed, family loyalty uneasily coexisted with national loyalty in the hearts and minds of even the most committed Southern Unionists. Strother's experience also shows, however, that the act of juggling family and national loyalty was fraught with dangerous consequences for those who demonstrated their loyalty in this most extreme form—and for their relatives as well.[3]

David Hunter Strother was born in Martinsburg, in Berkeley County, Virginia (now West Virginia), in 1816. He grew up in Berkeley Springs, in Morgan County, where his father owned a hotel at the resort town, well known throughout the region for its "spout, shower, plunge and swimming baths." The hotel had two hundred rooms to accommodate about four hundred guests.[4]

After a brief stint at Jefferson College in Canonsburg, Pennsylvania, David studied art and engraving in Philadelphia, traveled widely, and spent three years studying art and touring Europe. In 1853 he wrote and illustrated an article that appeared in *Harper's New Monthly Magazine* under the pen name "Porte Crayon," thus beginning a successful career that made that nom de plume a household name by the end of the 1850s. He became one of the magazine's best-known writer-artists, writing semifictionalized accounts of his travels and observations that regularly served as lead articles. Passers-by in public places often recognized Strother from his self-portraits in *Harper's*. By the end of his career, Strother had published more than seventy-two articles and eight hundred identifiable engravings.[5]

Before the Civil War, Strother embraced a conservative viewpoint that

David Hunter Strother, ca. 1864. Library of Congress.

favored law and order over the passionate fanaticism of Northern abolitionists and Southern fire-eaters. His biographer noted that whether considering abolition or manifest destiny, Strother "distrusted panaceas and schemes
which smelled of the pulpit or of newsprint." His feelings about John Brown's
trial, which he witnessed, illustrate his conservatism. During the proceedings Virginia Governor Henry A. Wise, Senator James M. Mason, and fire-
eater Edmund Ruffin, among others, met at the house of Andrew Kennedy,
Strother's uncle, on the outskirts of Charles Town to discuss the possibility
of forming a Southern confederacy. They invited Strother to this conference,

JONATHAN M. BERKEY

but he refused to have anything to do with the plotters, despite his aversion to Brown's extremism. After observing Brown's hanging, he proudly noted, "No man capable of reflection could have witnessed that scene without being deeply impressed with the truth that then & there was exhibited, not the vengeance of an outraged people, but the awful majesty of the law." By 1860 Strother held little confidence in the possibility that law and order would triumph over passionate fanaticism. "From a rationally conservative republic," he noted in his journal, "we have in thirty years degraded into a howling democracy, as a gentlemanly drinker degrades into a bestial sot." Strother believed that the solution for the United States was a stronger central government and a candid acknowledgment of inequality in human society.[6]

Virginia's secession from the United States in April 1861 greatly troubled Strother. Undoubtedly, he was not alone in his anguish. Inhabitants of the northern Shenandoah Valley could not easily resolve questions about national loyalty. Morgan County, the home of Strother's father, and Berkeley County, where David was born, bordered the Potomac River. Slavery played a minor role in both counties. In 1860 Berkeley's 1,650 slaves made up only 13 percent of the entire county's population. Census takers found only twenty-four slaves in Morgan County in the same year. Berkeley Springs and Martinsburg relied heavily on the Baltimore and Ohio Railroad, which linked their economic well-being to Baltimore and the eastern seaboard instead of Richmond or the Deep South. Geography dictated that the lower valley would become contested ground in the upcoming conflict. Strother knew that when war came to the region, "fair and fertile fields will be laid waste. . . . Kindred will be divided by the sword. Ancient friendships changed to bloody feuds; peace, security, and plenty [will] give place to war, watchfulness, and famine."[7]

In his inaugural address delivered on March 4, 1861, Abraham Lincoln asserted that "the central ideal of secession" was "the essence of anarchy." David Hunter Strother agreed. He believed that loyal Virginians had succumbed to the tyranny of impassioned secessionist leaders. In the struggle between what he perceived as the tyranny of the Confederacy and the lawful government of the Union, Strother's respect for order caused him to support the latter. However, he was reluctant to take the ultimate step from Unionist to Union soldier. Initially he favored "the idea of living in the mountains & organizing the neighborhood for local defence," but after thoughtfully considering his observations and experiences in the valley during the spring and early summer of 1861, he concluded that he would serve the best interests of the Old Dominion by taking up arms against the Confederacy.[8]

Virginia's secession suggested to Strother that passion had triumphed over reason and order. In the midst of the turmoil of the spring of 1861, he confided to his journal that he "felt like a sane man in a mad house." When visiting Charles Town before secession, he associated disunion with passionate individuals. "The politicians and tavern loungers are full of secession talk," he observed, "but, as far as I could learn, the more solid men and rural gentry were decidedly averse to it." When Strother returned to the town in May 1861, he found the situation worse. "The war spirit," he noted, "was in full blaze, and all traces of Conservatism or Unionism seemed to be rapidly disappearing before the terror of armed force and the irresistible current of social sympathy."[9]

According to Strother, the role that the more "passionate" sex played in the rebellion provided further evidence of its emotional nature. He observed that while some men bravely resisted the popular current of secessionist feeling, "mothers, wives, sisters, daughters & sweethearts threw themselves without reserve into the current wild excitement." Strother noted that men who refused to enlist in the Confederate army faced extreme social pressure from local women. A young man's sister became scornful and unfriendly; his feminine acquaintances refused to dance with him, favoring instead a Confederate recruit. "Alas!" Strother pondered, "poor boy, what sense of duty or prudent counsels could hold him in the whirl of this moral maelstrom?"[10]

Strother's observations of Harpers Ferry in the spring of 1861 convinced him that only something stronger than passive Unionism could save the Old Dominion. As the inhabitants of Harpers Ferry prepared to vote on Virginia's ordinance of secession, Strother observed men from various Southern states preparing for war in the region. Reflecting on this scene, he concluded, like other Virginians, that a foreign power threatened the Old Dominion. Unlike most of his contemporaries, however, Strother characterized the Confederacy as the threatening force. He observed, "The vote on the Act of Secession was taken amid the preparation for war & under the bayonets of southern troops collected from all parts of the slave states." Strother believed that any vote taken under such circumstances could not represent the will of the people. After observing the Virginia flag flying over Harpers Ferry, he mused, "Yesterday I was a citizen of the great American republic. . . . To-day, what am I? A citizen of Virginia. . . . What could she ever hope to be but a worthless fragment of the broken vase?"[11]

By July 1861 Strother had determined that his course of action came down to one choice. "To my mind it presented a simple choice between a

JONATHAN M. BERKEY

Government and Anarchy"—the law and order of the Union versus the cha-
otic passion of the Confederacy. Instead of retreating to the mountains, Porte
Crayon decided to battle actively against the rebellion. He later recalled that
by deciding to join the Union army he had "braved a moral tempest the fury
of which no man can conceive who has not seen and felt it." His father provided the inspiration that allowed Strother to move beyond a more passive
civilian Unionism and embrace direct military action.[12]

During his son's springtime of decision, Strother's father provided a shin-
ing example of staunch Unionism in the face of rebellion. During the War of
1812, John Strother resigned his commission in the Virginia militia to accept
one in the United States army, a strong indication of where his loyalty ultimately rested. After Lincoln's inauguration, John, although nearly seventy
years old, traveled to Washington to offer his services to the president. John
Strother provided the kind of solid example that his son would later emu-
late. "My Father's strong spirit," recalled David, "upheld the people in their
loyal instincts and encouraged resistance to the disloyal practices of the local
authorities." John Strother's enthusiasm was a double-edged sword, however.
David feared that his father's "zeal & courage had made him forget the discretion naturally belonging to age." Concern for his father made David hesi-
tant to abandon his family and join the Union army. He recalled, "I was held
in bondage by social and domestic ties that were hard to break. I was an only
son. My father was old and feeble, and appeared to need my presence and
support."[13]

Ultimately, David's respect for his father reinforced his desire for direct
action and contributed to his decision to enlist. An impassioned Fourth of
July oration by a local Confederate colonel proved to be the final inspiration
for David's enlistment, but his father played a crucial role in his decision.
His concern for John's safety had caused David to argue with him about
expressing Unionist views. David feared that John interpreted his caution
as evidence of a lukewarm Unionism. On the night of July 4, David admitted his determination to join the Federal army at the first opportunity. John
received this news with the "warmest satisfaction" and only regretted that
he was too old to accompany his son. On July 9, 1861, David rode into
Union-occupied Martinsburg and offered his services to General Robert
Patterson.[14]

David Hunter Strother had a varied wartime experience with the Union
army. During the summer of 1861, he accompanied General Patterson's
army as a civilian assistant in the topographical corps. David's anxiety over
financial support for his family, and his fear of being treated as a spy if cap-

tured, caused him to campaign for a military commission. In March 1862 Francis Pierpont, governor of "loyal" Virginia, commissioned David as assistant adjutant general of volunteers, with the military rank of captain. In June, David was commissioned lieutenant colonel of the Third Mounted Regiment of Virginia Volunteers. His companies were scattered among different military departments or existed only on paper; therefore, he essentially was a staff rather than a field officer. Since David was under the command of the loyal government of Virginia rather than the United States Army, he could serve under any Union commander who requested him. David was an advisor to Generals Nathaniel Banks and John Pope in 1862. He followed Banks to Louisiana that winter, and in 1864 he accompanied General Franz Sigel and later his distant cousin, General David Hunter, in the valley. In the fall of 1864, when General Philip Sheridan arrived on the scene, Strother resigned his commission, ending his military career. Throughout his active service Strother attempted to aid his neighbors and relatives while waging war upon the South.[15]

Strother struggled with his conscience over warring against relatives, friends, and neighbors, but he took comfort in the belief that he upheld the principles of a true gentleman. In reflecting on his decision to join the army, he realized he had sacrificed many things; however, he was "in a service that my Father had considered honourable and . . . it was one that I was proud of." Because Strother did not have many opportunities to prove his gentlemanly status on the battlefield, he tried to do so in other ways. Throughout the war he attempted to achieve the same goals that other Southern gentlemen strove for in the conflict—the protection of their communities and families. What made Strother's attempt so fascinating and difficult was that he was, in fact, a Yankee invader. He successfully served as a community guardian in the lower valley towns he invaded, but when the ebb and flow of war engulfed his own relatives, Strother became embroiled in a bitter dispute that destroyed the antebellum friendship of two entire families.[16]

Strother began his protective efforts early in his service. On the same day that he volunteered to assist the topographical corps, Strother carried a letter to General Patterson regarding some vandalism against an uncle's property. He later attempted to aid local civilians who had been arrested by the Federals. On his return to the valley with Banks, the concerns of local noncombatants kept him exceedingly busy. In March 1862 two women who ran a toll gate on the Opequon Creek asked Strother for protection; he gave them a pass that scared at least one unruly Union soldier away from the gate. After a May 1862 skirmish some Federals set fire to the town hall in Charles

JONATHAN M. BERKEY

Town. David attempted to get some soldiers and local citizens to put it out (he was guarding his mother-in-law's house at the time), but the soldiers were not interested and the civilians felt intimidated by the troops. Strother did manage to persuade the Eighth New York Cavalry to guard the streets and called upon the residents to bring out the fire engines. The hall burned to the ground, but the surrounding buildings escaped the conflagration.[17] Strother's wartime generosity had its limits, however. When his wife sent him a local secessionist's request for a pass to travel to Baltimore for a wedding dress, David replied, "So good a Southern rights girl ought to get married in Homespun." Conversely, some acquaintances expected too much of Strother. When traveling to Hancock, Maryland, in the fall of 1861, he encountered a woman whose secessionist husband was imprisoned at Williamsport. Strother agreed to use his influence in an attempt to free the man. He noted with disdain that "as soon as I promised the simple creature was overjoyed & said she would expect him [her husband] to morrow." Despite his attempts to minimize the significance of his influence, the woman was not satisfied until Strother set a date for her husband's release.[18]

By 1864 Strother's juggling act as protector and invader had become more difficult. He confessed to a friend in April: "I am constantly besieged with Clients by letter & in person—and my acquaintance with the country & people enables me to have some influence in modifying the hard condition of the region—not much however—but I can at least protect my own family & property and sometimes oblige my personal friends, & prevent outrages that are continually occurring through want of discipline in the troops & ignorance or rascality in the officers." In May Strother "determined to have no more social intercourse with the people of the country as it interferes with my military duties too much and brought me continually in view of outrage and distress which awaken my sympathies but which I could not prevent."[19]

As Union military policy toward civilians in the Shenandoah Valley became harsher, Strother found himself continually interceding with his cousin, General David Hunter, to protect property and people. He defended a Major Stearns who had used his discretion to save Newtown (now Stephens City), in Frederick County, from burning. Stearns feared Hunter's anger, but Strother "complimented Stearns and told him the chief's anger would blow over. I took an opportunity to speak on the subject and satisfied the General that Stearns was right." A Confederate veteran named Henry Beall recalled that Strother saved him from the wrath of General Hunter, who was about to "give me a sample of that roughness of manner and speech for which he had an unenviable notoriety." Strother invited Beall to his quarters, where he endorsed a packet of letters the prisoner was carrying from lower valley citizens.[20]

Although David usually succeeded in deflecting Hunter's orders, one notable exception reveals the stressful nature of Strother's private war. On July 18, 1864, Captain Martindale of the First New York Cavalry burned the house of Strother's uncle Andrew Hunter. David despaired in his journal, "A war of mutual devastation will depopulate the border counties which contain all my kindred on both sides of the question. I would fain save some of them but fear that all will go under alike in the end." While Strother could not prevent this burning, he did persuade the general to release Andrew Hunter from his arrest for disloyalty. Divided loyalties among families in the lower Shenandoah ensured that Strother could not protect all of his relatives, despite his best efforts to do so.[21]

While he was serving in Louisiana, Strother wrote to a friend that he felt discontented. He observed that an abstract patriotism should have been enough to satisfy him but admitted, "I miss the stimulous [sic] of personal feeling—the friendships and the enmities which gave zest to my Virginia Campaigns." Those friendships and enmities that Strother missed generally revolved around family relationships.[22]

Intense feeling for his family inspired Strother in his role as community protector. Early in his service he reacted strongly against a transfer from the lower valley to Washington. Not only was he moving to an area where his regional knowledge would be useless; his transfer would dash his hope "to be able to exercise a soothing influence" in the Shenandoah. Often Strother bestowed his care and protection upon his relatives. An incident in May 1862 illustrates his family devotion. When riding near Charles Town, Strother encountered a squad of Federal cavalry with a prisoner in tow. David recognized the prisoner as his "friend and cousin," Joe Crane. Joe had killed a trooper in a dispute over some of his horses. Strother "grasped his hand, [and] promised [his] best service." More direct family ties lay behind Strother's helpful inclination, as he admitted: "Joe was my father's favorite nephew and his best friend. He must be saved."[23]

The wartime ties between fathers and sons impressed Strother. He was at Neersville, Virginia, when Federal authorities arrested a county magistrate named Price for his allegiance to the Confederacy. When Price was placed under guard, his son immediately proclaimed his loyalty to the rebellion and joined his father in custody. Strother and the young man debated the question of where the magistrate's ultimate allegiance rested—to Virginia or to the United States. Although they advocated opposite positions, Strother

JONATHAN M. BERKEY

respected the younger Price's filial loyalty. He admitted, "I felt respect for the youth who had volunteered to share his father's evil fortunes and having expressed my sympathy & good wishes closed the conversation." The son's example probably reminded Strother of his obligations to his own father.[24]

While he occasionally observed examples of familial loyalty, more often Strother witnessed how his military position strained and disrupted his own family relations even as he tried to preserve them. Charles G. Halpine, in his humorous war memoir penned by the fictionalized persona of Private Miles O'Reilly, shows how difficult practicing family hospitality was for Strother while advancing with an enemy army. "O'Reilly" recalls:

> it was often ludicrously, though painfully, amusing, to hear Colonel David Hunter Strother, "Porte Crayon," . . . inquiring anxiously after the health of "Cousin Kitty," "Aunt Sallie," "Cousin Joe," or "Uncle Bob," from some nice old Virginia lady in smoothed apron, silver spectacles, and in tears, or some pretty young rebel beauty in homespun, without hoops and in a towering passion,—our soldiers meanwhile cleaning out the smoke houses and granaries by wholesale; and the end of the conversation, as the affectionate but politically sundered relatives parted, usually finding those of the rebel side without a week's food in the house, without a single slave to do their bidding, and with horses, cattle, sheep, bacon, pigs, poultry, and so forth, only to be recalled in ecstatic dreams.

Although his relatives might have appreciated his concern, it did not mitigate their loss in material possessions.[25]

Often Strother's Yankee status overshadowed his blood ties to his ardent Confederate cousins. On his first visit to Charles Town with the invading army, Strother had to convince unbelieving relatives that he was not a Federal prisoner. He created a scene with some relatives in the fall of 1862 when he entered his uncle Andrew Hunter's home. Several Federal officers were gathered in the library, speaking to Mrs. Hunter. David entered the room and gave a general greeting. "Mrs. Hunter," he recalled, "on recognizing me, jumped up with an exclamation and calling her daughter fled the room uttering some incoherent words like 'Good Lord—in my house.'" Strother prided himself on his cool reaction to Mrs. Hunter's outburst.[26]

David's encounter with other members of the Hunter clan in Louisiana further revealed the strain his military status placed on kin relationships, and he reacted more emotionally than he had to Mrs. Andrew Hunter's outburst. When near Jeanerette, Strother visited the home of his relative Alfred

Weeks to offer his protection to the household. On the porch he encountered Fanny Hunter and Mary Weeks, who coldly received him. Fanny addressed David as "Colonel Strother," and when he took her hand, he noted that she "accepted mine mechanically. It was as cold and lifeless as a dead hand. I have never seen as strong a picture of concentrated pride, anger and distress." Fanny would have rejected Strother's offer of protection, save for the helpless condition of her sister (who had just given birth) and her eight nieces and nephews. Fanny said she would prefer death to Federal protection if she could choose. Mary, the former playmate of David's daughter, could only compliment David by admitting her admiration for "a brave and generous enemy."[27]

Strother offered his relatives what protection he could. Usually they could not ignore his status as invader, which tempered any kindness they received from him. David handled intrafamily conflict over his military status fairly well; he reacted with compassion rather than anger toward his Rebel relatives. However, his conservative attempts to protect his family and neighbors were overshadowed by a feud between the McDonald and Strother families initiated by a conflict over national loyalties.

In August 1861 a squad of Confederate Colonel Angus McDonald's cavalry arrested John Strother in Morgan County, on a charge of treason. The troops marched their prisoner to Winchester, where they surprised McDonald with the captive. Coming home from church one day, Angus's wife, Cornelia, saw an old man in a carriage guarded by six cavalrymen at her gate. Upon entering her home, she saw her husband crouched over a table in the hallway, with his head in his hands. Dejectedly, he told his wife that the old man was John Strother, "his father's old companion-in-arms, and his own good friend. He was much distressed."[28]

The War of 1812 had joined the Strother and McDonald families. One of John Strother's comrades in that earlier conflict had been Major Angus W. McDonald, who died at Buffalo, New York, in 1814. John was present at Angus's death and brought his last messages to the McDonald family along with the major's sword and sash. McDonald's son was especially grateful for John's kind action. Fifty years later, in 1864, Angus observed of John, "He had been kind to my father, was his fellow soldier, tended him on his death-bed and was kind to me as his son. I never forgot it and was never ungrateful."[29]

Angus sent a communication to Richmond requesting Strother's release, and held a local tribunal rather than sending the prisoner on to the capital, as called for by common procedure. John Strother spent three days in a militia

Angus McDonald, 1864. *Blue and Gray Magazine.*

tent before a surgeon recommended his removal to a private home where his
daughter could attend to him. He was tried, acquitted, and released. Later
McDonald recalled that holding Strother as a prisoner and taking him to
trial was "the most painful duty I have been called upon to perform since the
war commenced."[30]

The news of his father's imprisonment shocked David Hunter Strother.
Because of the irregularity of the mail, David missed his wife's letter
announcing John's capture. A subsequent letter reported of "hearing from

our Prisoners at Winchester." This was all Strother's wife said on the subject, but he knew that his father was a prisoner. He struggled to master his fear and frustration. "The evil I had most apprehended had fallen upon me," he recalled. "I was haunted by visions of his feeble form and venerable face, bowed with unwonted privations and shameful indignities. . . . I deeply felt my own helplessness." Yet Strother also took comfort in the belief that his father's moral strength could overcome any outrage his captors might attempt.[31]

While on a visit to Washington, David was relieved to hear that the Confederates had released his father, who was enjoying good health back at home. Whatever relief David felt turned to grief in January 1862 when he learned that his father had died of pneumonia. The news stunned him; upon hearing it he asked, "What have I to live for now? what is success? what is honor? to me when my father's noble heart is cold—He for whom alone, it seems now, that I have sought distinction." Later that week he reported, "To night a heavy sleet is falling and a bitter storm wind howling around the camps. The fierce desolation of the night accords well with my soul."[32] David's grief subsided, but it returned when he made visits home. Arriving there in February 1862, a crowd of friends, relatives, and well-wishers lined up to greet him. He observed his wife and sister standing in the doorway of his home, "but the valiant and true hearted Father who should have shared my triumph was not there." He hurried into the house before losing control of his emotions. Just before the start of the Gettysburg campaign, Strother again returned home and wrestled with the grief of losing his father. He noticed John's portrait hanging in the parlor and reacted strongly: "I looked at it a moment and went away to prevent my heart from stirring. I hastily passed the closed door of his office. It will not do to dwell on those things."[33]

Even in death, John Strother provided a strong Unionist example for his son. John's last words were said to have been the patriotic but ultimately fruitless cheer, "Forward! Forward! M'Clellan!" John's death would have far-reaching consequences for both the Strother and McDonald families. Just as Major Angus W. McDonald's death in 1814 united the families, John Strother's imprisonment and death led to a series of events that embittered the families for the remainder of the war and beyond.[34]

The fortunes of war reversed in June 1864, and Colonel McDonald, formerly a captor, now found himself among the captured. General David Hunter's troops overtook McDonald as he attempted to escape from Lexington, where he had been serving on post duty. Hunter ordered him to

JONATHAN M. BERKEY

march with the advancing Federal column rather than to the rear with the other prisoners. McDonald's captors did not accord him any of the respect his rank deserved; they addressed him simply as "McDonald" (or worse) and served him a private's ration of food. The prisoner recalled: "I was . . . denounced as a bushwacker, bridge burner, and the cruel jailer of old Col. Strother. The field officers, whom I sometimes approached for food, all seemed averse to any intercourse with me, throwing up to me as true the alleged ill treatment of old Col. Strother." The circumstances of this war had thus tragically sundered two families formerly united by an earlier one.[35]

On June 16, 1864, a day after the prisoner arrived at Hunter's headquarters, the general informed Strother of McDonald's capture and offered to turn the prisoner over to him. David declined, not wishing to use his military status to his advantage in a private quarrel. He did allege, however, that Colonel McDonald had treated his father "in an insolent and inhuman manner." Upon leaving his quarters Strother encountered McDonald; the Confederate bade him good morning but received no reply. When McDonald attempted to address him again, Strother interrupted, asking, "Do you know me, Sir?" According to Strother, McDonald answered, "Yes, I know you and you know me very well." The captive apologetically continued, "And yet, Sir, you do not know me. No you do not know me." At this point in the encounter Strother emphatically replied, "I think I do know you, Sir," and turned away from McDonald in a last desperate attempt to keep up the appearance of a gentleman. He thought about his passionate feelings and convinced himself that he had acted with gentlemanly restraint:

> My blood boiled but I could not insult a prisoner, especially one with grey hair. Yet I remembered my father and bitter tears rolled down my cheeks. After three years the hour had at length come and this tyrannical old brute who had treated my aged father with such wanton indignity was himself a prisoner in my hands and I clothed with authority for life or death. That single look was vengeance enough for me. I could see remorse in his countenance when he recognized me and his aged appearance filled me with pity. If I had followed my impulses at the moment I should have liberated him.[36]

Strother did not liberate the prisoner, claiming his release would deny justice to both secessionists and Unionists who had accused Angus of "petty and vindictive tyranny." Apparently, Strother struggled to arrive at his enlightened reaction. Charles Halpine, writing as Miles O'Reilly, reported that upon hearing of McDonald's capture, Strother exclaimed, "I can only regret my civilization. Just for this one morning, Miles, I should like to be a Camanche or Sioux Indian, and have their privilege of vengeance." Halpine observed, "Not being a Camanche but a gentleman, however, he took no other notice of the prisoner than to see that he was no better and no worse treated than his fellow-captives of higher and lower rank."[37]

McDonald's capture initiated a family feud that contained a volatile mixture of family obligations and the circumstances of war. After the capture Major Edward H. McDonald of the Eleventh Virginia Cavalry found himself encamped near Berkeley Springs while Strother's wife, Mary Hunter Strother, was visiting. The major told his mother that he was tempted to capture Mrs. Strother and hold her behind Confederate lines until the Federals released Colonel McDonald. Only the knowledge that his father would consider the capture an "unmanly act" prevented him from attempting it. He did send her a letter pledging the lives of the nine McDonald sons to avenge their father. Confederate raids near Berkeley Springs allowed Edward to pursue a quarrel with Strother, but David's affiliation with the Union army hindered his ability to protect his family. In late July 1864 Strother learned that Edward had announced his intention to burn the Berkeley Springs property. He became upset at his inability to respond, and confided to his journal, "Thus while I am bound up with a large army in a cowardly retrograde protecting Washington against its own cowardice, a few thousand scoundrels are burning my property and insulting my family."[38]

Edward McDonald and David Strother did not get a chance to settle their feud. In November 1864 Angus McDonald was released from prison and sent to Richmond. The hardships he suffered had greatly weakened him, and he died about a month after his release. On his deathbed he ended the conflict by forgiving Strother and urging his sons not to avenge his suffering; they honored his request. A firm believer in his cause, like John Strother, McDonald urged that his younger children live in exile if the Confederacy met with defeat. The circumstances of war had tempered any rigid sense of personal honor in McDonald, but he retained his devotion to the Confederacy.[39] Angus's death also convinced David that the feud was over. On the day he learned that McDonald had died, Strother concluded his journal entry with the news, remarking, "Requiescat. That account is closed."[40]

After the war, Strother received no credit for his gentlemanly restraint and his aid of powerless civilians. In fact, Strother's role as Yankee soldier severely handicapped his efforts to temper the harshness of Union military activities in the valley. He sensed the bitterness of many postwar Virginians,

JONATHAN M. BERKEY

writing, "They talk as if I were commander in chief of the Union Armies."
Many held him responsible for General David Hunter's widespread destruction in the valley. As time passed, Strother distanced himself from postwar
sectional bitterness. A year after the war's end he wrote, "I abhor the South,
I despise the West, I ignore the East, and damn the North. I acknowledge
nothing but nationality and the American people, no country but the United
States."[41]

David Hunter Strother's private civil war, while unique in numerous ways,
broadly reflects the ambivalent experience of many individuals and families
in Virginia's lower Shenandoah Valley during the Civil War. In an area
that was not united in support of the Confederate cause, many individuals
faced wrenching decisions about what action they would take in the conflict.
Because the valley served as a transportation route for both armies, individuals found it difficult to retain a neutral stance. David Hunter Strother was
always a Unionist, but he faced a difficult decision about how to manifest
his Unionism. Ultimately he decided to become a Union soldier. As his case
shows, individual decisions about national loyalty and how one expressed it
affected broader family relations and could divide families. Private relationships became hopelessly entangled with questions of national allegiance and
military authority. Even when single families united behind one cause, their
loyalty could adversely affect friendly social relations with other families.
The ebb and flow of military activity in the region ensured that decisions
about national allegiance would have far-reaching and complex personal
consequences for inhabitants of Virginia's lower Shenandoah Valley.

NOTES

I would like to thank Peter Carmichael, Cecil Eby, Christian Keller, Sarah
Strother King, Robin King, and Robert Sandow for critiquing earlier versions
of this essay.

1. The first quote is from David Hunter Strother (DHS) Journal 9, "War Notes,"
the West Virginia and Regional History Collection, West Virginia University
(WVU), 2. The second quote is from DHS, "Personal Recollections of the War,"
Harper's New Monthly Magazine 33 (1866): 420, 138.

2. For an analysis of the antebellum concept of Union, see Paul C. Nagel, *One
Nation Indivisible: The Union in American Thought, 1776–1861* (New York: Oxford
University Press, 1964). Nagel discusses "absolute" Unionism on page 107. For a
discussion of the effect of Abraham Lincoln's call for troops on Southern Unionists

see Daniel W. Crofts, *Reluctant Confederates: Upper South Unionists in the Secession Crisis* (Chapel Hill: University of North Carolina Press, 1989), 334–35, 340–41. Many studies of Unionism attempt to categorize Unionists according to the strength of their commitment to the cause. In one of the earliest studies on Unionism, Georgia Lee Tatum applied the words *disloyal* and *disaffection* to characterize different levels of Unionist commitment; see *Disloyalty in the Confederacy* (Chapel Hill: University of North Carolina Press, 1934), viii. For a modern historian's effort to categorize Unionists, see Daniel E. Sutherland, ed., *Guerrillas, Unionists, and Violence on the Confederate Home Front* (Fayetteville: University of Arkansas Press, 1999), 4–5. In his study of Atlanta's wartime Unionists, Thomas G. Dyer also classifies Unionists according to their commitment to the cause but rightly notes that the expression of loyalty remained fluid throughout the conflict, often hinging on circumstance; see *Secret Yankees: The Union Circle in Confederate Atlanta* (Baltimore: Johns Hopkins University Press, 1999), 3, 267.

3. Carl N. Degler, *The Other South: Southern Dissenters in the Nineteenth Century* (New York: Harper and Row, 1974), 174; Richard N. Current, *Lincoln's Loyalists: Union Soldiers from the Confederacy* (Boston: Northeastern University Press, 1992), 146–47 (quote on page 146). For further discussion of the relationship between family and national loyalty, see the essays by Thomas G. Dyer, Kenneth Barnes, and John C. Inscoe and Gordon B. McKinney in this volume.

4. Information on John Strother's hotel was taken from an undated broadside and a floor plan dated April 29, 1848, in the Legal and Professional Papers of Edmund Lee, Shepherd College, Shepherdstown, W.Va. The U.S. Eighth Census, 1860, Morgan County, lists David Hunter Strother as part of his father's household. Neither David nor John Strother is listed as a slave owner in the 1860 slave census for Morgan County.

5. Cecil D. Eby Jr., *"Porte Crayon": The Life of David Hunter Strother* (Chapel Hill: University of North Carolina Press, 1960), 74; Jessie F. Poesch, "David Hunter Strother: Mountain People, Mountain Images," in *Graphic Arts and the South: Proceedings of the 1990 North American Print Conference*, ed. Judy L. Larson (Fayetteville: University of Arkansas Press, 1993), 64. Poesch discusses the scope of Strother's work on pp. 95–96 n. 3.

6. Eby, *Porte Crayon*, 109, 110–111; Boyd B. Stutler, "An Eyewitness Describes the Hanging of John Brown," *American Heritage* 6 (February 1955): 9.

7. Joseph C. G. Kennedy, ed., *Population of the United States in 1860* (Washington, D.C.: Government Printing Office, 1864); DHS, "Recollections," 6.

8. Lincoln's inaugural address quoted from Paul M. Angle and Earl Shenck Miers, eds., *The Living Lincoln* (1955; reprint, New York: Barnes and Noble, 1992), 386; DHS, "War Notes," 24.

9. Eby, *Porte Crayon*, 115; DHS, "Recollections," 5.

10. DHS, "Recollections," 141; DHS, "War Notes," 18.

11. DHS, "War Notes," 26; DHS, "Recollections," 16.

12. DHS to John Pendleton Kennedy, August 9, 1862, John Pendleton Kennedy Papers, microfilm, original collection at the Peabody Institute Library, Baltimore; DHS, "Recollections," 150.

13. Cecil Eby, "'Porte Crayon's' Quarrel with Virginia," *West Virginia History* 21 (January 1960): 71–72; DHS, "War Notes," 24, 29; DHS, "Recollections," 150.

14. DHS, "War Notes," 46–47; Eby, *Porte Crayon*, 115.

15. For a brief discussion of Strother's early military service, see Edwin C. Fishel, *The Secret War for the Union: The Untold Story of Military Intelligence in the Civil War* (New York: Houghton Mifflin, 1996); for a general outline of his military service, see Eby, *Porte Crayon*, 119–22.

16. DHS, "War Notes," 69.

17. DHS Journal 10, July 9, 19, 1861, WVU; Cecil D. Eby Jr., ed., *A Virginia Yankee in the Civil War: The Diaries of David Hunter Strother* (Chapel Hill: University of North Carolina Press, 1961), 14, 47–48. Strother saved Charles Town from burning on three separate occasions during the war. See Eby, *Virginia Yankee*, 280.

18. DHS Journal 10, October 11, 1861.

19. DHS to John Pendleton Kennedy, April 14, 1864, John Pendleton Kennedy Papers, microfilm; Eby, *Virginia Yankee*, 237–38.

20. Eby, *Virginia Yankee*, 241; War Reminiscences of Henry D. Beall, 1889, quoted in Hunter McDonald's Appendix to *A Diary with Reminiscences of the War and Refugee Life in the Shenandoah Valley 1860–1865*, by Cornelia McDonald (1875; reprint, Nashville: Cullom and Ghertner, 1934), 287–88.

21. Eby, *Virginia Yankee*, 285.

22. DHS to John Pendleton Kennedy, March 4, 1863, John Pendleton Kennedy Papers, microfilm.

23. DHS Journal 10, December 29, 1861; Eby, *Virginia Yankee*, 48.

24. DHS, "War Notes," 77–78.

25. Quoted in Julia Davis, *The Shenandoah* (New York: Farrar and Rinehart, 1945), 246–47.

26. DHS Journal 10, July 17, 1861; Eby, *Virginia Yankee*, 68, 122–23. This is the same Andrew Hunter whose home was burned in the spring of 1864.

27. Eby, *Virginia Yankee*, 170–71.

28. Cornelia Peake McDonald, *A Woman's Civil War: A Diary, with Reminiscences of the War, from March 1862*, ed. Minrose C. Gwinn (Madison: University of Wisconsin Press, 1992), 265. James B. Avirett, *The Memoirs of Turner Ashby and His Compeers* (1867; reprint, Gaithersburg, Md.: Butternut Press, 1984), 337; DHS, "Recollections," 422–23. David's cousin Edmund Pendleton was also captured on this expedition.

29. Avirett, *Memoirs of Turner Ashby*, 319; Angus W. McDonald to George Crook, September 6, 1864, printed in Hunter McDonald, Appendix, 280. See also Cornelia McDonald, *A Woman's Civil War*, 207.

30. Angus McDonald to George Crook, September 6, 1864, printed in Hunter McDonald, Appendix, 279–80.

31. DHS, "War Notes," 101; DHS, "Recollections," 416.

32. DHS Journal 11, January 17, 1862, January 24, 1862, WVU. A brief obituary of John Strother appears in *Harper's Weekly*, February 15, 1862.

33. DHS Journal 11, February 18, 1862; Eby, *Virginia Yankee*, 183.

34. DHS, "Recollections," 567.

35. R. D. Beall, "Col. Angus M'Donald," *Confederate Veteran* 17 (November 1909): 555; Angus McDonald to George Crook, September 6, 1864, printed in Hunter McDonald, Appendix, 282. McDonald's wife discusses his capture and treatment in *A Woman's Civil War*, 206–207.

36. Eby, *Virginia Yankee*, 260.

37. Ibid., 259–60; Miles O'Reilly [Charles G. Halpine], *Baked Meats of the Funeral* (New York: Carleton, 1866), 323. Angus McDonald's brief description of his encounter with Strother supports the latter's more detailed account described in the text. McDonald states that while he was waiting for General Hunter, "Col. Strother . . . opened the door, looked at me with apparent ferocity and hostility, insulted me by his manner and questions and closed the door." See Angus McDonald to George Crook, September 6, 1864, printed in Hunter McDonald, Appendix, 279.

38. Cornelia McDonald, *A Woman's Civil War*, 209; Eby, *Virginia Yankee*, 284–85.

39. Cornelia McDonald, *A Woman's Civil War*, 216. Avirett also discusses McDonald's death in *Memoirs of Turner Ashby*, 358. Angus McDonald's deathbed request failed to end the bitterness between his sons and Strother; most of the appendices of Hunter McDonald's edition of his mother's diary form a literary attack on Strother.

40. DHS Journal typescript, vol. 9, December 7, 1864, Harpers Ferry National Historical Park, Harpers Ferry, W.Va.

41. Eby, "'Porte Crayon's' Quarrel," 73, and *Porte Crayon*, 212.

Red Strings and Half Brothers

Civil Wars in Alamance County, North Carolina, 1861–1871

SCOTT REYNOLDS NELSON

One of the signal features of the eighteenth and nineteenth centuries was a division between the public world of politics and the private world of families.[1] Citizens' liberties depended in part on this distinction. Private communication, private control of one's person, and above all private property were liberties that were limited by this imaginary boundary between the family and the state. All of these rights were and are restricted at some outer margin. Some communication could be treasonous or libelous, those who had transgressed the law lost the right to control their person, and property could be confiscated for nonpayment of taxes.

Yet this elegant dichotomy between public and private was problematic from the very beginning. For most Southerners—white women, slaves, and children of both races—the divide between the hearth and the political stage meant that most liberties extended no farther than the patriarch, and thus their access to the political sphere was severely limited. Those without a claim to suffrage or full citizenship were folded under the care of the family. By this old definition, their concerns were not political, only social.

Social historians, concerned with the everyday lives of most people, have long sought to peer into this supposedly private world. We have done this much the way gossips and lawyers have done for generations, by reading private letters and diaries, gaping over the shoulders of census takers, and reading between the lines of public documents. The Civil War has served as a tremendous resource for such investigations. This is partly because so many people saved their personal letters and diaries during the war. But we also have more of these documents because both the Confederate and the Union governments sought to inspect and penetrate the allegedly private world of the family. The wartime search for conspiracy—literally, the whispered exchanges between two people—pushed the state further into the so-called private sphere. Opponents of the draft were sought out and jailed. Letters were censored or reprinted in public correspondence, or saved as evidence in trials. War is wonderful for historians, folks who love to rummage in the past of others, because the hazy line between public and private becomes nearly invisible. Private letters are preserved by families as public documents, and private correspondence is collected and saved by public officials. It is perhaps in studying war that the divide between social history and political history can be most easily crossed.

The wartime history of the Faucettes of Alamance County, North Carolina, allows us to see how artificial is the boundary between public and private, between political and social history. The Faucettes of Alamance included both black and white kin, and became bitterly divided as the war progressed. For them the war began in 1861 and ended not in 1865 but in 1871. Considering the Faucettes means considering not just their immediate families but the associations that the male Faucettes joined, secret societies of men that blurred the boundary between private association and public gathering. The Faucettes belonged to three such organizations—some were brothers in the Red Strings or Heroes of America, others joined the Loyal Republican League, and some joined a band called the White Brotherhood. All formed relationships with men whom they called brothers and traded their public and private secrets with one another. By 1871 many of their private secrets became public events in the life of the county and the state.

As early as 1830, Chesley F. Faucette—merchant, planter, and father—must have thought a great deal about a coming war. In the beginning of that year, fifteen months after South Carolina espoused the doctrine of nullification, the Faucettes named their second child Chesley Henry Clay Faucette, after the Whig Speaker of the House and architect of the Missouri Compromise. Few people in the Hawfields Church, where the baby was christened, would have doubted that the Faucettes were Unionists and Whigs. Twelve years later they named their eighth child William A. Graham Faucette, in honor of the best-known Whig in the state.[2] By the time his last child was born in 1855, Chesley Faucette had become a prominent slave-holding Whig in central North Carolina. The population around Faucette's plantation had grown so quickly, in part because of the construction of the nearby repair shops of the North Carolina Railroad, that in 1849 a new county, Alamance, was formed out of Orange County. By 1854 his part of the county was known as Faucette's Store.[3]

Chesley Faucette also had a secret that was not public but not entirely private either. It was the name of his oldest son, a name that did not appear in the family Bible. Sometime around 1820, four years before he married, Chesley Faucette became the father of an infant boy. The nineteenth-century term for the child's race was mulatto, because the boy's mother, Jemimah Phillips, was black. It is impossible to determine who chose the child's name, which was either White or Wyatt, depending on the source.[4] The census followed Chesley's younger sons, but Wyatt's status as a free black man made him almost invisible to county records. After the war his mother noted that county officials had not recorded his birth, his parentage, or his marriage.[5] Indeed, his absence from the public world of records was so complete that Wyatt apparently had no last name until after the Civil War. Through the 1840s and 1850s, Chesley Faucette bought a dozen or more slaves, men and women who cleared his land and filled his store with local goods, while his son Wyatt became apprenticed to a craftsman (probably in the nearby shops of the North Carolina Railroad).[6] While Chesley Faucette represented the new county of Alamance in North Carolina's House of Commons, Wyatt followed the trades of metal and wood, and became a cabinet maker, a mechanic, and a carriage maker.[7]

These family relationships, some public, some private, were drastically altered when President Abraham Lincoln called for troops in April 1861. Although that event did more than any other to unite whites in North Carolina and the upper South behind the Confederacy, this was not entirely true in Alamance County. Most of a regiment was quickly recruited from the farmers and mechanics of Alamance and organized into a unit later called the "Bloody Sixth"; yet many more stayed behind.[8] Indeed, shortly before North Carolina seceded from the Union on May 20, some men held a "Union Meeting" near the pre-Revolutionary battleground where Regulators had resisted troops sent by the British governor, William Tryon, to put them down in 1771. They resolved to raise an American flag on May 16, the ninetieth anniversary of the Regulator insurrection. To make sure that this statement would be understood as a public gesture of defiance against the Confederacy, they appointed a committee to advertise their actions to the county's most prominent secessionist.[9] Given Chesley Faucette's wartime career as a Unionist, it is likely that some of the Faucettes were among the men who raised the flag. Chesley had seven sons of recruiting age, but only two of the younger sons enlisted for Confederate service, and they did so rather later than 1861.[10]

Increased demands for troops by the end of the war's first year prompted the Confederacy to enforce enrollment with the Conscription Act of April 1862.[11] For the first time in American history, men were required to serve in a national army. It was this act, perhaps more than any other, that led the men of Alamance County to gather in secret societies. Governor Zebulon B. Vance ordered all conscripted men to report to their county seats for duty. Those who failed to do so were to be arrested as deserters.[12] By the end of 1862, Confederate troops and home guard units had begun arresting North Carolina deserters and confining them in the Confederate prison in Salisbury. Because President Jefferson Davis had declared martial law for a ten-mile radius around all Confederate prisons, men thus incarcerated could be imprisoned indefinitely without trial. To be more precise, writs of habeas corpus, demanding that a person be called forth and legally tried, were pointedly ignored by the commandant of the nearby prison camp in Salisbury.[13] That camp, the largest in the state and one of the most notorious in the Confederacy, housed both Union prisoners and Carolinian deserters and draft dodgers.[14]

In Alamance County the reaction to conscription and the arrests of those who resisted it ranged from surprise to outrage. In April 1864 Mary Jane Allen wrote her brother John that many Alamance men, even men who had previously paid for substitutes, had been forced to enroll and were marched under guard into the cars of the North Carolina Railroad. "The citizens," she wrote, "were very much displeased about it to see true men taken up and sent off in that way."[15] Although she supported the Confederacy, she wondered aloud about the fate of personal liberty under a Confederate state. "I hope the day will soon come when the last battle will be fought and we shall be free and happy people, but would we stay so?"[16]

By 1864 a secret organization had formed in central North Carolina to help men evade the conscription laws and to help Union prisoners escape across battle lines. The order was named the Red Strings, after an Old Testament story in which a woman named Rahab helped two Israelites

SCOTT REYNOLDS NELSON

evade the king of Jericho and escape over a mountain. When she asked the Israelites for protection when they returned with soldiers of God, they told her to hang a scarlet cord from her window, in memory of the cord that she hung from her roof to help them escape. Those people who displayed the red string would be spared when the armies of God returned.[17] In Alamance County the key members of the Red Strings were H. A. Badham, the first lawyer to try to use a writ of habeas corpus on behalf of a conscript; "Red-Eyed Will" Albright, a town commissioner in the county seat of Graham; and Chesley Faucette, who went on to represent the county in the state legislature in 1864. When Faucette was exposed as a member of the Red Strings, or Heroes of America, he publicly withdrew from the organization.[18]

The difficulty in describing a secret society like the Heroes of America is that it was, of course, secret. There are no published minute books or extended autobiographies of members. One way to get a closer look is to examine the most extreme public statements made by those who opposed the Davis administration and defended the Red Strings. Editorials such as these appeared in the *North Carolina Standard*, a newspaper reputed to be the organ of the Red Strings in the state's piedmont. Following a hallowed tradition, many editorialists for the *Standard* wrote under assumed names, which protected their privacy (and their necks) while allowing them to reach the wider public. "Palermo" (of Salisbury) and "Davie" and "Justice" (of Graham) opposed President Davis's system of impressment by imprisonment and echoed the question of Mary Jane Allen.[19] What was the fate of private liberty in the Confederacy, if the Confederacy declared martial law over its own citizens? They returned repeatedly to histories of England, and pointed to an almost unbroken tradition of personal liberty that stretched back to the "Magna Charter." Those liberties had been unbroken until the Davis administration. According to one such editorial: "The President has abused a power which has been recklessly conferred, and wantonly exercised dictatorial, tyrannical and offensive authority over a loyal and inoffensive people. *We fear that evil counsellors have got the ear of the President,* men who commend themselves to those in power by acting as panderers and pimps, and who keep out of battle by impugning the loyalty of men of more patriotism than themselves."[20]

These writers declared themselves inoffensive and, if not exactly patriotic, at least more patriotic than the evil counselors with the ear of the president in Richmond. They emphasized the evils of martial law: "Behold how it is managed!" wrote "Davie" in 1863. "The military go abroad, and without warrant or probable cause, supported by oath, they seize their prisoners, and with all possible speed, convey them to this place where the law is dead, and the sorrows of captivity fall on walls of stone."[21] "Justice" told North Carolinians to "denounce these attempts to betray our liberties and place [us] under a military despotism."[22] The general direction of their critique of state power was on behalf of personal liberty against a ruthless national power.

The demand for liberty against unjust power was a cry that played well in North Carolina, the state that had the largest number of enlistments and the largest number of casualties in this war, but was greatly underrepresented in the Confederate Congress.[23] But their demand for liberty also differed little from those made by certain Northern opponents of the war, or even of the Union. After all, the "Copperheads" in the North, who objected to a draft that forced them to fight to free slaves in other states, were so named because their members wore in their lapels copper pennies with the word *liberty* standing out. The Red Strings' demand for *personal* liberty against *political* power could seem politically inoffensive, not just because it relied on the binary division between public and private, a division that everyone understood, but because it sounded similar to the claim of the Davis administration that the liberty to hold slaves was under attack by a despotic power.[24]

By 1864 the Red Strings order had been exposed in administration newspapers. A furious search for Red Strings members expanded as rumors circulated of North Carolina troops with red strings on their lapels.[25] As Confederate authorities sought to jail theses subversives, Alamance County men who were secret members of the order stood up publicly in defense of liberty. H. A. Badham was the chief counsel of those imprisoned by Confederate government. Will Albright ran for state assembly in 1864 on a platform to forge a separate peace with the Union government. "Red eyed Will Albright talks of running for the legislature," Mary Jane Allen wrote in 1864. "I think if they send him there, the rest will think Alamance is getting scarce of bright metal."[26] Chesley Faucette kept a low profile, for he alone had been exposed as a member, perhaps a leader, of the Red Strings in Alamance.[27] He was elected a representative to the state assembly, but made few public speeches.[28]

Rhetorically, the supporters of the Red Strings emphasized the many ways in which public power robbed private citizens of their rights. They called themselves Conservatives and their enemies Destructives, men whose devotion to abstract principle had led to secession.[29] Their position was a defense of home and family, they asserted, while their opponents used public power to destroy both. Here again the personal (good) was arrayed against the political (bad). Thus when the editor of the *North Carolina Standard*, William Woods Holden, was accused of being a member of the Red Strings, he responded:

> No, we are guided in our steps by two entirely different strings, to wit, the latch string, which opens the doors of our friends and enables us to enjoy their confidence; and the apron string, girding the loins of the workingman who is our friend. . . . but the tortuous string which our opponents follow is steeped in blood, and leads through the ruined homesteads, desolated fields, and blazing cities. . . . [they] who live on the two governments, and grow rich while the people become poorer, follow this string at a safe distance, but they pull it till it is crimsoned with the blood of others. They are the red string party.[30]

In this way the Heroes identified themselves with home life—latch strings— and their opponents as political opportunists who used state power and politics to destroy others.

Whatever the rhetorical merits of the argument, it was a duplicitous one. The Red Strings was a political organization, not just a private group of friends. Many of its members were important political figures who were in a position to decide which citizens were exempted from Confederate service. Among its leaders were the manager of the state salt works and the superintendent of the North Carolina Railroad.[31] They employed hundreds of men who were thus exempted from service. Major General William A. Smith, another Red Strings member, commanded the Thirty-seventh Battalion of the North Carolina Home Guard. He was elected by his men for promising that soldiers under him would avoid direct conflict.[32] Ironically, the Thirty-seventh Battalion's responsibility was to find deserters in the state, an assignment that gave Smith tremendous latitude in particular cases. It is clear, too, that the Heroes of America had an expressly political purpose, to elect state representatives and a governor who would end the war.

It is probable that Chesley Faucette's son Wyatt joined a different brotherhood during the war. Indirect evidence suggests that in 1863 Wyatt crossed the line between North Carolina and Virginia and enlisted in the Second Regiment, Cavalry, of the United States Colored Troops. In that year he became Wyatt Outlaw. As a private, Outlaw saw action in the battles of Swift Creek and Fort Darling, and in the final assaults on Petersburg and Richmond.[33] During the war his wife died or disappeared, leaving him with two children to support. Wyatt, having become Wyatt Outlaw, would become an important leader in the Reconstruction of Alamance County.

By the war's end Outlaw had opened a shop—probably for carpentry and wagon repair—in the county seat of Graham. Will Albright, the former leader in the Red Strings, leased him the property.[34] The shop was one stop away from the North Carolina Railroad's repair shops. Wyatt Outlaw followed in the footsteps of his father, Chesley Faucette. Many people in Graham, black and white, thought Wyatt a respectable and honorable man. With his mother and children in adjoining rooms, Outlaw lived on the ground floor of the shop.[35] Many would have reflected that the fortunes of Wyatt Outlaw and his father moved in opposite directions, for by the late 1860s Chesley Faucette had been declared insane and moved into an asylum, while Wyatt Outlaw had prospered.[36]

Outlaw converted one of the private rooms of his shop into a public place for the sale of liquor. By 1868 railroad workers were paying cash for their drinks in Outlaw's semipublic barroom. Some of his customers were probably black men who worked in the nearby repair shops, given that a sizable number of shopmen and maintenance of way workers were men of color. White Republicans probably also frequented Outlaw's drinking room, since the other barroom (which stood closer to the shops) was run by a violent Democrat. Local courts had tried twice to close down Outlaw's shop for selling liquor without a public license, but he apparently refused the summonses of the county court.[37]

It was in his shops that Outlaw first organized the Alamance County chapter of the Loyal Republican League. "Mr. Outlaw was the man who started [the League]," one member said, "to try to build a school house and have a church." The owner of the shop, "Red-Eyed Will" Albright, was also a member, and so it should not be surprising that the Loyal League bore similarities to the Red Strings. Rather than Heroes, initiates in the Loyal League were known as Pioneers, the title given to black railroad workers who had rebuilt railroad lines for Union troops. Like the Union Leagues elsewhere in the South, the Loyal League sought to "cause voters to have courage to go to the polls and vote," according to one Pioneer. Members were posted at each of the polls during election time to see who voted, and how. Like Red Stringers, Loyal Leaguers wore small strips of fabric in their lapels to identify themselves to one another and discreetly tapped their lapels when passing brother members. Like the Red Strings too, Loyal League members identified one another with secret handshakes and code words. The biracial Outlaw could have been the ideal conduit between Unionists who had fought conscription and black men who had seized their liberty.[38]

SCOTT REYNOLDS NELSON

Like the Red Strings, the Loyal League stood somewhere between a private association and a political party. Reconstruction of the state broadened the franchise and made many more political posts elective.[39] William W. Holden, the former editor of the *North Carolina Standard* and the state's foremost leader of the wartime peace movement, became governor in the brief transition period between the old and new constitutions. The interregnum in 1868 allowed Holden to appoint county officers for positions that would become elective the following year. By building a corps of county incumbents, Holden hoped to establish a political constituency of white anti-Confederates and a few black leaders that would form the basis of a stable Republican Party in the state.[40] When appointing the town commissioners in Graham, Holden appointed former Unionists like Will Albright and H. A. Badham. The governor also named Albright as a director of the North Carolina Railroad, giving him free passage between Alamance County and the capitol in Raleigh. As both Albright and Chesley Faucette suddenly lost their citizenship and returned to private life (in an odd twist of fate, Albright too was declared insane and committed to the state asylum in 1868), Wyatt Outlaw was propelled even further into the public world as the town commissioner and representative for the area called Faucette's Store.[41]

There were many public men in Alamance who were unprepared to see Red Stringers or Wyatt Outlaw reconstruct the county. Among them were other Faucettes who also lived near Faucette's Store. George Faucette, a distant cousin of Chesley's, was a carpenter on the North Carolina Railroad. His brothers, Thomas and J. W., had died in the war. Wyatt Outlaw was well known to them.[42] In 1867, at the age of twenty-one, George joined an organization called the White Brotherhood, which he later recalled was formed "to strengthen the Conservative Party."[43] George and the other members of the White Brotherhood made their first demonstration in Graham in February of 1869. They marched with their weapons drawn and fired at local officials. It was a test of public authority for Wyatt Outlaw and the other members of the Red Strings who had been sworn in as town commissioners a few months earlier.[44] At the state level conservative Democrats claimed that Holden's Unionist appointees were usurpers. In some counties Democratic officials refused to turn over their offices to the new county officials and used force to prevent them from entering public buildings.[45]

Outlaw and the other local Republican officials responded to the white brotherhoods' violent demonstrations by establishing a patrol and a curfew. Armed Republicans, white and black, guarded the streets of Graham and stopped people traveling at night. To support the patrol, Governor Holden sent militiamen and state detectives into town. For some it was doubtless a relief, but for others it must have been an uncomfortable reminder of the visits by the North Carolina Home Guard in the years of conscription.[46] In the following year Klansmen attacked Republican leaders, most of them black men, in areas around the outskirts of Graham. In February 1870, on the anniversary of the White Brotherhood's first encounter with public authority, Klansmen entered Graham, seized Wyatt Outlaw from his offices, dragged him to the courthouse, and hanged him.[47]

The murder of Wyatt Outlaw was not a random act of violence but was calculated to draw the attention and anger of the Republican Party. So that all who went to church on Sunday morning would see the body, Klansmen threatened to kill anyone who cut it down from the tree in front of the courthouse. They told Will Albright, famous for his temper and just out of the asylum, that they had hanged Outlaw and had a list of other Republicans who would be hanged in Alamance.[48] These provocations led Governor Holden to declare Alamance County in a state of insurrection. He sent state troops to arrest suspected Klansmen, and writs of habeas corpus were once again suspended. Accused Klansmen were taken out of the county and imprisoned in Yanceyville. Some of the Klansmen were briefly tortured for their confessions.[49]

By carefully coordinating successive attacks on the Republican Party, Democratic newspapers succeeded in recasting the pages of Governor Holden's own anti-Confederate newspaper. They called the mass arrests the "Kirk-Holden War" and accused the governor of taking dictatorial powers. They claimed that Holden used public power to enter the homes of unoffending citizens and to rob them of their liberty. They called themselves conservatives and labeled Holden a radical.

The White Brotherhood was a peculiar mock-up of the Red Strings and the Loyal League. The first two organizations had acted as a bridge between private and public activities. They had relied on their private right of assembly to pursue political ends that were otherwise dangerous. One allowed public men to hide in a private organization, the other allowed private men to enter into public life. During Reconstruction the Klan successfully mimicked both organizations, but rather than connecting public and private, they used direct violence to attack voters, then cloaked themselves in the private security of a gentleman's organization.

Most significantly, the Klan skillfully drew the force of the state and federal government on their heads. They courted outrage at the state's penetra-

SCOTT REYNOLDS NELSON

tion of private affairs by pursuing arrest and imprisonment. They sought to prove to citizens that the Republican state, like the Confederate state before it, was a public entity that was bent on denying private citizens their liberties. Politically it was a successful strategy: a sufficient number of black voters were forced away from the polls, while many of the white voters who had elected Holden came to believe his administration was dangerous, if only because Democratic newspapers made his actions look so much like the tyrannies of the Confederate state.

During this decade-long civil war in Alamance, there were two ways in which the public and private worlds collided. Both turned Faucettes into outlaws. First, Confederate conscription had taken enlistment out of the hands of private men and placed it in the hands of a public entity. This shockingly unrepresentative body, the Confederate state, then turned opponents of the administration into felons who risked death in the prison camp at Salisbury. Opponents of conscription had to resort to private activities, conspiracies, to formulate their case against the government. They formed secret societies to map out strategy, they exchanged hidden signals to represent themselves to friends, they assumed names like "Justice" and "Palermo" to point out how far private liberties had been violated by state power.

By 1864 there was another way in which public and private collided. Emancipation for slaves *and* free blacks meant that people who had no standing in public courts or in public records became citizens, even if voting was still an open question. This emancipation was more than just personal freedom for those who had been enslaved. Black men and women emancipated themselves in much the same way Protestants were emancipated in France immediately before the French Revolution. They had a civil status, had their births and marriages recorded, and could sue and be sued. They cast off the claim that their lives were private concerns, the business only of their masters and mistresses, and they diligently pursued a public status as citizens.[50] Wyatt, the free black son of Chesley Faucette, became a full person with a political status. Wyatt, son of Chesley, became Wyatt Outlaw.

There was a final, fateful, brotherhood that some Faucettes created out of the crucible of Alamance. The White Brotherhood merged public and private by defining the public as a closed union of white men. They claimed to represent the true foundation of politics in Alamance by issuing public orders that ignored the county's vested authority. They claimed that black men's entrance into the public world was a violation that they would correct.[51]

This claim that black emancipation violated public order was difficult to sustain, and few North Carolinians would have accepted it on its face. It worked as a strategy only when one accepted that the first penetration of public and private—conscription, arrest, suspension of habeas corpus, and imprisonment—was directly connected to the second penetration of public and private—emancipation, expanded franchise, and a biracial Republican Party. If Governor William Holden could be made to look as repugnant as Jefferson Davis, only then could a white conservative party seize power in North Carolina and end Reconstruction.

As white voters embraced men who called themselves conservatives, Civil War and Reconstruction ended. It was Wyatt, the last Faucette to become an "outlaw," who paid the price.

NOTES

The Summer Research Grant at the College of William and Mary helped fund part of the research here, as did William and Mary's Charles Center, which provided funds for a summer research assistant. Robin Conner spent the summer of 1997 helping me cull information from the Tourgée Papers and trial transcripts. The author is grateful for useful comments and criticism of Catherine Clinton, Cindy Hahamovitch, Martha Hodes, and Michael P. Johnson about the version of this paper delivered at the "Families at War" conference in April 1998. Carole Troxler has also gracefully shared with me a draft of her work on Alamance County during the war.

1. On the idea of public and private see Jürgen Habermas, *The Structural Transformation of the Public Sphere: An Inquiry into a Category of Bourgeois Society* (Cambridge: MIT Press, 1989). Habermas's book was originally published in German in 1962 and has influenced a generation of historians. See, e.g., Mary Ryan, "Gender and Public Access: Women's Politics in Nineteenth-Century America," in *Habermas and the Public Sphere*, ed. Craig Calhoun (Cambridge: MIT Press, 1992).

2. On Alamance County's growth, see Durward T. Stokes, *Company Shops: The Town Built by a Railroad* (Winston-Salem, N.C.: John F. Blair, 1981); and Bess Beatty, *Alamance: The Holt Family and Industrialization in a North Carolina County, 1837–1900* (Baton Rouge: Louisiana State University Press, 1999). Thanks to Mark Faucette, a modern descendant and a math professor at the State University of West Georgia, who sent me his genealogical research about the Alamance Faucettes. Mark Faucette, "Genealogical Notes" (in the author's possession), copies the list of Chesley Faucette's children in the Faucette family

Bible. In the 1840s William A. Graham was a state senator. By the 1850s he became a national figure, as secretary of the navy under President Millard Fillmore and later governor of North Carolina.

3. *The South: The Southern Business Directory and General Commercial Advertiser*, vol. 1 (Charleston, S.C.: Steam Power Press of Walker and James, 1854), reprinted as fiche no. 1393 in *City Directories of the United States, 1960–1901* (Woodbridge, Conn.: Research Publications, 1983), 4.

4. *Hillsborough Recorder*, March 2, 1870 ["White"]; H. S. Rike to Andrew Jackson Rike, December 24, 1871, in Andrew Jackson Rike Papers, Southern Historical Collection, University of North Carolina at Chapel Hill ["Wiet"]; "For Commissioners of Town of Graham," July 28, 1868, in William W. Holden Papers, North Carolina Division of Archives and History, Raleigh ["Wiatt"]. On the family relationship between Wyatt and Chesley, see H. S. Rike to Andrew Jackson Rike, above.

5. Indeed, she noted that after the surrender, when "Wyatt" sought to register his children and his relationship to his mother, a county official (Monroe Cook) appeared to have inadvertently listed her relationship with her son as a marriage. See *Trial of William W. Holden, Governor of North Carolina, before the Senate of North Carolina* (Raleigh: Sentinel Printing Office, 1871), 1368, hereafter cited as Holden Trial.

6. U.S. Seventh Manuscript Census, 1850, Alamance County, N.C., Slave Schedule. It was only after the war that Wyatt chose the name Outlaw; he was known only as Wyatt before the war. Outlaw's connection to the NCRR is a guess, as it was a private letter between white railroad workers that revealed Wyatt's parentage to me. See H. S. Rike to Andrew Jackson Rike, December 24, 1871, Andrew Jackson Rike Papers.

7. Alamance County, 1870 Mortality Schedule, reprinted in http://www.rootsweb.com/~ncalaman/alms1870.html (as of July 2000); Testimony of Paul R. Hambrick, 1st Lieut. U.S. Army, in U.S. Congress, 41st Congress, 3d Session, Ex. Doc. no. 16, pt. 1, "Message of the President of the United States Communicating in Further Compliance with the Resolution of the Senate of the 16th of December, 1870, Information in Relation to Outrages committed by Disloyal Persons in North Carolina, and other Southern States," 60 ["mechanic"]; U.S. Congress, 42d Congress, 1st Session, Report No. 1, "Report of the Select Committee to Investigate Alleged Outrages in the Southern States," cxii ["carriagemaker"], hereafter cited as Committee on Alleged Outrages.

8. Stokes, *Company Shops*, 40–42.

9. J. G. de Roulhac Hamilton, ed., *The Papers of Thomas Ruffin* (Raleigh: Edwards and Broughton, 1920), 3:142.

10. Mark Faucette, "Genealogical Notes," April 1997.

11. Conscription by armies had taken place before that date. See Brigadier-General H. Marshall to Gen. Robert E. Lee, April 10, 1862, *Official Records*

of the War of the Rebellion, ser. 1 (Washington, D.C.: Government Printing Office, 1880–1901), 10:418; Allan R. Millett and Peter Maslowski, *For the Common Defense: A Military History of the United States of America* (New York: Macmillan, 1984), 196–97.

12. W. H. Younce, *The Adventures of a Conscript* (Cincinnati: Editor Publishing Co., 1899).

13. "The Writ of Habeas Corpus Resisted," *North Carolina Standard*, January 9, 1863; "Suspension of the Habeas Corpus Act in Salisbury and for ten miles around," *North Carolina Standard*, January 23, 1863.

14. B. F. Booth, *Dark Days of the Rebellion; or, Life in Southern Military Prisons* (Indianola, Iowa: Booth, 1897), 113–18.

15. Mary Jane Allen to John Mebane Allen, April 1864, John Mebane Allen Papers, Southern Historical Collection.

16. Ibid.

17. J. G. de Roulhac Hamilton, *Reconstruction in North Carolina* (Raleigh, N.C.: Edwards and Broughton, 1906); William T. Auman and David D. Scarboro, "The Heroes of America in Civil War North Carolina," *North Carolina Historical Review* 58 (October 1981): 327–63; the story of Rahab is found in the Book of Joshua, chap. 2.

18. Auman and Scarboro, "Heroes of America," 344–48.

19. "Justice" could have been Badham, Albright, or Chesley Faucette.

20. "Suspension of the Habeas Corpus Act."

21. "The Great Writ of Right," *North Carolina Standard*, January 30, 1863.

22. "Dangers to North Carolina," *North Carolina Standard*, January 1, 1864.

23. The *Standard* argued that although the number of legislators for the occupied states of Kentucky, Tennessee, Missouri, Arkansas, and Louisiana was based on the total population of the state, they were elected by a much smaller minority of Confederates. "Dangers to North Carolina," *North Carolina Standard*, January 1, 1864; "Habeas Corpus in the House," *North Carolina Standard*, May 27, 1864.

24. Thus the *North Carolina Standard* could approvingly reprint Alexander Stephens's states' rights critique of the Davis administration.

25. William T. Auman, "Neighbor against Neighbor: The Inner Civil War in the Central Counties of Confederate North Carolina" (Ph.D. dissertation, University of North Carolina, 1988), 123–57.

26. Mary Jane Allen to John Mebane Allen, April 1864, John Mebane Allen Papers. On Albright's vituperative qualities see Committee on Alleged Outrages, 340.

27. Auman and Scarboro, "Heroes of America," 348.

28. *North Carolina Standard*, August 9, 12, November 29, December 9, 1864.

29. *North Carolina Standard*, January 26, February 19, June 7, July 1, 5, 8, 1864.

30. *North Carolina Standard*, July 1, 1864.

SCOTT REYNOLDS NELSON

31. On the powers of the superintendent of railroads see "Proceedings of the House of Representatives in Secret Session on the Military Bill," *North Carolina Standard*, February 16, 1864. On Albert Johnson of the NCRR see "Proscription for Opinion Sake," *North Carolina Standard*, July 5, 1864; "Biographical Sketch of Albert Johnson," in William H. Richardson Papers, North Carolina Division of Archives and History. On members of the Heroes, see Auman and Scarboro, "Heroes of America," 350–51, 361.

32. William A. Smith to Kemp P. Battle, February 11, 1884, William A. Smith Papers, North Carolina Division of Archives and History.

33. His name appears as Wright Outlaw. Albion Tourgée gives an account of Nimbus Ware in his novel *Bricks without Straw* that led me to the U.S. Colored Troops roster. The name Nimbus is given him by his master, as a joke about the darkness of his skin, just as White or Wyatt may have been a joke about the whiteness of Wyatt's skin. In that story Nimbus DeSmit is the trusted servant who is asked to head a work gang that will be used by the Confederacy for fortifications. He escapes across Union lines and joins Company B of the Massachusetts Volunteer Infantry, where he assumes a different last name, Ware. It is possible that Wyatt Phillips/Faucette/Outlaw was a model for Nimbus DeSmit/Ware, in that Outlaw was the model of the central character in Tourgée's other novel of that same year, *A Fool's Errand*. The roster of U.S. Colored Troops is searchable on the National Park Service web site at http://www.itd.nps.gov/cwss/regiments.html (July 2000). A different account of the models for Tourgée's characters is given in Peter Jerome Caccavari, "Reconstructions of Race and Culture in America: Violence and Knowledge in Works by Albion Tourgée, Charles Chesnutt, and Thomas Dixon, Jr." (Ph.D. dissertation, Rutgers—The State University of New Jersey, 1993).

34. Committee on Alleged Outrages, 78–82.

35. Holden Trial, 619, 1133–34, 1198–99, 1363–68, 1917–18, 2051; Committee on Alleged Outrages, 270.

36. Holden Trial, 491.

37. In 1868 African Americans numbered 16 of 72 shop workers and 345 of the 455 (nearly 76 percent) maintenance workers. North Carolina Railroad, *Annual Report*, 1868, 27–39; Payroll Records, 1862, 1864, February 1871, North Carolina Railroad Collection, North Carolina Division of Archives and History; Minutes, December 1867, Court of Pleas and Quarter Sessions, Alamance County, North Carolina Division of Archives and History. The other barroom was owned by J. T. Trollinger and stood within sight of the train. Trollinger would later be an officer in the Ku Klux Klan. William W. Holden, ed., *Third Annual Message of Governor W. W. Holden* (Raleigh: Jo. W. Holden, State Printer and Binder, 1871), 182; testimony of E. M. Holt, Committee on Alleged Outrages, 252. These summonses are somewhat suspicious, as the pages from the years in which Outlaw was a

town commissioner were torn out and the back pages were placed in the ledger. It is these pasted-in back pages that are summonses for Outlaw. It is possible that after Outlaw was killed, the clerk of court doctored the records to give justification for the Klan's murder of Outlaw. In any case, because Outlaw served as commissioner but does not appear in the county records, it is difficult to trust the county records for these years.

38. Committee on Alleged Outrages, 41, 87, 97–99, 132, 144–47, 269; Holden Trial, 2039–51 ("courage" is from Committee, 146; "Mr. Outlaw" is from Holden Trial, 1198–99).

39. Paul D. Escott, *Many Excellent People: Power and Privilege in North Carolina, 1850–1900* (Chapel Hill: University of North Carolina Press, 1985).

40. In fact, Holden's right to make these appointments was by the military commander of the district. See E. R. S. Canby, Charleston, S.C., to W. W. Holden, July 17, 1868, William W. Holden Papers, North Carolina Division of Archives and History.

41. "For Commissioners of Town of Graham," July 27, 1868, in William W. Holden Papers, North Carolina Division of Archives and History; Holden Trial, 491, 1899–1901.

42. U.S. Sixth Manuscript Census, 1840, North Carolina, Orange County, 201, and Alamance County, 71; Robert Iobst, *The Bloody Sixth*, app. 1.

43. Payroll Records, February 1871, North Carolina Railroad Collection, North Carolina Division of Archives and History; Confession of George Faucett [December 1871], item 1568, Albion W. Tourgée Papers (microfilm), Swem Library, College of William and Mary.

44. Holden Trial, 625; W. A. Albright to Gov. Holden, August 19, 1868, W. W. Holden Papers. This note communicated that they were not yet ready to swear in all officers.

45. J. W. Schenk, Wilmington, to Gov. Holden, July 15, 1868; J. R. Bulla, Asheboro, N.C., to Gov. Holden, July 15, 1868, W. W. Holden Papers.

46. R. T. Bosher to His Excellency, March 25, [1869], Detective Reports, Box 10, General Assembly Session Records, 1870–71, North Carolina Division of Archives and History; *Greensboro Patriot*, June 6, 1872.

47. Confession of George Faucett. On the state detectives corps, see Stephen E. Massengill, "The Detectives of William W. Holden, 1869–1870," *North Carolina Historical Review* 62 (October 1985): 448–87.

48. "Grant & Wilson . . . Stirring Speech by Judge Tourgée of North Carolina," clipping file, item 1568, Albion W. Tourgée Papers (microfilm); Holden Trial, 1469–70.

49. Allen W. Trelease, *White Terror: The Ku Klux Klan Conspiracy and Southern Reconstruction* (New York: Harper and Row, 1971), 192–223; Scott Reynolds Nelson, *Iron Confederacies: Southern Railways, Klan Violence, and Reconstruction* (Chapel Hill: University of North Carolina Press, 1999).

50. I am indebted to Ronald Schechter for this understanding of the broader definition of emancipation.

51. A similar phenomenon, more explicitly sexualized, occurred in South Carolina. See Scott Reynolds Nelson, "Livestock, Boundaries, and Public Space in Spartanburg: African-American Men, Elite White Women and the Spectacle of Conjugal Relations," in *Sex, Love, Race: Crossing Boundaries in North American History*, ed. Martha Hodes (New York: New York University Press, 1999).

Highland Households Divided

Family Deceptions, Diversions, and Divisions in Southern Appalachia's Inner Civil War

JOHN C. INSCOE AND GORDON B. McKINNEY

*L*ate in 1863 Madison Drake, a Union captain from Wisconsin, escaped from a Confederate prison in Salisbury, North Carolina, and made his way with a group of fellow fugitives into the state's mountains toward the safety of Union-occupied East Tennessee. In a published account of that journey, he described an encounter he and his party had in Caldwell County, on the eastern slopes of the Blue Ridge. As they approached a small mountain homestead seeking food and directions, Captain Drake and his companions encountered a "vixen" of a woman who immediately recognized them as Yankee fugitives and gave them an impassioned tongue-lashing. Spewing her hatred of them and threatening to turn them in to local authorities, she assured them that they would hang from the same tree on which an earlier Northern fugitive had met his demise, and that she would gladly help carry out the execution.

Yet all hope of aid from this household was not lost, for the crippled husband of this "vixen" sat on the stoop and listened passively "while his spouse was declaiming against us so virulently." When she concluded her tirade, he winked at the men and, hobbling off the stoop, motioned for them to follow him. At a safe distance from the house, this "happy or unhappy husband," as Drake called him, married only six weeks, confided that he sympathized with their cause. He informed them that he had served in the Confederate army until he had been wounded and discharged. Two of his brothers, also Confederates, had been captured in battle, had "taken the oath," and were doing good business in the North. He was determined to do likewise and saw Drake and his companions as a means for his own escape. He "resolved to befriend" the fugitives and proposed guiding them across the mountains to Union lines if they would return with other forces and take him prisoner, thus allowing him to escape both impending conscription and his shrewish bride. Their conference was cut short by his wife's appearance, which sent the fugitives scurrying on their way, abandoning the "kind-hearted but unfortunate" husband to her supervision.[1]

Drake's story reveals three basic features of wartime Unionism in the mountain South: first, that it often took a very fluid form, the crippled husband having changed sides at least once since the war's outbreak; second, that the divisions between Union and Confederate loyalties were often localized, splitting not only communities and neighborhoods, but even families and households; and finally, that such divisions, and the tensions they generated, often meant some level of deception among family or household members.

If this particular scenario, of a husband concealing his sentiments from his wife, seems an extreme one, it was not unique. It is one of several documented accounts of Appalachian households in which family members—husbands and wives or parents and children—were divided in their loyalties to the Northern or Southern cause, and in which at least one party felt the need to keep his or her feelings concealed from those with whom they lived. This was part of a phenomenon Michael Fellman, in his study of the Civil War in Missouri, termed "survival lying." Individuals and families who lived in areas sharply divided and wracked by guerrilla warfare were often forced to practice extensive deception and role-playing to protect themselves and their households. "Loyalty was not the safest and most common presentation of self during this guerrilla war," Fellman noted; "prevarication was. Frankness and directness led to destruction more often than did reticence and withdrawal."[2]

Such was certainly true of southern Appalachia as well. Within the Confederacy, no region experienced more of such internal upheaval, and thus the need for deception and role-playing than did the mountain South.

With fewer slaves and more tenuous ties to the market economy, many—but by no means all—highlanders in North Carolina, Tennessee, Virginia, and Georgia found themselves increasingly alienated from the rest of their states as the sectional crisis unfolded. Some expressed vehement opposition to secession and remained firmly committed to the Union cause, either openly or more subversively, long after the war was under way. Many others resigned themselves to what they saw as the inevitability of the new nation into which they were forced by the vast majority of non–mountain residents who dominated their states, but they did so only halfheartedly. A North Carolina woman probably spoke for many, as she bemoaned that new reality: "The Union is gone and all these things follow it. . . . How quietly we drifted into such an awful night into the darkness, the lowering clouds, the howling winds, and the ghostly light of our former glory."[3]

Those political and ideological divisions, and the emotional baggage they often carried, were already established, if often still fluid, as the secession crisis played out and were exacerbated by the war that followed. A stronger political base and more effective leadership kept Unionist sentiment far more viable among East Tennesseans than among western North Carolinians, who quickly capitulated to the Confederate cause after the attack on Fort Sumter, though pockets of Unionist strength continued to exist there, just as Confederate enclaves emerged across the state line in the Tennessee mountains.[4] Thus many households and/or individuals quickly acquired minority status locally as either Confederate or Union sympathizers, depending upon the predominant sentiments of the communities of which they were a part. Some Appalachian families were made more vulnerable by the instability caused by the military and political power struggles that wracked certain highland regions. Such was particularly true of East Tennessee, where Confederate control over a hostile civilian majority during the war's first half capitulated to Union forces from mid-1863 on. The brutal harshness of early Rebel occupation policies led to equally harsh retaliation and vindictiveness, as once-oppressed Unionists became the oppressors of their disunionist neighbors and kinsmen.

From such divisions the war degenerated into a harrowing guerrilla conflict in much of the mountain South. As a Georgia Unionist escaping northward during the war noted as he moved into the Smoky Mountains, "I knew that we were now approaching the border country where some were Secessionists and others Union people, and with each step we took our danger from bushwhackers and scouts increased. . . . all showed me that we were gradually getting into the bloody ground of western North Carolina

JOHN C. INSCOE AND GORDON B. MCKINNEY

and East Tennessee, where neighbor fought with neighbor and brother slew brother."[5] In so volatile and uncertain an atmosphere, questions of allegiance and commitment were never far from the surface.

The scholarship on the Civil War in Appalachia is growing by leaps and bounds, and those same issues of identity and divided loyalties now preoccupy historians as much as they did those we study.[6] Although we know much about how highland Unionists fared as minorities and majorities in the context of region, of community, and even of neighborhood, we have not yet explored in any substantive way the extent to which divided loyalties penetrated that most intimate of social institutions: the family. These familial divisions—between spouses and between generations—highlight at its most basic level the uncertainties and fluctuations of ideological commitments among Southern highlanders. In examining the variety of motives and influences that pushed families into such awkward and on occasion destructive circumstances, we hope to reveal even more about the multifaceted nature of loyalty and patriotism and how they shaped the localized dynamics of family and kinship structure during this most divisive of American wars.

First, a look at several other examples of such household divisions. An Indiana officer who led a group of escapees from Camp Sorghum in Columbia, South Carolina, toward Union lines in Tennessee crossed paths with three sisters from the Hollinger family in Flat Rock, North Carolina. The fugitives presented themselves as Confederate troops in what they knew to be a predominantly pro-Southern neighborhood.[7] Only after the oldest, and boldest, of the three young women (who ranged in age from twenty-four to sixteen) vehemently denounced the men, the South, and the cause for which they were fighting, did the Indianans reveal their true colors. Once the Hollinger sisters were convinced that they were indeed Federal soldiers, they generously offered them aid. Over the next three days they fed the fugitives, provided them concealed shelter, and procured a guide to lead them across the mountains into Tennessee, as they had already done for other Union fugitives.

But the sisters too were engaged in "survival lying," for as they explained to the men in their care, two of them were married to Confederate soldiers. They also sought to shield their parents from their activities and refused to let the men in their charge approach their house. For although both parents were equally strong Unionists, the family lived as tenants on the summer estate of the Charlestonian Christopher Memminger, secretary of the Confederate treasury. The daughters believed that the less their father knew of their caretaking efforts, the safer his position was, both within this

Henderson County community and on Memminger's estate. Thus, in effect, these daughters and wives conducted an underground railroad operation for Northern troops and sympathizers without the knowledge of either their parents or their husbands, though the reasons for concealing their activity from the two differed.[8]

Despite the predominance of Unionist sentiment among Tennessee's highlanders, strong pockets of Confederate sympathy forced some Unionists there to engage in surreptitious activity, often at considerable risk, to oppose the cause for which other family members fought. Jeannette Mabry of Knox County was married to a Confederate colonel, and his family held strong Southern sentiments; yet she remained "unflinchingly true to the Union," and her actions as an informant and as a caretaker of Union soldiers and their families made her legendary among participants of a guerrilla war that devastated Tennessee's Smoky Mountains. Mabry made herself an indispensable contact for Union guides operating in and around Knoxville. No guide, it was said, considered his mission complete unless he stopped to trade intelligence with Mrs. Mabry. Her relative affluence and social position and the variety of charitable acts she undertook on behalf of refugees and indigents made her a particularly visible figure, and even an inspiration to other Unionists in the area. Oliver Temple, among her most ardent admirers, wrote of her impact in his decidedly partisan account of the war in East Tennessee: "Around the camp-fires in Kentucky, and in other distant fields where duty called them, no name left behind was uttered more frequently by the exiles, nor with a tenderer or more sincere invocation of a blessing on it, than that of Jeannette Laurimer Mabry."[9] Yet neither Temple nor the other accounts mention what her heroic actions meant to her Confederate husband or in-laws.

Another group of Federal fugitives encountered such deception across generations—a Unionist mother who kept her subversive activity secret from her Confederate son. West Virginian Michael Egan and two Ohio companions, fleeing across the remote wilderness of southwestern North Carolina, made contact with a Henry Grant, a "fire-tried Unionist." Grant, wrote Egan, wanted to "relieve our distress and give us the shelter of his hospitable roof at once, but there is a slight obstacle in the way—there is an armed rebel soldier in the house." This young Confederate was a neighbor, home on leave, and the dilemma was resolved only when Grant confided in the soldier's widowed mother, who lived in the adjoining house. To their surprise, they found that "she had no real sympathy with the Southern cause," despite the fact that her only son was fighting for it. She agreed to take the Union refugees under her roof, concealing both their presence and their identities from her son.[10]

Not all such ideological splits between spouses involved deception at that most intimate level; in some cases, deceiving others involved a partner's complicity. In the poignant case of a North Carolina highlander, related in a memoir he titled *The Adventures of a Conscript*, W. H. (or "Buck") Younce revealed the high price he paid romantically for his initial refusal to resort to "survival lying." As a committed Unionist in a predominantly Confederate neighborhood in Ashe County, Younce lay low during the war's first year. Only as the pressures of conscription loomed large in the fall of 1862 did he move with others across the state line into Tennessee, a mere six miles from his home, in order to enlist in a Union company. In so doing, he passed by the home of his fiancée, Edith Carroll, and despite the advice of his two companions, Younce separated from them to spend the first night of his trek at the Carroll home.

Younce, a mere twenty years old at the time, was fully aware that the Carrolls, including Edith, the youngest of three daughters, were strongly Confederate, even though they were among the few families so inclined in this northeasternmost corner of Tennessee. On earlier visits, according to Younce, Edith had "used all the persuasive powers at her command to influence me to volunteer in the Confederate army, but I always met her arguments with my side of the question, and her influence proved to no avail." Edith was surprised to see Buck on this particular night, and despite his efforts to obscure his reason for being in her neighborhood, she reached the correct conclusion and protested vehemently: "Oh, no; it can't be possible that you are fleeing for refuge! You can not only be turning your back upon your own country in the darkest hour of our peril, but by this act blasting every hope for an honorable and useful life in the future." Seeking to shame her young beau, Edith ended her speech by proclaiming: "O, if I were only a man, how I would teach you a lesson in patriotism by shouldering my musket and marching to the front!"

Buck responded with an equally impassioned denunciation of "the wicked and unjust cause" she represented and insisted that "the Government to which you refer so eloquently is not my country. . . . I cannot and will not fight for a government that seeks to enslave me and whose cornerstone is slavery." Edith resigned herself to the firm resolve of her betrothed, with a final speech assuring him of her personal loyalty to him. "It grieves me," she said, "that you have determined on this course, but I assure you that, come what may, not a word or deed of mine shall ever do you harm. I will shield and protect you so far as it is in my power to do so."

Alas, such assurances from his hostess proved worthless, when only minutes later a home guard force from Ashe County, having been alerted by some witness (Edith's father, perhaps?) to Younce's presence there, arrived at the house, where they were admitted by Mr. Carroll, who turned Buck over to them. In a dramatic confrontation with his Confederate captors, Edith tearfully inquired about his fate, which led the leader of the group, a Mr. Long, to recognize the reason for Buck's presence in this pro-Southern household. "You are insane, or perhaps worse, in love," he accused Buck. "I do not know which: but I do know you are not in love with your country." The young prisoner, still defiant, responded: "Yes, sire, I am in love with—Liberty."

Buck's captors escorted him back to North Carolina and into the Ashe County jail. A day later, an influential friend and Confederate captain approached Younce and offered the option of volunteering for service in his company, rather than face conscription or imprisonment as a deserter. Reluctantly, Younce agreed to do so and marched off to fight with fifty other recruits the next day.

"I was the hero of the occasion," he later wrote. "There was more rejoicing over one sinner that repented than over ninety and nine that went not astray." But, he continued, "they could not read my thoughts. My purposes were the same, and I believed that I would find refuge under the flag of my country someday," which he did indeed before the year was out.

This lapse into "survival lying" proved all too temporary and failed to serve Buck Younce's romantic interests, if indeed Edith Carroll ever heard of his celebrated conversion. These two young lovers were separated by their two very different senses of patriotism and a father who proved far less willing than did his daughter to tolerate those differences. Only at the end of Younce's memoir does Edith's name appear again. Writing in 1901, he informed his readers that she had married another man just after the war's end and was the mother of a grown family. "I have never seen her," he concluded, "since that midnight parting before mentioned"; he made no mention at all of a wife or family of his own.[11]

In some cases the tensions caused by these more open divisions within families led to violent consequences. The murder of a prominent Confederate in northwestern North Carolina was the result, in part, of a family squabble resulting from a marriage that linked two families on opposite sides. Late in the spring of 1864, in the North Fork community, which straddled Watauga

John Hunt Morgan's raiders. Daniel Ellis, *The Thrilling Adventures of Daniel Ellis* (1867).

and Ashe Counties, Isaac Wilson was plowing a field on his farm while home on furlough when he was shot and killed by members of the Potter family, into which his niece had married. Tensions between the Confederate Wilsons and the Unionist Potters had escalated as a result of the marriage that made them in-laws, with particular resentment on the part of the bride's family. As part of the local home guard, other Wilsons had been among those who had executed Jack Potter, the groom's father, several months earlier, and in feudlike retaliation other Potter men and their "bushwhacking" accomplices, lying in ambush in woods surrounding Isaac Wilson's farm, fired upon and killed their in-law and the community's most prominent Confederate soldier.[12]

Another death, resulting at least in part from divided allegiances within a Greenville, Tennessee, household, had even greater historical significance. Because the victim in that case was the Rebel raider and Confederate general John Hunt Morgan, the family in whose home he spent his last night alive remains the most famous, or perhaps infamous, divided house in the mountain South. Greenville was a major Unionist stronghold and the home of Andrew Johnson, but Morgan knew and often stayed with the town's most notable pro-Southern hostess, Catherine Williams. Williams, the widow of a physician, had two sons in Confederate service and a third who was a Federal officer. It may have been Morgan's misfortune that the wife of that third son, herself an ardent Unionist, was living with her mother-in-law when he and his staff took up quarters there on September 4, 1864.

Although historians disagree about the subsequent course of events, circumstantial evidence at the time suggested, and popular opinion quickly assumed, that Lucy Williams, the "Yankee" daughter-in-law, slipped away from the house as soon as she knew Morgan would be staying there and alerted Union forces about fifteen miles away. Early the next morning those troops surrounded the Williams house and killed Morgan as he tried to escape through a nearby vineyard. Lucy herself adamantly maintained her innocence in the affair, but her denials were suspect, given that her continued residence with her mother-in-law was probably dependent on how convincing she was in establishing her innocence in the events that brought such notoriety to that house and its residents. It is revealing that the presumption of her complicity in Morgan's death, as detested and feared as he was by most Greenville residents, led to Lucy's own social ostracism in this Unionist community. She was soon forced to move to Knoxville and later was divorced from Catherine Williams's Unionist son. Rather than being hailed as a heroine by her Unionist compatriots, it seems that Lucy Williams was shunned for betraying both a houseguest and the mother-in-law under whose roof she lived.[13]

Women's roles in these divided households were not always as active or subversive agents. In at least one highland household, a mother served merely as peacemaker between her Union and Confederate sons. A folk history of Tennessee's Smoky Mountains includes the story of Nancy Ghormley's family in Chilhowee. Visits home by two of her sons, one serving the South as Tennessee's provost-marshal, the other as a Confederate recruiting officer, were interrupted when three other sons and two grandsons, all wearing Union blue, also returned home. As the two groups encountered each other in the front yard, "talk became spirited," and "hands rested on sword hilts." At that point Nancy Ghormley took matters into her own hands by walking outside, announcing that dinner was ready, and instructing her offspring: "Gentlemen, leave your guns and swords in the yard and come in to dinner. You are all my children." The fact that the story ends there implies that these were boys who listened to their mother.[14]

Each of the divided households described above was an anomaly. No patterns emerge from this varied array of stories to suggest that such familial tensions were integral parts of the social upheavals that wracked the mountain South from 1861 to 1865. In fact, each of these cases flies in the face of what was perhaps the most obvious and universally agreed upon factor in Appalachia's war within a war—the remarkable extent of kinship solidarity in terms of wartime loyalties. If the strength of family bonds has long been

JOHN C. INSCOE AND GORDON B. MCKINNEY

recognized as a predominant characteristic of Southern society, it has been an even more conspicuous facet of Appalachia's image. From early stereotyping of the clannishness and even inbreeding of Southern highlanders to the myths and realities of the infamous feuds to sociological analyses of the 1960s and 1970s, family ties for better or worse have been central components in Americans' perceptions of "this strange land and peculiar people."[15]

The recent scholarship on the Civil War in the Southern highlands has also acknowledged the centrality of family bonds. Historians recognize—and debate—a number of determinants of loyalties of mountaineers: socioeconomic and slaveholding status, political partisanship, spatial patterns of settlement and market accessibility, migratory patterns and duration of residence, even religious affiliations. But of all the variables that help explain such allegiances, almost all scholars of the region seem to agree that the most immediate and consistent determinant of one's Unionist or Confederate identity lay in the allegiance of one's family.

Community studies make this point particularly well. Philip Paludan's book on the Shelton Laurel massacre in Madison County, North Carolina, Durwood Dunn's on Cades Cove, Tennessee, Martin Crawford's on the war in Ashe County, North Carolina, and Altina Waller's on the Hatfield-McCoy feud in the Tug Valley of Kentucky and West Virginia, along with work in progress by Ralph Mann on Sandy Basin, Virginia, Tracy McKenzie on Knoxville, Tennessee, and Jonathan Sarris on two north Georgia counties, all find kin networks to have been central in explaining the loyalty or disloyalty of individuals or households within neighborhoods or communities.[16] In the most detailed reconstruction of such localized loyalties, Mann contends that the residents of Sandy Basin looked back at the Civil War "as a war of family against family, or more precisely, family group against family group," and that within neighborhoods that included "a wide range of individual personalities and convictions. . . . ultimately kin pressure promoted family group solidarity on matters concerning the war."[17]

So how does one account for these splits within some highland households? No single explanation can account for the various situations described here. For several, though, the very fact of family solidarity serves to explain such divisions rather than contradict them. The ideological differences between married couples were, more often than not, due to the differing loyalties of the two families from which they came. It is telling that so many of these households were newly constructed and so many couples newlyweds; one of the most revealing such instances related here is that of the marriage that never took place because of such divisions. The star-crossed, and state-line-crossing, lovers Buck Younce and Edith Carroll each adhered to the ideological stance of their parents, despite the fact that the Younce family's Unionism and the Carrolls' pro-Confederate stance were minority positions in their respective communities.

Although such differences prevented Buck and Edith from becoming husband and wife, other marriages across similar lines did take place. The Caldwell County "vixen" and her crippled groom, whose story opened this essay, were only just married when he sought to make his escape from her and the Confederate war effort. The Hollinger sisters in Flat Rock adhered to the antislaveholding sentiments of their parents, into whose home they returned, rather than to the Confederate stance of their absent husbands. And the assassination of Isaac Wilson stemmed in part from resentment of his niece's marriage on the part of her Unionist in-laws.

The sheer tentativeness and fluidity of sentiment in areas characterized by partisan confusion may account for some of the differences among family members. Such wavering was evident from the war's beginning and became even more pronounced as the brutality and hardship of the conflict, or mere war-weariness, set in. In May 1861, in the midst of a Confederate rally in Wilkes County, North Carolina, until that time the area's acknowledged Union stronghold, an observer described the dramatic shift in the community's sentiments but noted the superficial nature of the change: "The people seem nearly united in the Cause of the South," wrote James Gwyn, "but I think if an influential man had got up and espoused the other side, he would have had a good many to join them."[18] Oliver Temple, the earliest chronicler of East Tennessee Unionism, also recognized local pressures as determinants of how individuals formed their allegiances. "Sympathy with friends and kindred," he wrote, "became the bond that united the South. Tens of thousands of men who had no heart for secession, did have heart for their neighbors and kindred. This almost universal fellowship and sympathy drew men together in behalf of a cause which one-half of them disapproved."[19]

It has taken a novelist to pinpoint an even more basic reason that young mountain men at least initially cast their lot with the new Southern nation within which they found themselves. In *Cold Mountain*, his celebrated epic of the war in the Carolina highlands, Charles Frazier suggests that baser instincts shaped those decisions. In reflecting on the reasons men go to war, and this war in particular, his central character, Inman, concludes that it was "change" or "the promise of it that made up the war frenzy in the early days. The powerful draw of new faces, new places, new lives. And new laws whereby you might kill all you wanted and not be jailed but decorated." Frazier elaborated: "Men talked of war as if they committed it to preserve what they had and what they believed. But Inman guessed that it was boredom with the repetition of the daily rounds that had made them take up weapons. . . . War took a man out of that circle of regular life and made a season of its own, not much dependent on anything else. He had not been immune to its pull."[20] If indeed it was the novelty of the experience that led highlanders to enlist, such sentiments were no doubt among the first to be abandoned as the war dragged on and the novelty quickly wore off.

The superficial and often fickle nature of those loyalties was fast becoming apparent by early 1862. Increasing desertion rates and other forms of disaffection began to expose what another highlander observed, that many who had sworn allegiance to the Confederacy did so "only from the teeth out."[21] Such shallow commitments may well have led one family member to abandon the cause for which others in the household continued to fight. Desertion was merely one indication of many highlanders' war-weariness and lack of enthusiasm for the cause they had fought for. While hardships at home often lured men back home, sometimes such desertion came sooner than wives or other family members found honorable or acceptable. Thus the crippled husband ready to accompany Madison Drake and company out of the South completely stemmed from war-weariness in battle, while his bride remained staunchly committed to the Southern cause that he, unknown to her, had abandoned. By the same token, those men facing more traditional military situations away from home were not subject to the same demoralizing home-front hardships, deprivations, or upheaval that made spouses, elderly parents, or younger siblings more susceptible to fluctuations in their loyalties and commitments to the war. The mother who agreed to shelter Michael Egan and his companions had undergone a thorough change of heart that her Confederate son, still in uniform, had not.

Equally significant, guerrilla warfare forced full families into a level of participation that more traditional warfare never did. In the process gender roles were blurred or even reversed. Women sometimes found themselves taking far more active, even dominant, roles in protecting their men or defending their property; they also found opportunities to provide military and other intelligence, to aid fugitives and refugees, and on occasion to betray enemies. In the fullest treatment of the subject, Michael Fellman wrote of Missouri's "inside war": "Disintegration, demoralization, and perverse adaptation engulfed women's behavior and self conceptions as it assaulted the

Appalachian women in guerrilla activity. Drake, *Fast and Loose in Dixie* (1880).

family and undermined male-female and female-female . . . relationships. Like male civilians in a guerrilla war theater, women were both victims and actors."[22]

Such was certainly the case in southern Appalachia as well. Both soldiers and civilians recognized the clout women wielded in waging the unconventional warfare in the mountains. Given the circumstances that later led to the death of his commander, there is a certain irony in the fact that it was one of John Hunt Morgan's officers who observed of East Tennesseans: "Did I stay long in this country, I should fear losing that respect and regard for the female sex, which I have been raised to have—here they unsex themselves, and by their conduct, lose all claim to be respected and regarded as ladies. . . . Was I in authority here, I should treat them as men."[23]

For some mountain women the responsibilities such localized warfare thrust upon them in their husbands' absence instilled an independence of spirit that led them to form loyalties different from those of the men who had left them. Or if other factors may have led to their differing loyalties, the new assertiveness either forced upon or granted to them led women to express their sentiments in visible or vocal ways. Although many engaged in "survival lying" for very practical reasons even within their own households, others spoke out or even lashed out, becoming like the "talking heroine" that a Winchester, Virginia, woman admiringly labeled a neighbor.[24] Given the volatility of local feelings and the levels of violence across gender lines, to

JOHN C. INSCOE AND GORDON B. MCKINNEY

speak one's convictions was often very risky. Other women, such as Jeannette Mabry, Lucy Williams, and the Hollinger sisters, did much more than talk. Through their actions in support of the Union and Federal troops, they actually shaped to varying degrees the dynamics of the conflict in their area.

Either articulating or acting upon their convictions, particularly when they differed from those of other family members, these women demonstrated another significant facet of their experience: they were not apolitical. The wives, mothers, and daughters in most of the households depicted in this essay not only made their views known to at least one observer, through whom they entered the historical record. They also took distinctive stands, adhered with great conviction to one cause or the other, and exhibited a strong sense of duty that sometimes put them and their households at considerable risk. It is telling that of all the examples cited here, only one woman ever took a neutral stand—Nancy Ghormley in her efforts to keep the peace among her sons at the dinner table.

Finally, one must acknowledge what is missing from most of these stories: how these household divisions were ultimately resolved. Although we have used the word *tensions* in describing these relationships, in most cases we have no direct evidence of that tension between spouses or between parents and children. This is in part because of the deception that prevented any open confrontation between family members, and in part, because family members were separated from each other, most often with a husband engaged in military service far from home. But what repercussions were there when the war ended, when these couples and other family members were reunited? Did love conquer all, and the joy of reunion override differing allegiances that by then would have been rendered irrelevant? Did "survival lying" perhaps extend through those reunions, with the hope that a lack of knowledge of a spouse's activities would allow a marriage to survive? The few answers we have from the couples we have dealt with here are not encouraging. The betrothal of a Unionist and his Confederate fiancée was broken as a result of these divisions. And in at least one instance, that of Lucy Williams, divorce resulted from her all too fateful betrayal against the Confederacy, or at least the notoriety attached to the assumption of betrayal. In the case of the Unionist cripple and his Confederate bride, one sees a marriage with very low odds of weathering the war-imposed tensions it would have had to endure. But we have no way of knowing the levels of deception, of forgiveness, or of affection that may have kept other marriages and households intact despite the tensions that had divided them during the war years.

A somewhat different scenario of household division is offered as a conclusion. If the practical necessities sometimes forced the "survival lying" of spouses, parents, and children, such duplicitous dual loyalties could, on occasion, provide unexpected benefits for those forced into such situations. Napoleon Banner and G. W. Dugger of Banner Elk, North Carolina, sent five sons between them into Union regiments in Tennessee but were themselves "detailed" by Confederate authorities to employment at the ironworks in nearby Cranberry. Such entanglements secured their safety, as Dugger's son later explained: "The Yankees passed over Napoleon for working for the South because he had three sons . . . in the Federal army, and the Homeguard let him off for being a Union man because he was hammering iron for the Confederacy." The elder Dugger was spared for the same reasons. "Thus," Shepherd Dugger summarized, "father and Napoleon sat on the top of a four-pointed barbed wire fence that divided the two armies, and so well did they balance themselves that they sat there four years and never got their hide split."[25]

Many Appalachian families found themselves perched precariously atop a barbed-wire fence during those four years of war. Some managed to maintain their balance better than others. In many parts of the Southern highlands, Unionists could not afford to flaunt openly their allegiance to what remained a minority cause and an enemy force for the region at large. The sheer variety of ways in which they maintained dual identities and the reasons they chose to do so—ranging from conscientious and ideological to opportunistic and mercenary—testify both to the variables in human nature and to the vacillations in loyalties and commitments toward the war and the fluidity with which they exerted themselves. For the most part, family bonds provided a vital resource in Southern highlanders' attempts to survive the multiple pressures—social, economic, military—the conflict imposed on the region. Yet the fact that, at least on occasion, such pressures forced families to fall on opposite sides of that conflict, often in deceptive or subversive ways, adds to our appreciation of the momentous local impact of this most uncivil of wars on that part of the South in which the bonds of kinship and family otherwise proved most durable.

NOTES

1. J. Madison Drake, *Fast and Loose in Dixie* (New York: Authors' Publishing Co., 1880), 140–41.

JOHN C. INSCOE AND GORDON B. MCKINNEY

2. Michael Fellman, *Inside War: Guerrilla Conflict in Missouri During the Civil War* (New York: Oxford University Press, 1989), 48–49.

3. Gordon B. McKinney, *Southern Mountain Republicans, 1865–1900: Politics and the Appalachian Community* (Chapel Hill: University of North Carolina Press, 1978), 19.

4. The literature on East Tennessee Unionism is vast. Among the most recent assessments of sentiments there during the secession crisis are Jonathan M. Atkins, *Parties, Politics, and the Sectional Conflict in Tennessee, 1832–1861* (Knoxville: University of Tennessee Press, 1997), chap. 8; Noel C. Fisher, *War at Every Door: Partisan Politics and Guerrilla Violence in East Tennessee, 1860–1869* (Chapel Hill: University of North Carolina Press, 1997), chap. 2; Peter Wallenstein, "'Helping to Save the Union': The Social Origins, Wartime Experiences, and Military Impact of White Union Troops from East Tennessee," and W. Todd Groce, "The Social Origins of East Tennessee's Confederate Leadership," both in *The Civil War in Appalachia: Collected Essays*, ed. Kenneth W. Noe and Shannon Wilson (Knoxville: University of Tennessee Press, 1997); and Robert Tracy McKenzie's essay in this volume. On the minority Confederate presence in that region, see W. Todd Groce, *Mountain Rebels: East Tennessee Confederates and the Civil War, 1860–1870* (Knoxville: University of Tennessee Press, 1999); and Daniel E. Sutherland, ed., *A Very Violent Rebel: The Civil War Diary of Ellen Renshaw House* (Knoxville: University of Tennessee Press, 1996).

On secession sentiment in western North Carolina, see John C. Inscoe, *Mountain Masters: Slavery and the Sectional Crisis in Western North Carolina* (Knoxville: University of Tennessee Press, 1989), chaps. 8 and 9. For a comparison of the two regions, see Inscoe, "Mountain Unionism, Secession, and Regional Self-Image: The Contrasting Cases of Western North Carolina and East Tennessee," in *Looking South: Chapters in the Story of an American Region*, ed. Winfred B. Moore (Westport, Conn.: Greenwood Press, 1989).

5. W. H. Parkins, *How I Escaped* (New York: Home Publishing Co., 1889), 114–15.

6. In addition to other work cited throughout these notes, the first four essays in Noe and Wilson, *The Civil War in Appalachia*, focus specifically on this issue. The eleven essays in that volume reflect the extent and range of current scholarship on the war in the highland South, as do several essays in Daniel E. Sutherland, ed., *Guerrillas, Unionists, and Violence on the Confederate Home Front* (Fayetteville: University of Arkansas Press, 1999).

7. The fugitive narratives of Union soldiers or escaped prisoners provide rich and underutilized sources on the war and its impact on the areas through which they moved. For an analysis of those moving through the southern Appalachians, see John C. Inscoe, "'Moving through Deserter Country': Fugitive Accounts of the Inner Civil War in Southern Appalachia," in *The Civil War in Appalachia*, ed. Noe and Wilson, 158–86.

8. J. V. Hadley, *Seven Months a Prisoner* (New York: Charles Scribner's Sons, 1898), 180–86. In the final paragraph of his memoir, Hadley stated that in the summer of 1897, he returned to North Carolina and visited the Hollinger sisters, "and found them all alive—all married and happy in their mountain homes, with large families about them" (258).

9. Oliver P. Temple, *East Tennessee and the Civil War* (1899; reprint, Freeport, N.Y.: Books for Libraries Press, 1971), 426–27. For other references to Jeannette Mabry, see Georgia Lee Tatum, *Disloyalty in the Confederacy* (Chapel Hill: University of North Carolina Press, 1934), 151; Paul A. Whelan, "Unconventional Warfare in East Tennessee, 1862–1865" (M.A. thesis, University of Tennessee, 1963), 139; and William A. Stasser, "'A Terrible Calamity Has Befallen Us': Unionist Women in Civil War East Tennessee," *Journal of East Tennessee History* 71 (1999), 74.

10. Michael Egan, *The Flying Gray-Haired Yank; or, The Adventures of a Volunteer* (Marietta, Ohio: Edgewood Press, 1888), 325–28. On the strains that generational differences within households often put on mothers and wives, see Gordon B. McKinney, "Women's Role in Civil War Western North Carolina," *North Carolina Historical Review* 69 (January 1992): 52–53, 55.

11. W. H. Younce, *The Adventures of a Conscript* (Cincinnati: Editor Publishing Co., 1910), 5–16, 105. For a discussion of the authenticity of Younce's memoir, see Martin Crawford, *Ashe County's Civil War: Community and Society in the Mountain South* (Charlottesville, University Press of Virginia, 2001).

12. The fullest and clearest account of this tangled affair, interpreted as an example of the power of family solidarity in the face of divided allegiances, is found in chap. 5 of Crawford, *Ashe County's Civil War*. For an earlier, far less complete version of Isaac Wilson's murder, see John Preston Arthur, *A History of Watauga County, North Carolina, with Sketches of Prominent Families* (Richmond: Everett Waddey, 1915), 170–71. The same book includes a detailed account of another, similar set of tensions that led to a violent break between Keith Blalock and his stepfather and stepbrothers, pp. 163–64.

13. The most detailed accounts of Morgan's death and Lucy Williams's role in the incident are Cecelia Fletcher Holland, *Morgan and His Raiders: A Biography of the Confederate General* (New York: Macmillan, 1942), 339–48; and James A. Ramage, *Rebel Raider: The Life of John Hunt Morgan* (Lexington: University Press of Kentucky, 1986), 232–40. For a more recent historiographical discussion of the incident, see Fisher, *War at Every Door,* app. B, "Union Informants and the Death of John Hunt Morgan," 186–87.

14. Alberta and Carson Brewer, *Valley So Wild: A Folk History* (Knoxville: East Tennessee Historical Society, 1975), 170.

15. A mere sampling of the literature on Appalachian families and kinship includes John C. Campbell, *The Southern Mountaineer and His Homeland* (New York: Russell Sage Foundation, 1921); Patricia D. Beaver, *Rural Community in*

JOHN C. INSCOE AND GORDON B. MCKINNEY

the Appalachian South (Lexington: University Press of Kentucky, 1986); Jack E. Weller, *Yesterday's People: Life in Contemporary Appalachia* (Lexington: University Press of Kentucky, 1965); *We're All Kin: A Cultural Study of a Mountain Community* (Knoxville: University of Tennessee Press, 1981); Dwight B. Billings and Kathleen M. Blee, *The Road to Poverty: The Making of Wealth and Hardship in Appalachia* (New York: Cambridge University Press, 1999); and most of the works cited in the following notes.

16. Philip S. Paludan, *Victims: A True Story of the Civil War* (Knoxville: University of Tennessee Press, 1981); Durwood Dunn, *Cades Cove: The Life and Death of a Southern Mountain Community, 1818–1937* (Knoxville: University of Tennessee Press, 1988), chap. 5; Altina L. Waller, *Feud: Hatfields, McCoys, and Social Change in Appalachia, 1860–1900* (Chapel Hill: University of North Carolina Press, 1988), 29–33; Ralph Mann, "Family Group, Family Migration, and the Civil War in the Sandy Basin of Virginia," *Appalachian Journal* 19 (summer 1992), 374–93; Mann, "Guerrilla Warfare and Gender Roles: Sandy Basin, Virginia, as a Test Case," *Journal of the Appalachian Studies Association* 5 (1993): 59–66; Martin Crawford, "Confederate Volunteering and Enlistment in Ashe County, North Carolina," *Civil War History* 37 (March 1991): 29–50, and "The Dynamics of Mountain Unionism: Federal Volunteers of Ashe County, North Carolina," in *The Civil War in Appalachia*, ed. Noe and Wilson, 55–77; Jonathan D. Sarris, "Anatomy of an Atrocity: The Madden Branch Massacre and Guerrilla Warfare in North Georgia, 1862–1865," *Georgia Historical Quarterly* 77 (winter 1993): 679–710; and Sarris, "An Execution in Lumpkin County: Localized Loyalties in North Georgia's Civil War," in *The Civil War in Appalachia*, ed. Noe and Wilson, 131–57; and Robert Tracy McKenzie's essay in this volume. See also John W. Shaffer, "Loyalties in Conflict: Union and Confederate Sentiment in Barbour County," *West Virginia History* 50 (1991): 109–28.

17. Mann, "Family Group, Family Migrations," 374, 385.

18. James Gwyn to Rufus T. Lenoir, May 2, 1861, Lenoir Family Papers, Southern Historical Collection, University of North Carolina, Chapel Hill. For more on the tentativeness of Unionist sentiment, see John C. Inscoe and Gordon B. McKinney, *The Heart of Confederate Appalachia: Western North Carolina in the Civil War* (Chapel Hill: University of North Carolina Press, 2000), chap. 4.

19. Oliver P. Temple, *Notable Men of Tennessee, from 1833 to 1875: Their Times and Their Contemporaries* (New York: Cosmopolitan Press, 1912), 243.

20. Charles Frazier, *Cold Mountain* (New York: Atlantic Monthly Press, 1997), 218.

21. Quoted in Paludan, *Victims*, 64.

22. Fellman, *Inside War,* 193. Fellman's chapter 5 is devoted to women's roles in Missouri's guerrilla war. On the role of women in Appalachia's Civil War, see McKinney, "Women's Role"; Dunn, *Cades Cove*, chap. 5, esp. pp. 135–38;

Mann, "Guerrilla Warfare and Gender Roles," 59–67; John C. Inscoe, "Coping in Confederate Appalachia: Portrait of a Mountain Woman and Her Community at War," *North Carolina Historical Review* 69 (October 1992): 388–413; David H. McGee, "'Home and Friends': Kinship, Community, and the Role of Elite Women in Caldwell County during the Civil War," *North Carolina Historical Review* 74 (October 1997): 363–88; and Stasser, "'A Terrible Calamity.'"

23. G. W. Hunt to John Hunt Morgan, November 26, 1864, quoted in Fisher, *War at Every Door,* 117.

24. Quoted in Drew Gilpin Faust, *Mothers of Invention: Women of the Slaveholding South in the American Civil War* (Chapel Hill: University of North Carolina Press, 1996), 200.

25. Shepherd M. Dugger, *War Trails of the Blue Ridge* (Blue Ridge, N.C.: n.p., 1932), 204–5.

Prudent Silence and Strict Neutrality

The Parameters of Unionism in Parson Brownlow's Knoxville, 1860–1863

ROBERT TRACY McKENZIE

*D*uring the Civil War, few individuals did more to acquaint Northerners with Southern Unionism than the "Fighting Parson of East Tennessee," William G. Brownlow. Charged with treason against the Confederacy and ultimately exiled from its borders in March 1862, the Knoxville newspaper editor immediately embarked on a triumphal speaking tour of the North that lasted well into the fall of the year. The "martyr missionary" addressed packed houses from Cincinnati, Ohio, to Portland, Maine, enthralling his audiences with tales of Confederate "atrocities" and emotional pleas for the deliverance of Southern loyalists. For those who could not hear him in person, the celebrated exile penned *Sketches of the Rise, Progress, and Decline of Secession,* a colorful account of "his adventures among the rebels." Sales of the volume, known popularly as *Parson Brownlow's Book,* rapidly approached one hundred thousand.[1]

So widespread was Brownlow's audience that the historian Richard B. Drake identifies the Parson as the prime architect of one of the first popular stereotypes of the Southern mountaineer, the image of the "hard-pressed

William "Parson" Brownlow, 1860. Frontispiece from Brownlow, *Sketches of the Rise, Progress, and Decline of Secession* (1862).

lover of freedom who held strongly to the Union."[2] Like most stereotypes, Brownlow's portrayal of Southern Unionism was long on evocative power and short on complexity. With a penchant for "piling up epithets," as he himself put it, Brownlow spent most of his energy on ad hominem attacks against the "Satanic" Confederacy in general and the malevolence of local Confederate leaders in particular. The latter, for reasons of personal ambition rather than principled conviction, had rebelled against the best government on earth and inaugurated a "reign of terror" over the "multitudes of ever-true and now suffering patriots."[3] The loyal victims of this oppression were characterized by three distinguishing features, collectively epitomized in the person of Brownlow himself: "uncompromising devotion" to the Union, "unmitigated hostility" to those who would destroy it, and a willingness to risk life and property "in defense of the glorious Stars and Stripes."[4]

Brownlow's rhetoric played well in front of Northern audiences who had little experience of civil war within Civil War. Whether it helps us actually to understand Southern Unionism in its local context is another question entirely. With Brownlow's stereotypical "ever-true patriot" as a backdrop, this essay sketches the parameters of Unionism among leading citizens in Brownlow's adopted hometown, focusing primarily on the period of the secession crisis and the twenty-seven months of Confederate occupation that followed, that is, from November 1860 through early September 1863.

In addition to its tie to Parson Brownlow, two factors make Knoxville a particularly attractive subject for a study of Southern Unionism. The first is the rich historical record that has survived from the town's Civil War years, including a range of sources that offer unusually extensive insight into how the sympathies of individual civilians were perceived by contemporaries. To begin with, there was Brownlow himself. Both before his exile—in the pages of the *Knoxville Whig*—and after his return to Knoxville—in the columns of *Brownlow's Knoxville Whig and Rebel Ventilator,* Brownlow relished identifying specifically his friends and, in particular, his enemies. A second informative resource is *East Tennessee and the Civil War,* an 1899 study focusing heavily on Knoxville, written by a local attorney named Oliver P. Temple, a prominent Unionist and arguably Brownlow's most trusted friend.[5] Like Brownlow, Temple also had a penchant for naming names. Of greater value still are a variety of military records generated in the Union provost marshal general's office during the Federal occupation of Knoxville between September 1863 and the end of the war.[6]

Knoxville is also an appealing subject for study simply because of the compelling story that unfolded there. With a population of approximately four thousand on the eve of the Civil War, Knoxville was the largest town and the leading commercial hub in the Valley of East Tennessee. Often labeled the "Switzerland of America," the Valley of East Tennessee was a prosperous mixed-farming region containing few large slaveholders or plantations; both literally and figuratively, it was a world far removed from the cotton South.[7] When the secession crisis came, the inhabitants of this economically distinct region of the future Confederacy asserted their political distinctiveness by opposing Tennessee's separation from the Union by more than two to one in a statewide referendum on June 8, 1861. The opposition to separation was even stronger in Knoxville's immediate environs—rural Knox County rejected disunion by a margin greater than four to one.[8]

In contrast to the overwhelming opposition to separation surrounding the town, Knoxville itself was quite closely divided, ultimately rejecting separation by the slender margin of 377 to 341 (52.5 percent to 47.5 percent).[9] Despite its slim Unionist majority, the town's comparatively large support for disunion made Knoxville a leading center of Confederate influence in an otherwise predominantly Unionist region, and its size and strategic significance as a transportation center led to its evolution as the primary administrative seat of Confederate authority in the Department of East Tennessee. As a result, the town was perpetually under Confederate military occupation from June 1861 until its "liberation" by Ambrose Burnside's Army of the Ohio in September 1863. For Knoxvillians, the meaning of "Unionism" would be pragmatically defined under the watchful eye of Confederate soldiers.[10]

To gauge the contours of Unionism among Knoxville's leading citizens, this study focuses on those Knoxvillians (including William Brownlow) who ranked among the top 5 percent of property holders in Knox County on the eve of the Civil War.[11] Although wealth was by no means a perfect indicator of social position in the nineteenth-century South, it was nevertheless "a basic defining characteristic of social class" and "the surest sign of social, as well as of economic, position."[12] Predominantly merchants, lawyers, and physicians, these seventy individuals—sixty-five men and five women—owned an average (median) of thirty-eight thousand dollars in real and personal property in 1860. Four out of five were slave owners, owning approximately seven each. Although their wealth would have been deemed modest by the standards of the Black Belt, they towered over their own community, where the median household reported only five hundred dollars' worth of property. Collectively, they controlled over four-fifths of the total wealth of the town. Not surprisingly, they also dominated the boards of Knoxville's largest businesses, as well as of its leading educational institutions and charitable organizations. To round out their influence, they also held most of the political offices above the level of alderman.[13]

When the Civil War ultimately divided their community, this elite disproportionately sided with the Confederacy. Although Southern Unionism was nowhere stronger than in East Tennessee, Unionists were a small minority among Knoxville's leading citizens. Evidence exists to categorize with some confidence some fifty-eight (83 percent) of the town's top seventy wealthholders. Based on the testimony of Brownlow, O. P. Temple, and the Union provost marshal general for East Tennessee, only eighteen of these should be considered Unionists; the remaining forty were specifically singled out as pro-Confederate. This finding raises a number of questions that go beyond the scope of this essay, including the obvious query why wealth seems to

ROBERT TRACY MCKENZIE

have correlated so strongly with Confederate sympathies.[14] The question of the moment, however, is different: what did these labels signify in terms of individual *belief* and *behavior*? How did Unionists differ ideologically from secessionists as the nation lurched toward disunion and war? After separation was accomplished, what did it mean to be a Unionist in a Confederate-occupied town?

If an initial lack of enthusiasm for secession was tantamount to Unionism, then almost all of Knoxville's leading citizens would have qualified. In the common parlance of the day, no more than a half dozen were "original secessionists," that is, individuals who advocated secession immediately after the election of Abraham Lincoln. Less than three weeks after the election, a Knoxville attorney called attention in his diary to the secessionist ardor of John H. Crozier and C. W. Charlton. Crozier, a former two-term Whig congressman who had recently converted to the Democratic Party, and Charlton, the Democratic postmaster of Knoxville and sometime minister and journalist, were "bent on dissolution of the union *now*, in spite of the world, the flesh and the devil."[15] Another Democrat, J. G. M. Ramsey— physician, banker, railroad booster, and historian—had been arguing for the inevitability of separation for years and claimed two months before Tennessee's secession to "have done all that one man can do to produce her severance with the (late) United States." Ramsey himself identified William G. Swan, a former state attorney general and future Confederate congressman; William H. Sneed, another former Whig congressman; and Joseph A. Mabry as other prominent Knoxvillians who were early leaders in the fight for secession.[16]

Unlike the tiny clique of "original secessionists," most of the Knoxville elite who ultimately sided with the Confederacy arrived at that position much later and with considerable misgivings. This far larger group generally held *both* North and South responsible for the current political crisis. Faced with an agonizing decision between imperfect options, they put off taking sides as long as possible. For some, it was the secession of other Southern states that prompted a final decision. The attorney William G. McAdoo, for example, was convinced that "vile politicians" from both regions had "brought ruin on the country. . . . The maddened masses of both extremes of sectional feeling" were threatening to plunge the nation "into a general and bloody war." To forestall this tragedy, McAdoo advocated that the slave states seek redress of their grievances within the Union; he deplored South Carolina's threats of secession and expressed a willingness "to go with spade and pick axe and work a month to ditch around her and float her out into the Atlantic a thousand miles." The subsequent "precipitate and uncompromising withdrawal" of South Carolina and six other Deep South states, however, forced Tennesseans to decide whether they would go with the North or with the South, and McAdoo pragmatically saw no choice but to go with the South. "Sooner or later, we *must*; it is our geographical necessity. The laws of trade compel us. Every mans [*sic*] pocket binds him there."[17]

More frequently, Knoxville's elite Confederates cast their lot with the Confederacy only after Tennessee formally separated from the Union. David Deaderick, for example, chose to side with the South but continued to agonize over his decision as late as 1862. Granted, the North had "for years intermeddled with the subject of slavery, which very remotely concerned *them*." But on the other hand, Deaderick could not help noting, Abraham Lincoln had been constitutionally elected, and the South, rather than submitting for four years, had "precipitated war upon us by the first hostile attack."[18] Similarly, the prominent Knoxvillian Hugh Lawson McClung did not vote in favor of separation and struggled mightily before converting to support of the Confederacy. "I hesitated, long hesitated," the Whig McClung explained to a former political ally, citing "a belief that our difficulties might have been averted" and the suspicion that "they were brought upon us by . . . a party who preferred a disruption of the Union to a loss of office. . . . But, when convinced that it was narrowed down to a sectional strife, that I had to take sides either with the South or the North, I could no longer hesitate." Rather than condone the coercion of their homeland, such reluctant Confederates grimly cast their lot with the Confederacy in an avoidable war that the South had helped to start.[19]

Ideologically, the deepest dividing line among Knoxville's leading citizens was not that between Confederates and Unionists per se, but rather that between the handful of original secessionists and everyone else. Indeed, during the secession crisis the community's leading Unionists closely resembled in attitude their reluctant Confederate peers. Throughout the winter and spring of 1861, Unionists' standard position was that the conflict was the bitter fruit of extremism on both sides. Thus, although they ultimately sided with the Union, they found much to blame in the conduct of the North. In February 1861, for example, Horace Maynard, a Knoxville attorney and Whig congressman, called attention on the floor of Congress to a small group of Southern fire-eaters who were "disunionists for the sake of disunion." These demagogues benefited from popular discontent stimulated by the decades-long "anti-southern crusade," Maynard maintained. Although he believed that many of the secessionist leaders were selfishly motivated,

ROBERT TRACY MCKENZIE

the Knoxville congressman argued that Southerners were justifiably alarmed by Republican aggression against slavery and staunchly advocated passage of proslavery amendments to the Constitution to assuage Southern fears.[20]

Oliver Temple professed similar views. Temple denounced the "Secession Party" of the South, a cabal of Democrats who, for partisan reasons, were working systematically to divide the country. In their despicable designs, however, they were matched by the Northern abolitionists—fanatics who, with "superlative madness and folly," were willing to overthrow the Union and the Constitution to gratify their "sickly sympathy for an abstract slave." Both groups of extremists grew and were strengthened "by the nourishment afforded by the other. If either could have been kept silent for four years," Temple maintained, "the other would have died of inanition."[21]

William Brownlow's position was identical, albeit a bit more vividly stated. Unquestionably, the rights of the South had been violated by the North's "personal liberty laws," the Parson opined in March 1861, yet the appropriate response was to seek redress within the Union, thus pursuing a course "midway between the ultraism of the hell-deserving Abolitionists of the North, and the God-forsaken Disunionists of the South." After his exile to the North, Brownlow told a delegation from the Ohio legislature, "If fifty years ago we had taken one hundred Southern fire eaters and one hundred Northern Abolitionists and hanged them up, and buried them in a common ditch, and sent their souls to hell, we should have had none of this war."[22]

In sum, while Knoxville's leading Unionists heartily detested fire-eating secessionists, they simultaneously deplored the election of Abraham Lincoln and agreed that the South's rights had been violated. And yet, when forced to choose, they ultimately clung to the Union. Brownlow explained this decision to Northern audiences by stressing the unconditional Unionism of East Tennessee patriots. Knoxville's leading Unionists, however, appear to have been influenced by a host of pragmatic considerations: (1) disproportionately former Whigs, they equated the Confederacy with "a revival of corrupt Southern Democracy" and recoiled before the prospect of an alliance with their chief political rivals; (2) inhabitants of a grain-growing and stock-raising region, they discerned little common economic interest with the cotton states; (3) though granting that the South had serious cause for complaint against the North, they denied that secession would ameliorate any existing evil; (4) unconvinced that the North would permit the Southern states to depart without a fight, they worried that secession would bring a cruel war to the South and eventuate in the destruction of slavery.[23]

This last concern deserves special emphasis. One of the most striking similarities between leading Unionists and Confederates in Knoxville was their common unquestioning commitment to the preservation of slavery. The views of William Brownlow, who owned two slaves on the eve of the Civil War, were characteristically extreme. Slavery was "a blessing to the master, a blessing to the non-slave-holders of the South, a blessing to the civilized white race in general, and a blessing to the negro slaves in particular," the Parson asserted in a debate in Philadelphia in 1858. Both the Bible and the Constitution protected Southerners' rights to "Hamitic servitude," he averred, "and these rights we intend to enjoy, or to a man we will die, strung along Mason and Dixon's line, with our faces looking North!"[24] Horace Maynard's position was less dogmatic. Maynard had denounced slavery as a "curse to the country" when he first came to Knoxville from Massachusetts in 1839, yet by 1850 he was a slave owner himself, having discovered in the interim "a bright as well as a dark side to the picture of slavery." As he explained to his father, who was still living in Massachusetts, the slaves' "servitude is no more a burden to them, than is the service of our children until they arrive at twenty one years of age."[25] Unlike Maynard, Oliver P. Temple was the son and grandson of slaveholders and never experienced any qualms about the rectitude of human bondage. "My conscience did not trouble me on the subject," he recalled years later. "I was a friend to the Union, because in part, I was a friend of slavery." If Temple's memory was correct, "every prominent Union leader" in East Tennessee was similarly a "friend" of the institution.[26] Such friendship was not merely theoretical, for Knoxville's leading Unionists were even more likely to own slaves than their Confederate counterparts. Thirty-one of forty known Confederates (78 percent) were slave owners, averaging six slaves each, whereas sixteen of eighteen Unionists (89 percent) were masters, owning eight slaves each on average.[27]

Unionists' determination to preserve slavery must be borne in mind in assessing the last—and least pragmatic—reason for their loyalty to the Union: the abstract conviction that secession was unconstitutional. This belief, widely held in East Tennessee, has earned for the region a misleading reputation as one of the rare bastions of "unconditional Unionism" in the future Confederacy. In the strictest sense, opinions on the legality of secession became moot in May 1861 when the Tennessee General Assembly passed, not an ordinance of secession, but a "declaration of independence." According to the resolution, which was submitted to a statewide referendum in early June, the people of Tennessee explicitly "waiv[ed] any expression of opinion as to the abstract doctrine of secession" and asserted instead "the right, as a free and independent people, to alter, reform, or abolish our form of government in such manner as we think proper."[28] Although they denied the constitutionality of secession, East Tennessee Unionists, like most Americans—including even Abraham Lincoln—recognized the inalienable, natural right of revolution. Even Brownlow explicitly conceded it, although he denied that circumstances called for it.[29] Others similarly condemned it as unwarranted or attacked the motives of its supporters, but none denied the right of revolution per se.

Even before the action of the state legislature shifted the relevant question from the legality of secession to the right of revolution, there is good reason to doubt that East Tennessee Unionism was unconditional. Theoretical constitutional arguments aside, a commitment to unconditional Unionism meant only one thing to Southerners in the concrete historical context of 1860–61: a hypothetical willingness to sacrifice slavery to Northern abolitionism rather than jeopardize the Union. During his tour of the North, Parson Brownlow identified himself as an "unconditional Union man" in precisely such terms. If the question dividing the nation was that of "no slavery and the Union or no Union and slavery," he told Northern audiences, "I am for the Union if it exterminates every institution in the South."[30] Years after the war, the Knoxville Unionist Thomas W. Humes remembered such views as characteristic from the beginning of the war among East Tennesseans, who "were satisfied to let men of the South keep serfs at pleasure, but they counted it no business of theirs to help in the work. If the perpetuity of the Union or that of slavery were the question at issue, they would have no hesitation in deciding. Let slavery perish and the Union live."[31]

By the latter half of the war, such sentiments were clearly ascendant among East Tennessee Unionists, yet it would be a mistake to assume that they were widespread during the secession crisis.[32] To do so is to ignore how the momentum of events unleashed by the war carried Southern Unionists to ever more radical positions concerning slavery. Such an assumption also disregards how the beginning of the war changed the nature of the rhetorical debate between Unionists and secessionists. Before the war commenced, the central question in East Tennessee was not whether secession was legal or revolution an inalienable right, but rather whether constitutional safeguards were sufficient to protect slavery against *Northern* aggression. After the war began, in contrast, Unionists could blame emancipation on *Southern* aggression by castigating secessionist extremists for foolishly provoking an unnecessary war. It is no coincidence that William Brownlow never asserted a willingness to sacrifice slavery until the war was nearly a year old. Indeed, during the secession crisis he explicitly disavowed such a position (a detail he failed to reveal later to Northern audiences), telling his Southern readers that he differed from fire-eating extremists only "as to the *time* and *mode* of resistance." In the early weeks after Lincoln's election, the Parson counseled patience and urged Southerners to exhaust every constitutional means to protect their rights before resorting to disunion and, in all likelihood, the sword. If the latter eventuality should prove necessary, he would go with the South "to the death." Brownlow was not alone. I have been unable to unearth evidence of a single instance during the secession crisis in which a leading Knoxville Unionist openly avowed a willingness to submit to Northern antislavery sentiment rather than disturb the Union. Such a position was simply untenable. Rather than professing an "unconditional" Unionism that valued Union above slavery, they emphatically denied that slavery was in danger and argued that Southerners need not choose between the Union and their peculiar institution. If they genuinely subscribed to an unconditional Unionism, they went out of their way to avoid declaring so publicly.[33]

Whatever the foundation of their loyalty, East Tennesseans' Unionism was numerically insufficient to offset lopsided disunionist majorities across the rest of the state, and Tennessee became the eleventh and final state to withdraw from the Union in June 1861.[34] In the immediate aftermath of Tennessee's formal separation, most of Knoxville's leading Unionists hoped, above all, to be left alone. With a large Confederate force already at Knoxville and little realistic hope of military assistance from the North, overt resistance to Confederate authority seemed futile and even foolhardy. Thus, when East Tennessee Unionists met in convention at nearby Greeneville less than ten days after the state's withdrawal, Knoxville delegates successfully opposed a series of resolutions that called for East Tennesseans to arm themselves and fight rather than submit to Confederate rule. In August, Brownlow argued forcefully against resistance in the *Whig*; he noted that Unionist leaders were doing everything in their power to calm the masses in the belief that "it is madness to rebel, and the worst of folly to contribute to the getting up of a Civil War in East Tennessee." A month later, a number of prominent Knoxville Unionists—including Brownlow, Temple, and four other members of the Knoxville elite—wrote an open letter to the Confederate commander in East Tennessee, Brigadier General Felix Zollicoffer. In the letter they expressed their opposition to any activities calculated to provoke conflict and urged area Unionists to pursue their vocations quietly and refrain from acts of resistance that might inaugurate civil war in their midst.[35]

Initially, Confederate civil and military authorities pursued a policy of

ROBERT TRACY McKENZIE

conciliation in East Tennessee that was all that Knoxville's leading Unionists could have desired. When local Confederate leaders appealed to Governor Isham Harris for sterner measures, Harris replied that he preferred to give East Tennessee's Unionists "every opportunity and inducement to come in and submit gracefully to the will of the majority." General Zollicoffer concurred in this course of action, even after East Tennesseans (including a slender majority of Knoxvillians) exercised their "right of free speech and free thought" in an August election for the provisional Confederate Congress by electing a Unionist, Horace Maynard, who slipped through the mountains and went to Washington, D.C., instead.[36]

Confederate leniency came to an abrupt halt in late 1861 when, on the night of November 8, small bands of Unionists burned five strategic railroad bridges between Bristol and Chattanooga and attempted to destroy four others, including one spanning the Holston River east of Knoxville.[37] Although few Knoxvillians were implicated (and leading Knoxville Unionists were quick to disavow the act), the uprising prompted immediate repression by Confederate authorities. With the support of the Confederate War Department, local military authorities swiftly imposed martial law in the region, established a court martial in Knoxville for the trial of alleged conspirators, and began to fill Knoxville's jails with political prisoners, including William Brownlow, who, after hiding out for several weeks in the mountains, surrendered in early December. Although not technically illegal, public expressions of support for the Union largely vanished; since every Unionist was now a suspected saboteur, they were simply too dangerous.

Thereafter, with Horace Maynard in Washington and William Brownlow in jail, later in exile, Knoxville's leading Unionists followed what Oliver Temple called a path of "prudent silence." Temple recalled that only one man in Knoxville—Colonel John Williams, a four-time state senator and member of one of the town's oldest families—publicly acknowledged his affinity for the Union. No other leading Unionist dared to do so.[38] In public, at least, most Unionists affected a posture of strict neutrality.[39] In cases when prison seemed the likely alternative, however, they were generally willing to make public declarations of loyalty to the Confederacy, or at least of acquiescence to Confederate rule. When the wealthy merchant and slave owner Abner Jackson was arrested and charged with disloyalty, for example, he refused to swear an oath of loyalty under compulsion, but wrote local authorities from jail to say that since Tennessee's secession he had been a "loyal citizen of the Confederate States, and would allow his arm to be severed before he would raise it against this government." Similarly, when suspicions were aroused about Temple's loyalty, he asked the editor of the *Knoxville Daily Register* to inform the public that he had "already taken the oath to support the Confederate States, and intends to demean himself as a loyal citizen thereof. He wishes quietly to pursue the practice of his profession, without being drawn into the arena of public discussion."[40] Both declarations were made under duress, of course, and may have been examples of what one historian has termed "survival lying."[41] One thing is clear, however: in Knoxville such pronouncements did not necessarily violate community standards for Unionism, for neither Jackson nor Temple were discredited as Unionist leaders after the arrival of Burnside's army in September 1863.

No individual case better illustrates the complexity of Unionism under Confederate occupation than that of John Baxter. A prominent Knoxville attorney, banker, and Whig politician, Baxter was one of the town's most forceful opponents of secession until Tennessee's formal separation in June 1861. Oliver Temple doubted whether "any man in the state . . . was so bitter in denunciation of secession and its leaders." His contempt for the Confederacy continued into July, when, according to the *Knoxville Daily Register,* Baxter boasted that "in a few weeks we will have the rebels like partridges in a trap, and I expect to be obliged to go to Richmond to use my influence with Mr. Lincoln to prevent my secession relatives in Virginia from being hanged."[42] The Confederate victory in late July at Bull Run evidently changed his perspective dramatically, however, for from that point Baxter appears to have adopted the position that Confederate independence was inevitable. The most sensible course for sincere Unionists, he maintained, was to resign themselves to Confederate rule and work within the system to minimize the power and abuses of "original secessionists" in the new government. Baxter voluntarily took an oath of loyalty to the Confederacy in mid-September, nearly three months before the bridge burnings, at least in part to be able to defend Unionists in the local Confederate court. That same month he ran unsuccessfully for a permanent seat in the Confederate Congress against an original secessionist, William G. Swan. Early the next year he briefly published a newspaper in Knoxville, the *East Tennessean,* which, according to its editorial statement, attempted to "harmonize the discordant elements among us, and reconcile the disaffected to the Government of the Confederate States."[43]

The range of responses to Baxter's strategy is instructive. Temple counseled against it and considered Baxter to have converted to secessionism. Although a year later Brownlow would describe Baxter as a "moderate secessionist," in the fall of 1861 he publicly endorsed Baxter's candidacy for the

ROBERT TRACY MCKENZIE

Confederate Congress, exclaiming that "a more honorable, high-minded and patriotic gentleman than he, never presented himself as a candidate to the people of Tennessee." In private, Brownlow maintained that Baxter was "making a good impression" in the campaign and lauded his brave defiance of Confederate soldiers who tried to break up his speeches.[44] Baxter's law partner, the Confederate senator Landon Carter Haynes, on the other hand, praised Baxter's courageous, if tardy, stand with the South, while the pro-Confederate *Daily Register* was suspicious if not outright dismissive of his purported submission to the Confederacy. "How many believe in the sincerity of his new faith and would trust him in the new position to which he now aspires?" the *Register* asked contemptuously.[45] The Confederate general Edmund Kirby Smith, who was still receiving "repeated accusations" against Baxter some six months after he took the loyalty oath, was similarly skeptical. Fearing that Baxter might be attempting to communicate with Unionists in West Tennessee, and incensed by a recent "disloyal if not treasonous" speech in which Baxter held out "not one hope for the future success of the Southern cause," Smith wrote to General Albert Sydney Johnston in late March 1862 to suggest that Baxter be arrested and searched while en route to Memphis on business. Angered by such insulting treatment (and possibly impressed as well by Union military victories during the first half of 1862), by June 1862 Baxter had switched course again. Temple described his new path as a reversion to "stalwart Unionism." J. Austin Sperry, editor of the *Daily Register*, characterized Baxter's behavior as "that of strict neutrality of conduct, though of secret preferences for the Federal cause." In the context of Confederate-occupied Knoxville, "stalwart Unionism" and "strict neutrality" were apparently synonymous.[46]

Again, it is significant that such dramatic political shifts during the period of Confederate occupation did not disqualify Baxter from a position of influence as a leading Unionist after the arrival of Burnside's army in September 1863. Only a month after the Confederate evacuation, the *Knoxville Daily Register* (now located in Atlanta) wryly noted the report of a recent refugee that Baxter had already delivered a half-dozen Union speeches. The Union provost marshal's office readily accepted him as loyal, and less than six months later he became a charter member of the East Tennessee Relief Association, a charitable organization created to publicize the sufferings of Unionists in the region. Although Brownlow ultimately broke bitterly with Baxter and was wont to ridicule the latter's "treason" during the period of Confederate rule, the rift between them stemmed mainly from partisan rivalry. Baxter's real crime, in Brownlow's eyes, was his shift to the

Democratic Party in protest of the Emancipation Proclamation. Both O. P. Temple and Thomas Humes—less politically radical and personally vindictive than the Parson—persisted in classifying Baxter as a sincere Unionist, albeit with "a mental agility that is somewhat remarkable."[47]

Given the range of political behavior reconcilable with Unionism, it is not surprising that Unionists among the Knoxville elite pursued a variety of economic strategies as well. Some traded openly—and apparently willingly—with the Confederate government. John S. VanGilder, a New Jersey–born boot- and shoe- and hatmaker, started the Knoxville Leather Company during the war—in partnership with one of the town's Confederate elite, Frank Scott—and manufactured infantry brogans and cavalry boots for the Confederate military. By December 1862 the future Knoxville mayor was selling between two thousand and twenty-five hundred pairs of boots and shoes to the local Confederate quartermaster. Yet after the Federal occupation of the town, VanGilder was immediately accepted as a "respectable Union man," according to the records of the Union provost marshal general. Furthermore, it is clear that his business continued to prosper. By 1869 VanGilder was not only president of the Knoxville Leather Company but principal owner of the Bank of Knoxville as well, and his net worth had increased from fifteen thousand dollars at the beginning of the war to approximately one hundred thousand dollars.[48] Although the historical record does not afford a detailed account of VanGilder's business dealings during the period of Confederate rule, a poem sent to his son and future business partner, Thomas VanGilder, by an ardently pro-Confederate female friend is suggestive:

> Oh! Tommy dear, you used to talk
> Ere Blue Coats came this way
> As if you were the best of Rebs
> Why are you Yank today?
>
> And you were always wont to say
> You loved the Rebels dearly.
> So a man may change his politics
> As he does his dress coat—yearly.
> I think that all you want just now
> Is to make plenty money.
> Whichever army should be here
> You'd call them dearest honey.[49]

Other Unionists among the elite were more discreet than VanGilder. Although evidence is inconclusive, there is good reason to suspect that Oliver Temple also had business dealings with the Confederate government, albeit less openly. Temple's brother, Major S. Temple, had a contract worth $150,000 annually to manufacture salt at Saltville, Virginia, for the Confederate state government of Georgia. Major Temple wrote to his brother in September 1862 to describe the arrangement and to invite him to "unite your destinies with me at this place." Oliver's response to this invitation has not survived, but William McAdoo, who had relocated to Georgia in early 1862, insisted in his diary in December of that year that both Temples were extensively involved and asserted that Oliver was spending most of his time at Saltville. The contract was "immensely profitable," according to McAdoo, and would "make millionaires of these Temples of Mammon."[50]

McAdoo was undoubtedly predisposed to think the worst of Oliver Temple, and there is no definite proof that he was involved with the Saltville project. On the other hand, there is no question that he later bankrolled the efforts of his brother to buy both cotton and tobacco behind Confederate lines in upper East Tennessee, with an eye to eventually selling those precious goods in the North. In April 1864 Major Temple wrote to his brother from Greeneville, still under Confederate control at the time, to report that their "joint account" was now approaching "95 to 100,000 rated at Confederate prices." Among various investments, he noted new acquisitions of seventeen bales of cotton and a railroad car of salt currently "out of view" near the village of Limestone in Greene County, noting that they were "now called mine & will at the proper time be called yours." Major Temple asked his brother what he thought "of a pretty heavy additional investment in *cotton*," observing that "passports to visit & return at pleasure [across Union lines] will be necessary for personal security & proper protection of property."[51]

The risk involved in such investments was great, of course, in that the entire sum involved would be lost unless the goods could be transported safely into Federally occupied territory. For the rest of the year, Union and Confederate armies contended for control of upper East Tennessee while bands of guerrillas roamed across the region. As late as October, Major Temple sent an anxious letter to his brother expressing concern that all would be lost.[52] The historical record is silent about whether the Temple brothers succeeded in salvaging their various stockpiled commodities. If they failed, however, it was not for lack of assistance from the United States Army. In September 1864 Colonel John B. Brownlow of the Ninth Tennessee

Cavalry, United States Army—the Parson's son—wrote to Oliver Temple while on an expedition in Greene County and explained that his commanding officer had authorized him to impress three teams of horses from Rebel civilians in order to haul the Temples' tobacco to Knoxville. "At all events I will get the property out without its costing you anything," Brownlow assured him. "You have done a great deal for Uncle Sam and there is no reason why he should not do something for you."[53]

Temple's economic opportunism was far from unique among Knoxville's leading Unionists. John Baxter requested and received permission from the Union provost marshal general for East Tennessee to cross into Confederate-held territory for the purpose of purchasing cotton and tobacco with Confederate scrip he had received while the Confederates held Knoxville. A subsequent reference in the provost marshal general's records suggests that he was prepared to ship eighty-nine bales of cotton to Louisville by early June. There is compelling evidence, however, that not all of the stockpiling of staples occurred after the onset of Federal occupation. As early as the spring of 1862, the *Knoxville Daily Register* printed a letter charging "East Tennessee Lincolnite Cotton Speculators" with buying cotton in Georgia and South Carolina and shipping it to East Tennessee, where they intended to store it until the region was overrun by the Union army. The letter claimed that such men were making everything they could out of the Confederacy while all the time proclaiming Union sympathies. Although the newspaper never named names while it was operating in Knoxville, after it relocated in Atlanta the *Register* identified one of the chief offenders as the wholesale firm headed by prominent Unionists James Cowan and Perez Dickinson. Writing only a month after the evacuation of Knoxville by Confederate forces, editor J. A. Sperry alleged that Cowan and Dickinson, as well as "other noted Unionists," had already shipped several hundred bales of cotton to the North. Sperry explained that Cowan and Dickinson, as well as other prominent "Tories," had initially refused to accept Confederate currency in their business dealings. They then began to accept it and, as a hedge against depreciation, used it to buy cotton, which they stored in Knoxville in anticipation of its eventual liberation. Sperry claimed to have seen cotton piled conspicuously near the railroad depot when he took one of the last trains out of town before Burnside's arrival. Apparently, the evacuating Confederate forces made no effort to destroy it, prompting Sperry to complain that "the traitors of East Tennessee have thus profited by the mistaken leniency of our military authorities."[54]

Such profits could be considerable. It is unknown just how much cotton

Cowan and Dickinson had under their control at the time of the Confederate evacuation, but Union military records show that in October 1863 the firm forwarded at least 111 bales of cotton to Cincinnati and New York, and by early November they had another 256 bales ready for shipment north. A conservative estimate is that these 367 bales could have sold in New York for between $140,000 and $150,000 in gold, promising a fair rate of return for goods that were, in all likelihood, purchased with now worthless Confederate paper. Unfortunately for Cowan and Dickinson, before the 256 bales could be shipped they were confiscated by order of General Burnside and used on the fortifications of Knoxville. The firm seems to have survived in fine shape, however. After the war's end the local agent of the R. G. Dun Mercantile Agency rated Cowan and Dickinson as the strongest commercial house in town and confirmed that the business had "made money on cotton" during the war. The agent noted that both of the principal members of the business were worth as much as or more than they were when the war began, and the firm was strengthened even more by the addition of two silent partners from among the Knoxville elite—Confederates Frank and Charles McClung.[55]

The point of these examples of economic opportunism is not to question the loyalty of purported Unionists such as VanGilder, Temple, Baxter, Cowan, or Dickinson, but rather to show clearly the range of economic behavior consistent with local perceptions of Unionism. Northern audiences cheered when William Brownlow told them that "a man who would not sacrifice his property" in defense of the Stars and Stripes "deserves not the protection of that flag."[56] As a rule, the leading citizens of Knoxville were able to reconcile profit-taking with Unionism and did not accept the Parson's criterion of loyalty. Nor did Brownlow himself when he was in Knoxville, one might add. Upon his return from exile, the Parson continued to have the highest regard for O. P. Temple and later, as governor, offered him a seat on the state supreme court. Similarly, he joined with Union General Burnside in endorsing the loyalty of both James Cowan and Perez Dickinson and in supporting their claim for damages from the federal government for the confiscated cotton.[57] Brownlow's uncompromising standard for loyalty played well at patriotic Northern rallies far removed from the theater of war, but, as he himself seems to have understood, it was ill suited to the realities of life in a bitterly divided community under Confederate occupation.

A more nuanced understanding of Unionism in Brownlow's Knoxville awaits the opportunity to investigate attitude and behavior across the entire socioeconomic spectrum of the town's population. This study of Knoxville's leading Unionists strongly suggests, however, that when the Parson educated Northern audiences about Southern Unionism, he considerably exaggerated the ideological chasm between Unionists and Confederates and obscured complex patterns of political and economic behavior under Confederate rule. Excluding an extremely small group of "original secessionists," the division that emerged among Knoxville's leading citizens during the secession crisis stemmed more from differences in judgment than of philosophical conviction. Both groups agreed that Southern rights had been violated; both detested Northern extremism and deplored the election of Abraham Lincoln; both sought to keep war from the South and preserve slavery; both recognized the right of revolution if slavery could be preserved in no other way. In 1860–61, they primarily disagreed about whether such drastic action was yet called for. When their more cautious position lost out, Knoxville's leading Unionists largely refused to follow Brownlow's lead and acquiesced to Confederate rule. Their Unionism was manifested primarily in "prudent silence," "strict neutrality of conduct," and a willingness to make money while awaiting Federal deliverance.

NOTES

1. For examples of Brownlow's speeches, see *Chicago Tribune*, April 11, 1862; *New York Times*, April 1, 3, May 14, 22, 1862; *New York Daily Tribune*, May 16, 20, 1862; *National Anti-Slavery Standard* (New York), May 24, 1862; *Philadelphia Public Ledger*, April 19, June 14, 1862; *Boston Daily Evening Transcript*, May 24, 1862; *Parson Brownlow and the Unionists of East Tennessee* (New York: Beadle, 1862); and *Portrait and Biography of Parson Brownlow, the Tennessee Patriot* (Indianapolis: Asher, 1862). For the Parson's published account of his Knoxville experiences, see W. G. Brownlow, *Sketches of the Rise, Progress, and Decline of Secession* (Philadelphia: George W. Childs, 1862). For Brownlow's perspective on his northern tour, see Brownlow to publisher George Childs, June 26, September 15, November 10, 1862, William G. Brownlow Papers, Special Collections Division, University of Tennessee Libraries, Knoxville; Brownlow to Childs, August 7, 1862, Brownlow to Dr. Sprague, October 2, 1862, William G. Brownlow Papers, Library of Congress (hereafter LC); Brownlow to Miss C. M. Melville, June 28, 1862, Crosby Noyes Autography Collection, LC. For detailed sketches of Brownlow's Civil War career, see E. Merton Coulter, *William G. Brownlow: Fighting Parson of the Southern Highlands* (Chapel Hill: University of North Carolina Press, 1937); Steve Humphrey, *"That D——d Brownlow"* (Boone, N.C.: Appalachian

ROBERT TRACY MCKENZIE

Consortium Press, 1978); and James C. Kelley, "William Gannaway Brownlow," pt. 2, *Tennessee Historical Quarterly* 43 (1984): 155–72.

2. Quoted in Humphrey, *That D——d Brownlow*, viii. On the development of Appalachian stereotypes before the Civil War, see David C. Hsiung, *Two Worlds in the Tennessee Mountains: Exploring the Origins of Appalachian Stereotypes* (Lexington: University Press of Kentucky, 1997).

3. *Chicago Tribune*, April 11, 1862; *Knoxville Whig*, September 21, 1861; Brownlow, *Sketches of Secession*, 7.

4. Brownlow, *Sketches of Secession*, 5; *Chicago Tribune*, April 11, 1862. See also *Philadelphia Public Ledger*, April 19, 1862; *New York Daily Tribune*, May 14, 1862.

5. Years after his father's death, Brownlow's son wrote to O. P. Temple, "I am sure you were for a longer period an intimate friend of my father than any man in Tennessee, and that friendship was more intimate and substantial than ever existed between himself and any other person." See John B. Brownlow to O. P. Temple, January 31, 1891, O. P. Temple Papers, Special Collections Division, University of Tennessee Library, Knoxville.

6. Chief among these is a list of disloyal civilians who sought to avail themselves of President Lincoln's December 1863 amnesty proclamation and the proceedings of a commission appointed by General Ambrose Burnside to evaluate claims filed by local Unionists for commissary stores appropriated by the Union army. See RG 393, U.S. Army Continental Commands, entry no. 2764, District of East Tennessee, Records of the Provost Marshal, 1863–65, vol. 1, "Oaths of Allegiance," National Archives and Records Administration, Washington, D.C. (hereafter NARA); RG 393, entry no. 2759, District of East Tennessee, Endorsements Sent by the Provost Marshal General, September 1863–July 1864, NARA; RG 92, Records of the Office of the Quartermaster General, E. 881, "List of Loyal and Disloyal Claimants," NARA.

7. Hermann Bokum, *The Tennessee Handbook and Immigrants' Guide* (Philadelphia: J. B. Lippincott, 1868), 8; Thomas W. Humes, *The Loyal Mountaineers of Tennessee* (Knoxville: Ogden Brothers, 1888), 19–35; J. B. Killebrew, *Introduction to the Resources of Tennessee* (Nashville: Tavel, Eastman and Howell, 1874), 423–47; Robert Tracy McKenzie, "Wealth and Income: The Preindustrial Structure of East Tennessee in 1860," *Appalachian Journal* 21 (1994): 260–79.

8. *Knoxville Daily Register*, June 11, 1861.

9. The Knoxville vote is based on the tally reported in the June 11 issue of the prosecession *Knoxville Daily Register*, altered to exclude the votes of 436 Confederate soldiers from other counties who were training on the outskirts of Knoxville at the time of the state referendum and were allowed to vote. The *Register* included the soldiers' votes in its tally and reported that the town had given secession a resounding endorsement. Figures on ballots cast by nonresident soldiers

are contained in RG 87, Tennessee Election Returns, roll 1861–62, Tennessee State Library and Archives, Nashville.

10. Monographs that include extensive coverage of Knoxville's Civil War include Charles Faulkner Bryan Jr., "The Civil War in East Tennessee: A Social, Political, and Economic Study" (Ph.D. dissertation, University of Tennessee, 1978); Wilma Dykeman, *The French Broad* (New York: Rinehart, 1955); Lucille Deaderick, ed., *Heart of the Valley: A History of Knoxville, Tennessee* (Knoxville: University of Tennessee Press, 1976); Digby Gordon Seymour, *Divided Loyalties: Fort Sanders and the Civil War in East Tennessee* (Knoxville: University of Tennessee Press, 1963). For a good introduction to recent scholarly literature on the Civil War in southern Appalachia generally, see Kenneth W. Noe and Shannon H. Wilson, eds., *The Civil War in Appalachia: Collected Essays* (Knoxville: University of Tennessee Press, 1997). A helpful overview of the behavior of border-state Unionists in 1860–61 is Daniel W. Crofts, *Reluctant Confederates: Upper South Unionists in the Secession Crisis* (Chapel Hill: University of North Carolina Press, 1989).

11. I have included in this definition of the Knoxville elite individuals who worked primarily in Knoxville without residing there; twelve of the seventy did not reside in Knoxville according to the Federal population census but had professional offices or businesses there. Information on place of business was obtained in *Williams' Knoxville Directory, City Guide, and Business Mirror, 1859–'60* (Knoxville: C. S. Williams, 1859). Figures on wealthholding are garnered from the manuscript population schedules of the Eighth Census (1860).

12. Gavin Wright, *The Political Economy of the Cotton South* (New York: W. W. Norton, 1978), 37; Edward Pessen, "How Different from Each Other Were the Antebellum North and South?" *American Historical Review* 85 (1980): 1130. See also Gail O'Brien, "Power and Influence in Mecklenburg County, 1850–1880," *North Carolina Historical Review* 54 (1977): 134; and Paul D. Escott, *Many Excellent People: Power and Privilege in North Carolina, 1850–1900* (Chapel Hill: University of North Carolina Press, 1985), 19.

13. *Williams' Knoxville Directory*, 20–30.

14. For works that investigate the socioeconomic correlates of Unionist and Confederate sympathies in East Tennessee, see Walter Lynn Bates, "Southern Unionists: A Socio-Economic Examination of the Third East Tennessee Volunteer Infantry Regiment, U.S.A., 1862–1865," *Tennessee Historical Quarterly* 50 (1991): 226–39; "'Helping to Save the Union': The Social Origins, Wartime Experiences, and Military Impact of White Union Troops from East Tennessee," in *The Civil War in Appalachia*, ed. Noe and Wilson, 1–29; and W. Todd Groce, *Mountain Rebels: East Tennessee Confederates and the Civil War, 1860–1870* (Knoxville: University of Tennessee Press, 1999), chap. 3.

15. William Gibbs McAdoo Diary, entry for November 30, 1860, Floyd-McAdoo Papers, LC.

16. William B. Hesseltine, ed., *Dr. J. G. M. Ramsey: Autobiography and Letters* (Nashville: Tennessee Historical Commission, 1954), 93–95, 100; J. G. M. Ramsey to A. Porter Esq., April 16, 1861, in J. G. M. Ramsey Papers, Southern Historical Collection; Mary U. Rothrock, *The French Broad–Holston Country: A History of Knox County, Tennessee* (Knoxville: Knox County Historical Society, 1946), 403–4, 487–88, 493–95. Sneed's position is aptly summarized in his circular to Knox County voters in *Knoxville Whig*, February 2, 1861.

17. McAdoo diary, entries for November 8, 13, December 12; italics in original. See also McAdoo to Hon. John Bell, April 18, 1861, William G. McAdoo Papers, LC. For additional biographical information on McAdoo, see John W. Green, *Bench and Bar of Knox County, Tennessee* (Knoxville: Archer and Smith, 1947), 61–63.

18. David Anderson Deaderick Diary (typescript), McClung Collection, Knox County Public Library, Knoxville, 53, italics in original. For more information on Deaderick, see Daniel E. Sutherland, ed., *A Very Violent Rebel: The Civil War Diary of Ellen Renshaw House* (Knoxville: University of Tennessee Press, 1996), 223; Rothrock, *French Broad–Holston Country*, 409–10.

19. Hu. L. McClung to Thos. A. R. Nelson, Esq., October 7, 1862, Thomas A. R. Nelson Papers, McClung Collection, Knox County Public Library, Knoxville. See also McClung's amnesty application in Amnesty Papers, NARA.

20. "Speech of Hon. H. Maynard of Tennessee in the House of Representatives, February 6, 1861," *Appendix to the Congressional Globe*, 30(2):165. See also Maynard to George S. Hillard, November 16, 1860, Maynard Papers; Maynard to O. P. Temple, January 8, 1861, Temple Papers; Maynard to William G. McAdoo, February 11, March 1, 1861, McAdoo Papers; *Knoxville Whig*, January 26, March 9, 1861.

21. Temple, *East Tennessee and the Civil War*, 246–53; see also *Knoxville Whig*, January 5, 1861.

22. *Knoxville Whig*, March 30, 1861; *New York Times*, April 3, 1862. See also W. G. Brownlow to the editors of the *New York Weekly*, June 28, 1862, Brownlow Papers, LC.

23. *Knoxville Whig*, January 26, March 23, 1861; Temple, *East Tennessee and the Civil War*, 547–49.

24. *Ought American Slavery to Be Perpetuated? A Debate between Rev. W. G. Brownlow and Rev. A. Pryne* (Philadelphia: J. B. Lippincott, 1858), 102, 263. Brownlow's views on slavery changed considerably between the 1830s and the 1850s. As late as 1834, Brownlow accepted "the truth of the proposition . . . that slavery is an evil, and a great evil at that." The same year he signed an antislavery petition to the state constitutional convention which condemned the peculiar institution as "the bane of American prosperity" and a "canker that is fast corroding republican institutions." See Brownlow, *Helps to the Study of Presbyterianism* (Knoxville: F. S. Heiskell, 1834), 110; Legislative Petitions, no. 38, 1834, Tennessee

State Library and Archives. My thanks to Professor Durwood Dunn for calling to my attention the antislavery petition bearing Brownlow's signature.

25. Horace Maynard to Ephraim Maynard, January 23, 1839, August 15, 1850, December 7, 1850, March 7, 1851.

26. Temple, *East Tennessee and the Civil War,* 545–46.

27. Eighth Census, Slave Schedule, Knox County. Works that analyze the proslavery sentiments of Southern Unionists include John Inscoe, *Mountain Masters: Slavery and the Sectional Crisis in Western North Carolina* (Knoxville: University of Tennessee Press, 1989), and "Race and Racism in Nineteenth-Century Southern Appalachia," in *Appalachia in the Making: The Mountain South in the Nineteenth Century,* ed. Mary Beth Pudup, Dwight B. Billings, and Altina L. Waller (Chapel Hill: University of North Carolina Press, 1995), 103–31; and Kenneth W. Noe, *Southwest Virginia's Railroad: Modernization and the Sectional Crisis* (Urbana: University of Illinois Press, 1994).

28. The latter phrase was taken verbatim from the "declaration of rights" in Article I of the 1834 Tennessee state constitution. Both the 1834 constitution and the "declaration of independence" are reprinted in *The Official and Political Manual of the State of Tennessee* (Nashville: Marshall and Bruce, 1890), 80–106.

29. *Knoxville Whig,* February 9, 1861. For Lincoln's affirmation of the right of revolution, see Roy P. Basler, ed., *Abraham Lincoln: His Speeches and Writings* (Cleveland: World, 1946), 209.

30. *Boston Daily Evening Transcript,* May 24, 1862; see also *Chicago Tribune,* April 11, 1862.

31. Humes, *Loyal Mountaineers of Tennessee,* 31.

32. On the growing support for emancipation among East Tennesseans by 1863, see the newspaper clippings enclosed in W. G. Brownlow to Abraham Lincoln, March 27, 1863, and Andrew Johnson, Horace Maynard, and Allen A. Hall to Abraham Lincoln, March 27, 1863, Robert Todd Lincoln Collection of the Papers of Abraham Lincoln, Springfield, Ill.

33. *Knoxville Whig,* January 19, 1861, November 24, 1860, January 5, 1861.

34. Only 31 percent of East Tennessee voters supported secession in the June 1861 referendum; in contrast, the proportion of voters supporting secession was 88 percent in Middle Tennessee and 83 percent in West Tennessee. See Mary E. R. Campbell, *The Attitude of Tennesseans Toward the Union, 1847–1861* (New York: Vantage Press, 1961), 291–94.

35. *Knoxville Whig,* August 17, September 21, 1861.

36. Isham Harris to Gen'l. W. G. McAdoo, June 10, 1861, McAdoo Papers, LC; Bryan, "The Civil War in East Tennessee," 74–80, and "'Tories' Amidst Rebels: Confederate Occupation of East Tennessee, 1861–1863," *East Tennessee Historical Society's Publications* 60 (1988): 3–22; Fisher, *War at Every Door,* 42–48. Maynard outpolled his pro-Confederate opponent, James H. Shields, by twenty-six votes

in Knoxville. For Zollicoffer's proclamation to the people of East Tennessee, see *Knoxville Whig*, August 10, 1861.

37. On the bridge burners see Temple, *East Tennessee and the Civil War*, 375–85; Bryan, "The Civil War in East Tennessee," 85–91; David Madden, "Unionist Resistance to Confederate Occupation: The Bridge Burners of East Tennessee," *East Tennessee Historical Society's Publications* 52–53 (1980–81): 22–39.

38. Temple, *Notable Men of Tennessee* (New York: Cosmopolitan Press, 1912), 114–17.

39. McAdoo Diary, June 9, 1862.

40. *Knoxville Daily Register,* November 25, August 1, 1862.

41. Michael Fellman, *Inside War: The Guerrilla Conflict in Missouri during the American Civil War* (New York: Oxford University Press, 1989), 49.

42. Temple, *Notable Men of Tennessee*, 69; *Knoxville Daily Register,* February 28, 1862.

43. *Knoxville Whig*, September 21, 28, 1861; *Knoxville Daily Register,* February 28, 1862; Temple, *Notable Men of Tennessee*, 70–72.

44. Temple, *Notable Men of Tennessee*, 70–71; Brownlow, *Sketches of Secession*, 294; *Knoxville Whig*, September 28, 1861; Brownlow to Robertson Topp, October 1, 1861, Robertson Topp Papers, Tennessee State Library and Archives.

45. Landon Carter Haynes to Jefferson Davis, April 19, 1862, in RG 109, War Department Collection of Confederate Letters, Letters Received by the Confederate Secretary of War, NARA; *Knoxville Daily Register,* October 5, 1861.

46. Major General E. Kirby Smith to Gen. A. S. Johnston, March 25, 1862, Smith to Samuel Morrow, April 13, 1862, in RG 109, chap. 2, vol. 51, District of East Tennessee, Letters and Telegrams Sent, NARA; *Knoxville Daily Register,* February 28, 1862. On Baxter's shift toward neutrality, see McAdoo Diary, June 9, 1862. The pro-Confederate Knoxville attorney Henry Elliott described Baxter in September 1862 as "one of the most notorious of the Tories." See Elliott to McAdoo, September 15, 1862, William G. McAdoo Papers.

47. *Knoxville Daily Register,* October 9, 1863; *Brownlow's Knoxville Whig and Rebel Ventilator,* February 13, 1864; RG 393, entry no. 3513, Department of Ohio, Register of Letters Received, February 13, June 22, 1864, NARA; Temple, *Notable Men of Tennessee*, 53, 73 (quote on p. 73); Humes, *The Loyal Mountaineers of Tennessee*, 108ff., 245–46. On the postwar rivalry between Brownlow and Baxter, see W. G. Brownlow, *To Whom It May Concern* (Washington: n.p., 1871), in Samuel Mayes Arnell Collection, Special Collections Divisions, University of Tennessee Libraries; John Baxter, *The Harmon Case: Reply of Colonel John Baxter to the Speech of Senator W. G. Brownlow* (Knoxville: Chronicle Job Printing Office, 1871); and Humphrey, *That D——d Brownlow*, 351–56.

48. Rothrock, *French Broad–Holston Country*, 499–500; *Knoxville Daily*

Register, December 10, 1862; Confederate Papers Relating to Citizens or Business Firms, RG 109, War Department Collection of Confederate Records, NARA; R. G. Dun Mercantile Agency, Tennessee, 18:24, Baker Library of Business Administration, Harvard University.

49. Sutherland, *A Very Violent Rebel,* 123–24.

50. Confederate Papers Relating to Citizens or Business Firms, RG 109, NARA; M. S. Temple to O. P. Temple, September 9, 1862, Temple Papers; McAdoo Diary, December 6, 1862, Floyd-McAdoo Papers.

51. M. S. Temple to Col. O. P. Temple, April 9, 1864, Temple Papers.

52. M. S. Temple was twice robbed and threatened by guerrillas in late August. See M. S. Temple to O. P. Temple, August 31, 1864, Temple Papers.

53. M. S. Temple to O. P. Temple, April 19, October 4, 1864; John B. Brownlow to O. P. Temple, September 9, 1864, Temple Papers.

54. RG 393, entry no. 3513, Department of Ohio, Register of Letters Received, February 13, June 22, 1864, NARA; *Knoxville Daily Register,* March 14, 1862, October 10, 1863.

55. RG 92, Records of the Office of the Quartermaster General, entry no. 963, Records of Special Claims, NARA; Tennessee 18:27, R. G. Dun and Co. Collection.

56. *Chicago Tribune,* April 11, 1862.

57. Green, *Bench and Bar of Knox County,* 69; RG 92, Records of the Office of the Quartermaster General, entry no. 963, Records of Special Claims, NARA.

They Had Determined to Root Us Out

Dual Memoirs by a Unionist Couple in Blue Ridge Georgia

KEITH S. BOHANNON

*T*housands of Unionists in southern Appalachia endured trials and suffering during the American Civil War, although very few left written accounts of their experiences. Horatio and Margaret Hennion are exceptional in this regard; both of them dictated reminiscences to their children, he in 1892 and she in 1900, calling on their exceptional memories to create detailed narratives of their Civil War experiences. Together, these narratives from the perspective of husband and wife provide insight into the dynamics and survival strategies of a Unionist household in the mountain South.

The Hennions, as Unionists living in a region in which they were minorities, were persecuted relentlessly for their loyalties in a guerrilla war that wracked the north Georgia mountains. The exigencies of the conflict periodically forced a reversal of traditional gender roles within the Hennion family. When Horatio went into hiding, Margaret became the provider and protector of the household. Not surprisingly, when husband and wife looked back on their experiences, they held different perspectives and sometimes imbued events with different meanings. What emerges is a rich portrait of a marriage and how it survived, as experienced, perceived, and recalled in similar and distinct ways by both partners.

Horatio Hennion was born in Parsippany, New Jersey, in 1827. Although tutors prepared him for college, Horatio decided instead "to see something of the world and learn a trade." In 1848, at the age of twenty-one, he set off on a lengthy trip that took him across the Great Lakes to a number of western cities. Horatio returned home with hopes of going to California in the Gold Rush, but when those plans fell through he apprenticed in his father's buggymaking shop in Parsippany.

After working with his father for a short time, Horatio moved to Virginia, where he found employment clerking for a man interested in establishing ironworks. Hennion became knowledgeable in the ironworking trade and spent several years in the early 1850s traveling throughout the Midwest and upper South, testing ores and putting up cold and hot blast furnaces. In 1854 he traveled with a partner to the mountainous Blue Ridge region of northeast Georgia to look at the Mossy Creek Ironworks, located along Mossy Creek in Habersham County. (Iron resources were abundant in Habersham, according to an 1855 gazetteer of Georgia.) Hennion and his partner purchased the ironworks and fifty surrounding acres for $460 and, after repairing a dam on Mossy Creek, began producing iron.[1]

Soon after his move to Georgia, Hennion met Margaret Jane Service, a seventeen-year-old girl born and brought up in upstate South Carolina near the village of Coopersville. Margaret's father died when she was a girl, and in 1853 she and her mother moved to Mossy Creek at the request of Margaret's sister Eliza Gilmer. After a year of courting, Horatio and Margaret were, in her words, "foolish enough to get married" in what became their log cabin near Mossy Creek on July 29, 1855. Over the next six years the couple had four children: William Norcross (born 1856); Julian Wilson (born 1858); Horace Victor (born 1860); and Alice Victoria (born 1861).[2]

Horatio's marriage tied him into a network of families in the Mossy Creek neighborhood. Margaret's oldest sister, Eliza, had married Andy Gilmer, who in 1854 abandoned his wife and their four children to head west and find gold in California. Eliza's other sister, Mary Ellen, married one of Horatio's antebellum business partners, Hamilton Ferguson, and had several children. The sizable Ferguson clan, noted Horatio, had all moved to northeast Georgia from Kentucky and "were of Revolutionary stock" with "good fighting qualities."[3]

Horatio Hennion's intelligence and leadership abilities earned him a degree of popularity among his wife's many relatives and the other inhab-

KEITH S. BOHANNON

Horatio Hennion, probably from the 1850s. Courtesy of Marilyn Hennion, Smiths Grove, Kentucky.

itants of the rural community of Mossy Creek. In 1857 Mossy Creek became part of newly created White County, carved out of a portion of Habersham County. Like most of southern Appalachia, White County remained heavily wooded in the mid–nineteenth century; only 15,000 out of 80,105 acres in the county appear on the 1860 census as "improved" farmland.

White County in 1860 was primarily a renter and yeoman society. Roughly 37.5 percent of the white farmers living there in 1860 owned no land and worked as tenants, probably renting for cash or working for shares or a fixed quantity of the crops raised during the year. The remaining landholding yeomen owned 274 small farms, half of them under fifty acres in size. Indian corn was the county's principal commodity, followed by grain crops, tobacco, and cotton. Few farmers owned or used slave labor; only 263 slaves (7 percent of 3,578 persons) lived in White in 1860.[4]

The creation of White County prompted some of Hennion's neighbors to suggest that he run for a local or state office. (Margaret Hennion remembered that people told her husband "he was a smart man if only he would let it be known.") Horatio declined the suggestions, claiming that such jobs paid little and that he intended to spend only another year or two in northeast Georgia before moving back north.[5]

Numerous problems with business partners and workers forced Horatio to rent out his portion of the Mossy Creek Ironworks and revert to his earlier occupation of making buggies and wagons. By 1860 the Hennions had moved a few miles south of Mossy Creek to the town of Gainesville in Hall County, where Horatio and a partner operated a wagonmaking shop. The census enumerator that year noted that Horatio owned $350 in personal estate and $700 in real estate, modest holdings for a member of the artisan class. When Hennion's partner "failed in his contract" in late 1860, Horatio went to work with "the principle manufacture[r] of buggies and wagons" in Gainesville.[6]

Business occupied only part of Horatio's attention in 1860. He had a keen interest in politics and in the presidential election that year supported the national Democratic candidate Stephen Douglas, who warned Southerners against the dangers of secession. Although neither of the Hennions explained Horatio's reasons for being "a strong Union man," his Northern upbringing, education, and continuing ties to family members in New Jersey were undoubtedly factors in shaping his political beliefs and patriotic attachments.[7]

During the secession crisis in the winter of 1860–61, many citizens in Gainesville and northeast Georgia remained conditionally loyal to the Union. One observer in Gainesville noted that there "seems to be still some among us disposed to act with the Black Republican party. It is uncertain which [party] has the power in our county." Hall County's three popularly elected delegates to Georgia's secession convention mirrored the sentiments of many of their constituents when they unanimously voted against the ordinance of secession.[8]

The formation of the Southern Confederacy, the firing on Fort Sumter, and Lincoln's subsequent call for volunteers to put down the rebellion deci-

KEITH S. BOHANNON

sively tipped the balance of power in northeast Georgia against the diehard Unionists. With secessionist excitement sweeping through the region, and local Confederate military companies forming and drilling, many people who had earlier expressed Unionist sentiments switched sides or became silent. Since he remained openly Unionist, Horatio Hennion soon became the target of threats. When he learned that the secessionists planned "to mob him and ride him on a rail," he took his gun and dog and went to Mossy Creek, leaving the keys to his business with a Unionist friend in Gainesville.

Two weeks after his move, Hennion persuaded his wife's brother-in-law Ham Ferguson and a friend to settle his business in Gainesville, sell some furniture, and move Margaret and the children to her sister Eliza Gilmer's house in Mossy Creek. The Hennions lost many of their possessions in the move. They had moved to Gainesville with five wagonloads of belongings but left with only one.[9]

Threats of violence continued after Horatio's return to Mossy Creek. "Rumors came every day of different companies getting ready to come after me," he remembered, "but I paid no attention to it." He did begin carrying a gun when he went to work repairing and painting buggies at a neighbor's blacksmith shop. The situation grew worse after John E. Caldwell, a former business partner of Hennion's, made a speech in Gainesville denouncing Horatio for flying a United States flag over his house and raising a company of one hundred Unionists.

The people in Gainesville responded to Caldwell's accusations by sending two companies to Mossy Creek before dawn one day in late June 1861. One of the armed groups turned around when a Mossy Creek resident denied Caldwell's assertions, but the other company, Captain William H. Mitchell's Gainesville Light Infantry, continued toward Hennion's residence. Mitchell and a dozen of his men surrounded the Hennion home but did not find Horatio. The Confederates questioned Margaret Hennion and her sister Eliza about Horatio's whereabouts, then confiscated a powder horn and a tiny American flag that Margaret had made on perforated cardboard. Fearing for her husband, Margaret sent her nine-year-old nephew, Andy Gilmer, off on the pretense of getting some wood for a fire. The boy's real mission was to warn Horatio, who had spent the night at a neighbor's house in anticipation of helping harvest a wheat crop.

Horatio responded to his nephew's warning by circling around the Confederates, rounding up two or three of his Unionist neighbors, and proceeding to the point where a small group of Southern soldiers had remained with some wagons. After scaring them off, Horatio's group disbanded, and he returned home for dinner. Later that afternoon, his wife's twelve-year-old niece, Ann Jane Ferguson, came in and announced that the soldiers had returned. The Hennions looked out the door and saw a group of Confederates running toward their house.

The charging soldiers terrified Andy Gilmer, who "had heard that they were going to whip him to death" for warning his uncle. The boy immediately "sprang out and ran like a deer." Margaret Hennion, who had been sewing on Horatio's clothes, shoved her husband out the door, remembering that she "wouldn't give him time to get anything but his gun." "Ratio," as Margaret called her husband, bounded out of their cabin holding up his pants with one hand and his gun and powder horn in the other.

Horatio sprinted several hundred yards before crossing Mossy Creek on a foot log and scampering up the other bank to some bushes. The pursuing soldiers fired two shots at him, barely missing both times. When Horatio saw that the Confederates were not going to cross the creek, he headed for Ham Ferguson's house to warn him of the soldiers' return. The shots left Margaret Hennion thinking that Horatio had been killed. "I screamed," she recollected, "for I thought, what would become of us all." Some of the Ferguson clan and other Unionist neighbors gathered to retaliate but disbanded when they found that the soldiers had left and Horatio was unhurt.[10]

Horatio and Margaret both believed that he had avoided capture or death as a result of her quick thinking and the assistance of her nephew and niece. Although no one had been injured, these and other subsequent terrifying events left deep impressions on the Hennions, including at least one of the children. Margaret remembered that the war "sickened" her oldest son, five-year-old Bill, who asserted that "he didn't want to grow up to be a man" and go to war.[11]

The foiled attempt to capture Hennion and his neighbors created considerable excitement in White County, with rumors "flying thick and fast" that other Confederate companies would attempt to round up Unionists. Horatio continued to express his political opinions despite such reports. At a large public gathering in early July 1861 on the "law ground" near Mossy Creek, Judge E. Jules Houston of the White County Inferior Court accused Hennion of being a Unionist and a spy and repeatedly asked the Northerner if he would fight for Jefferson Davis. Hennion replied that he "would see old Jeff Davis in hell" before he would fight for the Confederacy and pointed out that the judge, like many others in the region, had been a Unionist until the outbreak of war. Although Houston was armed and had supposedly boasted that he would kill Hennion if he openly declared his sentiments, he did nothing. Horatio later claimed that the judge knew that "he would never have escaped from my friends alive if he had shot me."

In mid-August 1861 Horatio left Mossy Creek and went north to Cherokee County, North Carolina, to establish and operate a hot blast furnace. Although the decision resulted in a long separation from Margaret and the children, Horatio later stated that he made it at least in part to keep his wife from worrying about his safety. By late summer he had been the target of so many threats that he no longer felt safe spending nights at home and had started camping out. Local Confederates also had maligned Horatio to his children, attempting to turn him into a "bugbear."

With the exception of two brief trips to visit his family in January and May 1862, Horatio remained in North Carolina for a year, building and operating two furnaces. Although the extended separation was undoubtedly hard on Margaret, she had the support of her mother and two older sisters, who lived in Mossy Creek. She probably had experience functioning in a family without an older male head of the household. When she had moved with her widowed mother to Mossy Creek, the two lived for at least a year with Margaret's abandoned sister, Eliza Gilmer, and her young sons.[12]

Horatio returned to Mossy Creek in August 1862 to make arrangements for his wife's brother-in-law, Ham Ferguson, to look after Margaret and the children while he tried to get through the lines to join the Union army, as other Unionists in the area had done. Margaret apparently acquiesced to her husband's decision, making a pair of gray woolen pants to disguise him as he passed through Confederate lines.

Horatio canceled his enlistment plans after learning about a recent act of violence committed by the Confederates. Three days before he planned to leave Mossy Creek, Hennion heard that a Union man named Thompson had been shot to death in adjacent Habersham County by a party of armed men that included a Confederate conscription agent. The killing spurred Horatio and Ham Ferguson to organize local Unionist men of conscription age to hunt down Thompson's killers. Although the conscription agent got away, Hennion claimed that the Unionists gave many Confederates "a piece of our minds." Hennion's apparent success in foiling any further activities of the conscription agent and his followers persuaded him to remain in White County. Keeping men out of the Confederate army, Hennion believed, was as important a contribution to the Union cause as regular military service and involved less bloodshed.[13]

Hennion's followers included roughly two dozen white men from Mossy Creek in White County and the nearby communities of Argo and Polksville in Hall County who shared his opposition to Confederate conscription. Some of these men might have been among those who appeared at a muster of the White County militia on March 4, 1862, called for the purpose of raising a company for Confederate service. Young Davis, a militia officer and former business partner of Horatio Hennion, wrote Georgia's Governor Joseph E. Brown that although seventy-two men had volunteered at the meeting to serve in the Confederate army, around one hundred "hale harty single and newly married men" had refused to enlist.

Davis also complained to Brown that there were "a great many young men standing in idleness some halling whiskey and speculating" while others claimed they had no reason to "fight for the secessionist bayonet." These uninterested and disaffected individuals, along with growing numbers of army deserters, represented a significant minority of White County's white male population by the late summer of 1862, when Horatio Hennion formed his band.[14]

In most respects Hennion's followers differed little from their more numerous pro-Confederate neighbors. The Unionists were farmers or students in their late teens or twenties, and all except Hennion had been born in Georgia or the Carolinas. Hennion's men were all nonslaveholders of limited means; several were young tenants or farm laborers who owned no land and lived in or near their parents' households. Those who owned land had no more than a few hundred dollars in personal and real estate.[15]

Kinship ties, many scholars assert, were extremely important in determining and reinforcing the political allegiances and courses of action chosen by mountain Unionists in the Southern Confederacy. An analysis of the men in Hennion's band supports this contention. The group included at least two sets of brothers, as well as three men named Ferguson, two named O'Kelley, and two named Myers. None of the men lived alone in 1860; all either had wives and children or were in households with their parents. Some of the men had extensive kinship networks that included married siblings, uncles, aunts, and cousins. Horatio's ties through marriage to the Fergusons, one of the most prominent Unionist families in Mossy Creek, undoubtedly made it easier for the New Jersey native to assume a leadership role and cultivate trust with native Southerners who shared his convictions.[16]

Although these connections suggest the importance of kinship in determining allegiances, ideological differences sometimes tore families apart. One of Hennion's men, Jacob W. "Jake" Wofford, had a brother living near him in Hall County who was a staunch Confederate. When in November 1863 a mob of citizens accused Jake Wofford of murder and lynched him,

KEITH S. BOHANNON

the pro-Confederate sibling "expressed the opinion that his brother had only received justice."[17]

Hennion's "boys" had several encounters with Confederate conscription agents and soldiers in the fall of 1862. In almost every instance, the Unionists fired only a few shots at their opponents before running away. This was probably wise, since many of the Unionists carried antiquated flintlock rifles. Hennion also noted that his men were "a minority in the enemies' country" and that if they went on the offensive they "would be exterminated sooner or later and nothing accomplished."

Hennion's men scored their biggest success in the late fall of 1862 when twenty-two of them made a nocturnal foray into the county seat of Cleveland to rescue one of their members placed in the White County jail by Confederate conscription authorities. Although the Unionists expected the jail would be guarded, Hennion and his men were determined to rescue their comrade "or kill a few of the Rebs." When the Unionists arrived in Cleveland around 2:00 A.M., they found the jail unguarded. After stationing men around the courthouse and adjacent jail, Hennion directed two stout young individuals to break down the foot-thick wooden jail door with a sledgehammer and ax. The subsequent hammering and cutting "could be heard for miles around." After half an hour the door yielded, and the Unionists released their comrade. Although the jailer and other townspeople had rallied with pistols during this time, Hennion "told them to retreat & they did in a hurry."[18]

News of the jailbreak caused consternation throughout northeast Georgia. Realizing that he could no longer safely remain at home, Horatio spread the rumor that he had moved to North Carolina but instead took his men to a "natural shelter of rocks" overlooking the Chattahoochee River only a mile and a half from his house. The cave, dubbed "Fort Hennion," was large enough to shelter some twenty or thirty men. It had a long natural fireplace in front and was completely "brushed in" with young pine trees.

Hennion's men camped at the cave from the first week of November through Christmas 1862, making occasional forays out to fight conscription agents and to vote one of their members into the office of bailiff for their militia district. The absence of Confederate voters, who were "off to the war," resulted in the Unionist victory and a subsequent nullification of the election by Confederate authorities. Shortly thereafter, Hennion's followers left their cave, which became a refuge for army deserters.[19]

The soldiers who moved into "Fort Hennion" represented only a small number of the hundreds of Confederate deserters seeking refuge that winter near their homes in northeast Georgia. Since the deserters had arms and ammunition, Hennion's men decided to unite with them. At a meeting in White County, Hennion and forty of his followers signed "an agreement of mutual protection" with the deserters. Afterward, the group sent negotiators to other counties in northeastern Georgia and western North Carolina to look for more members. As Hennion's men and the deserters sought to complete their organization, a group of approximately one hundred of them (not including Hennion) decided to march on the town of Dahlonega.[20]

By the second week of January 1863, Governor Brown knew about the organization of deserters and "disloyal citizens" and their plans to seize Dahlonega. The governor responded by sending state troops, reinforced by several companies of Confederate cavalrymen, to the threatened town. At the same time, the governor issued a public proclamation claiming that the Unionists were "robbing loyal citizens of their property, and threatening to burn their dwellings and do other acts of violence." The proclamation instructed local militia officers, sheriffs, and constables to arrest all soldiers who could not justify their absence from the army and warned "disloyal citizens" who harbored deserters or encouraged desertion that they would be arrested and placed in jail.

When Brown's state troops and the Confederate cavalrymen reached Dahlonega, they found that the "Tories" and deserters marching on the town had dispersed rather than face local authorities and defiant townspeople. Confederate Colonel George W. Lee, commander of the military post at Atlanta, took charge of the forces in Dahlonega. He soon issued a declaration of clemency for those deserters willing to return to their commands and ordered squads of soldiers into the surrounding mountains to "scour the whole country and arrest every lawless man." At least one party of Lee's men went repeatedly to Mossy Creek, which had gained a reputation for being filled with Unionists, deserters, and those wishing to avoid conscription. The Confederates captured three of Hennion's men on January 28, 1863, but failed to locate any other Unionists.[21]

By the time of Lee's expedition, Horatio and Margaret Hennion had moved their family into a house near Mossy Creek which they rented from a neighbor named Brock. Here members of Horatio's band established a distillery in some bushes along the creek only two hundred yards from the house. (Horatio sold his share in the Mossy Creek Ironworks around this time and had no source of income.) The still became a rendezvous point for the men, who found themselves once again poorly armed and woefully out-

KEITH S. BOHANNON

Margaret Jane Service Hennion, ca. 1880s. Courtesy of Marilyn Hennion, Smiths Grove, Kentucky.

numbered after many of their allies who had deserted from the Southern army turned themselves in to Confederate authorities in Dahlonega.[22]

The events of January 29, 1863, when at dawn a small contingent of Colonel Lee's Confederate cavalrymen approached the Hennion home, yielded a story that both Margaret and Horatio told repeatedly with few changes for years afterward.[23] The horsemen dismounted and approached the house, hailing Margaret and asking for Horatio. She replied that he was in North Carolina, but the soldiers didn't believe her. After searching in, under, and around the house, the Confederates started toward the spring and still house, where Horatio and several other men had spent the night.

Earlier, the married men in Hennion's group had arranged signals with their wives, so as not to go home and walk into a trap. "Ratio" and Margaret decided that she would warn her husband of danger by calling repeatedly for their dog, Rolla. When the Confederate cavalrymen first approached her house, Margaret went to the front door and began shouting in earnest for Rolla. Horatio heard the warning, and he and the half-dozen men with him at the still house hid their belongings "and went off a short distance and kept a lookout."[24]

The soldiers returned to the house and asked Margaret who had cut the wood in the yard. She answered her nephew. They then noticed the large amount of "sweet Indian bread" in the house and asked why she had baked so much. She replied simply "to eat." The frustrated soldiers then said they would take one of the Hennion children if Margaret did not disclose her husband's whereabouts. She responded by calling again for Rolla. Her son Billy, uninformed of his parents' signals, pointed out that Rolla was already in the house. Although Margaret claimed that the family owned two dogs, Billy had already identified the one in the house as Rolla, and the soldiers remained convinced that Horatio was nearby. After threatening to burn Margaret out of her house, the officer in charge began talking to Billy, "debating whether they would take him or Alice." The officer eventually seized thirteen-month-old Alice, claiming that he would "as [soon] have a little Hennion as a big one."

Margaret remembered being outwardly calm during the ordeal; despite being "scared out of her wits," she refused to disclose Horatio's location. "I suppose they thought I would holler and scream," she recalled, "and thus call my husband out of hiding." The departing Confederates told the frightened woman that they would drown Alice, but Margaret didn't believe it and thought that they would leave the baby someplace nearby instead. A neighbor who had been acting as a guide for the Confederates soon returned Alice.[25]

Margaret's belief that her infant daughter would not be harmed reveals her conviction that the Confederates, even when filled with anger and frustration, would remain bound by the traditional limits of gender behavior. As several recent studies suggest, Civil War soldiers were willing to invade homes and threaten, torment, and arrest white women but would seldom physically injure them or their children. Margaret and Horatio Hennion and the other Unionists in Mossy Creek realized this and used it to their advan-

KEITH S. BOHANNON

tage, with the result that the women often became the temporary protectors of their households and families.[26]

Subsequent Confederate patrols forced Horatio's band to camp across the Chattahoochee River in Habersham County for several weeks. Eventually the Unionist group broke up, most of the men establishing smaller camps near their homes. The Confederate soldiers and their civilian sympathizers became more vigilant, noted Horatio, forming parties to watch the houses of Unionists and "driving the woods for us" in groups sometimes numbering several hundred.

This intensified pressure forced Horatio's men to change their living arrangements. Instead of "large, comfortable camps" with fires, they built eight-foot-square shelters that provided bed space for two or three men. Horatio located his camp in some open woods not far from the house of a Confederate. Southern "hunters," as Hennion termed them, passed near the shelter almost daily for several weeks but failed to discover it.

When reminiscing, Horatio claimed that he and his boys generally had "a very pleasant time" engaging in trials of skill with the Rebels. Hennion's band met frequently at different locations to discuss where the Confederates would conduct their next sweep. Occasionally "some of the boys would get shot at," Horatio remembered, "but seldom was any damage done." Several of the Unionists attempted to venture to North Carolina or Kentucky, but Hennion believed that Confederates intercepted and captured them all.[27]

While Horatio recollected an "interesting game" of life and death between his men and the Confederates, Margaret Hennion's memoir displays no hint that her Civil War experiences constituted a pleasant time. The Confederate search parties made her so uneasy that she often refused to let Horatio stay at home. (Margaret's decisions in this regard go unmentioned in her husband's memoirs.) Her husband's extended absences left Margaret feeling lonesome, and she often took the children a short distance away to her landlord's house to spend the night.

Horatio's seclusion forced Margaret to provide for their entire family, something that proved to be an enormous task. Every two or three days, Horatio acknowledged, his wife brought food to his camps. At one point Margaret bought a pig for twenty Confederate dollars, fattening it by feeding it swill from Horatio's still house. When it came time to slaughter the hog, she sent her nephew into its pen with an ax. As the boy swung at the pig it leapt over the fence and disappeared into the woods. The hog's loss made Margaret "feel savage." "Meat was scarce," she remembered, "and I had to get along any old way."[28]

Although she makes no mention of it in her memoirs, Margaret's extended family undoubtedly provided material and moral assistance to her and Horatio. They also probably helped shape Margaret's Unionist sentiments. Neither of Margaret's sisters supported the Confederacy, despite having spent their adult lives in South Carolina and Georgia. When Confederate authorities came to take Eliza Gilmer's eldest son, James, into the army, she instructed the youth to "be a good boy . . . and read your Bible, but don't come back until the War is over." Eliza made this statement in the presence of the Confederates, but her son knew that she really "wished me to make my way to the Union lines as quick as possible." Margaret's other sister, Mary Ellen, presumably followed her husband, Ham, to Kentucky, where they were refugees behind Union lines for the rest of the Civil War.[29]

The activities of Horatio's band, which included several of the Fergusons, prompted threats from Confederates that were an increasing source of concern for Margaret Hennion. Frustrated Southern soldiers often harassed her after searching in vain for Horatio, knowing that he and his men could not remain in the area without help from their wives. The Confederates finally warned Margaret that they would give her ten days to leave or burn down her house. Earlier threats of a similiar nature had so worried her that she stored most of the family's valuables at her sister's residence.

Horatio told his wife not to move as "the burning game was a new one," and that "the Rebs had more houses to burn than we had." Eventually Horatio decided to move the family away, since they lived in a rented house and Margaret was having an increasingly difficult and risky time acquiring provisions. He also hoped in vain that his departure might mean that the Confederates "would not hunt the other boys so much." Whether Margaret also wanted to leave is not mentioned in her memoir.

Around April 1, 1863, Horatio and several other men went to Persimmon Creek Forge in western Cherokee County, North Carolina. Although the group "got afoul of a Rebel party" and had to scatter, Hennion made it to the forge and accepted a position there. He then returned to Mossy Creek with another man and a four-mule team to get Margaret and the children. Under the cover of darkness, the Hennions loaded a few of their belongings into the wagon and started northward without telling anyone their destination. Horatio traveled apart from his family, but they all arrived at their destination on April 13.

Margaret Hennion's departure from Mossy Creek was a heartrending affair. She had only recently moved her family out of the house rented from Brock into "a nice new house" owned by Jake Ferguson, a local Unionist.

KEITH S. BOHANNON

(Ferguson, a twenty-six-year-old farmer with a wife and small daughter, was a friend of the Hennions and probably a relative of Margaret's brother-in-law Ham.) When Horatio appeared in the wee hours of the morning to move the family, Margaret was with her mother. Margaret never forgot leaving her mother in the empty house, "where she was to stay until daylight, when she was to go back to my sister's, a mile out from Mossy Creek." It was November 1874 before Margaret saw her mother again; by that time the older woman was paralyzed, near death, and barely recognized her daughter.[30]

Despite her separation from her mother, Margaret Hennion's nuclear family survived the war intact. The same cannot be said for many of the Hennions' former neighbors in Blue Ridge Georgia. After Horatio's departure, the men in his band found themselves trapped in a bloody cycle of violence.[31]

Throughout the fall of 1863, detachments of local home guards and militiamen scoured the "mountain fastness" of White County, hunting down and killing several of Horatio Hennion's associates. The Unionists, by this time under the leadership of Jake Ferguson, struck back, ambushing and killing one of their antagonists. Southern newspaper editors dehumanized the "tories," portraying them as outlaws who were "constantly committing depredations upon the loyal citizens." The editor of the *Athens Southern Banner* wrote, "We hope the people of that section will continue to work until they exterminate the whole gang."[32]

Horatio Hennion's move to extreme western North Carolina provided only a temporary escape from the violence destroying the households of his former neighbors in northeast Georgia. Horatio's occupation as an ironworker at Persimmon Creek initially exempted him from conscription in North Carolina. He claimed that "old enemies" in Georgia "were afraid to come up after me, although they would frequently threaten to come up and hang me." He worked at the forge, remembered Margaret, "until the country became all torn up and full of Rebs, and every Union man had to scatter." After a group of men chased down and stabbed to death the boss at Persimmon Creek Forge, Horatio once again began camping out.

Horatio's memoirs and letter extracts end with his family's move across the state line from Georgia to North Carolina. Unfortunately, only brief, undated vignettes appear in Margaret's memoir to illuminate her family's trials in North Carolina. She related that at one point Horatio had been "on a mountain with some of the Union boys" when Confederates began shooting at them. While running from the Confederates, Horatio tripped over a log and sprained his arm but got away. On another occasion a party of "hard looking" Confederates that included several Cherokee Indians ransacked the Hennions' house at the forge, "throwing some things out of doors." Once again fearing for her possessions, Margaret put "some of her best things" in a trunk and hid it in the woods. She also had a table with a false bottom that she crammed full of things. No one found either hiding place.

Despite the suffering she endured at the hands of Southern soldiers, Margaret Hennion did not shun them to the same degree that her husband did. When a group of Confederate infantrymen from Gainesville, Georgia, passed her house in North Carolina, Margaret remembered that they "behaved nicely." Although she lied to them about Horatio's whereabouts, Margaret seemed to enjoy their brief company and the news they had concerning her former female acquaintances. Years later she remembered how one of the men had coaxed her three-year-old daughter, Alice, into talking to him.[33]

Margaret's difficulties in procuring provisions continued in North Carolina. After work ceased at Persimmon Creek Forge and supplies stopped coming from Tennessee, her family "almost starved to death." Salt and sugar became nearly unobtainable, and for two weeks the Hennions lived on what Margaret called "sick flour" which they could eat "only a very little at a time."[34]

Things undoubtedly improved for the Hennions in the fall of 1864, when Horatio traveled westward to Chattanooga, Tennessee, seeking employment. On November 1, 1864, he signed a contract to work as a civilian wheelwright for the United States Army for seventy-five dollars a month. The job kept him busy through the spring of 1865 working with dozens of other wheelwrights to repair the large number of army vehicles that continually passed through Chattanooga.[35]

Margaret Hennion saw her husband only twice during his six-month stay in Chattanooga. During this final wartime separation, Margaret had a degree of autonomy she may not have known before. When the children of the family she was living with became unbearable, Margaret moved into another house. She also decided in April 1865 to walk fifty miles to Chattanooga, having been told by a neighbor named Minnie Ingram that Horatio had money and wanted her to come there. Margaret left all of her children, except her newborn daughter, with a neighbor and set out for Chattanooga accompanied by two other women.

When the women arrived in Chattanooga, Margaret found her husband "very much put out" for her traveling so far on foot. She discovered that Minnie Ingram had lied about Horatio's sending a message "so as to get me there so she could borrow some money . . . with which to get coffee." After a short stay in Chattanooga, the women boarded a wagon for the trip back to North Carolina. En route they all came down with a case of measles contracted from another passenger in the vehicle.

After the surrender of the two main Confederate armies in April 1865, the United States Army laid off many of its civilian employees. Horatio received a discharge on May 9, 1865. He returned to his family in North Carolina but "didn't feel quite safe," thinking that "some of the old Confederates might wreak revenge on him." Fortunately, the ex-Rebels left the Hennions alone.

In the fall of 1865, Horatio decided, partly at the urging of his father, to move his family to his hometown in New Jersey. (Horatio may have been concerned about his father's health; the elder Hennion died less than six months after his son's return home.) After traveling westward in a wagon to Cleveland, Tennessee, the Hennions sold what few possessions they had and boarded a northbound train on the East Tennessee and Virginia Railroad. Margaret admitted that her husband "had his hands full" on the trip looking after her and their five small children. Their journey took them through central Virginia, where they viewed a number of the shell-torn battlefields. The scenes of devastation "made one's blood run cold," remembered Margaret.

Sometime in October 1865 the Hennions arrived in north central New Jersey and ran into Horatio's father on the road to Morristown. The elder Hennion did not at first recognize his son, but after becoming reacquainted and meeting the rest of the family, the party arrived at the Hennion house, where all the relatives received them in what Margaret described as "a warm and friendly manner."[36]

Horatio Hennion had planned on moving back north since the late 1850s. His frustrating antebellum associations with the Mossy Creek Ironworks and the buggy shop in Gainesville left him with low opinions of Southern business practices and the "inefficiency of the Georgia laws." By 1862 he had sold his share of the Mossy Creek Ironworks and had to remain in hiding most of the time. He remembered that the Confederates "were determined to root us out" and that he remained in Blue Ridge Georgia "only to spite them."

Horatio's memoirs display pride in his leadership of the White County Unionists and his contributions to the Union cause. At times he inflated his importance, as when he asserted that people in Gainesville wanted him arrested more than anyone since he "was considered the cause of the [Unionist] rebellion." Like many Civil War veterans, Horatio created a heroic identity for himself based on his willingness to face the physical dangers of war. He even remembered enjoying the high-stakes game of skill between his men and the Confederates, despite the many concomitant hardships. "If there had been no danger," he boasted, "it would have been a tiresome business."

Such dangers apparently did not extend to Margaret and the Hennion children; neither husband nor wife expressed serious fears about her physical safety or that of their children. Horatio did, however, feel the need for a degree of male supervision in the household during his frequent absences. He almost always found a trusted male neighbor to "look after" his family while he was gone.[37]

Margaret Hennion's memoirs contain no evidence that she enjoyed any aspect of the internecine warfare that tore apart the Appalachian communities in which she had lived. She consistently supported her husband and displayed pride in his leadership role, but the long periods of separation from him, the burden of providing for her entire family, and the harassment and threats she endured at the hands of Confederates were for her no source of excitement or pleasure. Although she had no deaths to mourn as did the families of other mountain residents, the war took its toll on her. "I had grown ten or more years older in looks," she remembered, a change so dramatic that her mother did not recognize a photo of Margaret sent in the mail shortly after the end of the war.[38]

Unlike her husband, Margaret Hennion made no mention of wanting to leave the South. She also left no indication about whether she objected to the family's moving to North Carolina and then New Jersey. Her exodus from northeast Georgia had resulted in a long-term (and, in the case of her mother, a permanent) separation from her extended family and friends. She also missed the beauties of nature that had surrounded her in upstate South Carolina, Blue Ridge Georgia, and North Carolina; her memoirs contain many detailed descriptions of Southern flora and fauna.

In some ways the Civil War experiences of the Hennions as targets of prolonged harassment were typical of Unionist families living in areas of southern Appalachia where Confederate sentiments predominated. Yet the Hennions also differed in some significant ways from their Appalachian neighbors. Horatio Hennion was an outsider, a well-traveled and well-educated Northern-born man with unique job skills. When the Hennions left Appalachia in the fall of 1865 they never returned, remaining in north central New Jersey the rest of their lives and bringing up a family of ten children. Horatio Hennion died in Littleton, New Jersey, in 1905, and Margaret died in Hinsdale, Massachusetts, in 1923. Both are buried in the Vail Cemetery in Parsippany, New Jersey.[39]

KEITH S. BOHANNON

The family of Horatio and Margaret Hennion had been fortunate to survive the Civil War, a period many north Georgia Unionists later referred to as the "reign of terror." The Hennions' strong partnership, Margaret's determination and resourcefulness, and Horatio's unique job skills helped them to survive ordeals that destroyed the families of many of their neighbors. While their devotion to each other is clear in their memoirs, the events of the Civil War took on different meanings as they related their life stories years afterward.[40]

NOTES

1. Horatio Hennion memoir entitled "Account taken at my Father's dictation at Boxwood Lodge (Dec. 14, 1892) Parsippany, N.J." (hereafter cited as H. Hennion memoir), Horatio Hennion Papers, U.S. Army Military History Institute, Carlisle Barracks, Pa., 1–3, 44. The page numbers cited are from a typescript of the Hennion Papers produced by George M. Glover of Lilburn, Ga., a copy of which is in the White County Public Library, Cleveland, Ga.; Habersham County, Ga., Superior Court Records, Deeds and Mortgages, vol. 5 (1853–58), 214, 340, Drawer 179, Box 17 (microfilm), Georgia Department of Archives and History, Atlanta; George S. White, ed., *Historical Collections of Georgia* (New York: Pudney and Russell, 1855), 490.

2. H. Hennion memoir, 4. Margaret Hennion dictated her memoirs to her daughter Alice Dixon in 1900. Margaret Hennion memoir entitled "Copy of Mother's notes and account of her early life and some events during the war" [hereafter cited as M. Hennion memoir], 26, 27.

3. Horatio and Margaret both claim that Elizabeth Gilmer had only four children, but the 1860 census lists five in her household. H. Hennion memoir, 4, 23; M. Hennion memoir, 26; U.S. Eighth Census, 1860, Schedule 1, Free Inhabitants, White County, 490, 505; Service Family Genealogy, courtesy Cheryl Hennion Hahn, Hackettstown, N.J.

4. Frederick A. Bode and Donald E. Ginter, *Farm Tenancy and the Census in Antebellum Georgia* (Athens: University of Georgia Press, 1986), 93, 131; Joseph C. G. Kennedy, *Agriculture of the United States in 1860* (Washington, D.C.: Government Printing Office, 1864), 28–29, and *Population of the United States in 1860* (Washington D.C.: Government Printing Office, 1864), 60, 61, 64, 65, 68, 69.

5. H. Hennion memoir, 14; M. Hennion memoir, 27.

6. H. Hennion memoir, 3–4, 14–15; U.S. Eighth Census, 1860, Schedule 1, Free Inhabitants, Hall County, Ga., 90; James E. Dorsey, *The History of Hall County, Georgia 1818–1900* (Gainesville, Ga.: Magnolia Press, 1991), 1:112–13.

7. For references to the intensely patriotic educations received by many Northern-born Southern Unionists, see Thomas G. Dyer, *Secret Yankees: The Union Circle in Confederate Atlanta* (Baltimore: Johns Hopkins University Press, 1999), 54–55; see also Dyer's essay in this volume.

8. Horatio Hennion believed that many of the Georgia Secession Convention delegates "were bribed or talked over" to vote for secession, including Hall County delegate Ephraim Malone Johnson. Hennion was wrong about Johnson, who voted against secession. H. Hennion memoir, 4–5; A. M. Evans to Howell Cobb, March 20, 1861, in *The Correspondence of Robert Toombs, Alexander H. Stephens, and Howell Cobb*, ed. Ulrich B. Phillips (Washington D.C.: Government Printing Office, 1913), 551; Dorsey, *History of Hall County*, 155–56; Ralph Wooster, "The Georgia Secession Convention," *Georgia Historical Quarterly* 40 (March 1956): 46.

9. M. Hennion Memoir, 27; H. Hennion memoir, 5.

10. While running, Horatio found he could not sling his powder horn over his shoulder, so he threw it into a potato patch, where the soldiers found it. Hennion later got the horn back. H. Hennion memoir, 6, 7, 8, 15, 16; M. Hennion memoir, 28; U.S. Eighth Census, 1860, Schedule 1, Free Inhabitants, White County, Ga., 505.

11. H. Hennion memoir, 6; M. Hennion memoir, 28. For speculation on the heavy psychological toll that the Civil War took on children, see James Marten, *The Children's Civil War* (Chapel Hill: University of North Carolina Press, 1998), 153, 167–70.

12. H. Hennion memoir, 4; M. Hennion memoir, 26, 27.

13. H. Hennion memoir, 8–11, 16–17. The April 1862 passage of the Confederate Conscription Act prompted many north Georgia Unionists to flee northward, where several thousand enlisted in the U.S. Army. Robert S. Davis Jr., "Memoirs of a Partisan War: Sion Darnell Remembers North Georgia, 1861–1865," *Georgia Historical Quarterly* 80 (spring 1995): 14; Jonathan D. Sarris, "Anatomy of an Atrocity: The Madden Branch Massacre and Guerrilla Warfare in North Georgia, 1861–1865," *Georgia Historical Quarterly* 77 (winter 1993): 679–710.

14. Colonel George W. Lee suggested to Governor Joseph E. Brown on January 27, 1863, that the state arm and station in White County a local company known as the Chattahoochee Rangers (later Company G, First Georgia State Line) since there were "a large number of Torys &c in that and adjoining counties." Young Davis to Joseph E. Brown, March 1862, Georgia Governor's Incoming Correspondence, RG 1-1-5, 3335-01, Box 28, Georgia Department of Archives and History; C. H. Sutton, "The Troubles in North-East Georgia," *Atlanta Southern Confederacy*, February 22, 1863; George M. Glover, comp., "Partial Roster of Confederate Soldiers from White County," copy in author's possession; Lillian Henderson, *Roster of the Confederate Soldiers of Georgia, 1861–1865* (Hapeville, Ga.: Longino and Porter, 1960), 3:21–30, 5:452–62; Kennedy, *Population*

in 1860, 60; George W. Lee to Joseph E. Brown, January 27, 1863, Georgia Governor's Incoming Correspondence, RG 1-1-5, 3335-06, Box 38, Georgia Department of Archives and History.

15. A partial list of the men in Hennion's group appears in H. Hennion memoir, 11. U.S. Eighth Census, 1860, Schedule I, Free Inhabitants, White County, Ga., 453, 460, 461, 493, 504, 505; U.S. Eighth Census, 1860, Schedule I, Free Inhabitants, Hall County, Ga., 43, 51, 57, 61; "The Slayer of Lewis Pitchford Hung," *Athens Southern Banner,* November 28, 1863. For other similiar composite portraits of mountain Unionists, see Martin Crawford, "The Dynamics of Mountain Unionism: Federal Volunteers in Ashe County, North Carolina"; and Peter Wallenstein, "'Helping to Save the Union': The Social Origins, Wartime Experiences, and Military Impact of White Union Troops from East Tennessee," in *The Civil War in Appalachia*, ed. Kenneth W. Noe and Shannon H. Wilson (Knoxville: University of Tennessee Press, 1997), 1–29, 56–57; Walter L. Bates, "Southern Unionists: A Socio-Economic Examination of the 3rd East Tennessee Volunteer Infantry Regiment, U.S.A.," *Tennessee Historical Quarterly* 50 (1991): 226–39; Richard N. Current, *Lincoln's Loyalists: Union Soldiers from the Confederacy* (Boston: Northeastern University Press, 1992), 133, 138; Noel Fisher, *War at Every Door: Partisan Politics and Guerrilla Violence in East Tennessee, 1860–1869* (Chapel Hill: University of North Carolina Press, 1997), 64.

16. For studies that stress the importance of kinship ties, see Bates, "Southern Unionists," 226–39; Ralph Mann, "Ezekial Counts's Sand Lick Company: Civil War and Localism in the Mountain South," in *The Civil War in Appalachia*, ed. Noe and Wilson, 79–80; and John C. Inscoe and Gordon B. McKinney's essay in this volume.

17. "Slayer of Lewis Pitchford Hung."

18. H. Hennion memoirs, 11–12, 17–18. Confirmation of Hennion's success in breaking O'Kelley out of jail appears in a November 12, 1862, entry in the White County Inferior Court Minutes. The court agreed to pay $47.25 to repair and reinforce the door of the county jail. White County, Ga., Inferior Court Records, Drawer 149, Box 76 (microfilm), Georgia Department of Archives and History. For concern over future jailbreaks, see the January 17, 1863, proclamation of Governor Joseph E. Brown in *Athens Southern Banner,* January 28, 1863.

19. H. Hennion memoirs, 12, 18–19; "Resisting the Law," *Athens Southern Watchman,* November 12, 1862.

20. The *Dahlonega Signal* claimed that the well-armed band of one or two hundred deserters and tories approaching the town was motivated by revenge and "the hope of rescuing friends from jail." H. Hennion memoirs, 19; *Dahlonega Signal,* January 17, 1863 article, reprinted in the *Augusta Constitutionalist,* January 21, 1863; "From Colonel Lee's Expedition," *Atlanta Southern Confederacy,* February 3, 1863; "Col. Lee's Expedition to N. E. Georgia," *Atlanta Southern Confederacy,* February 4, 1863.

21. William H. Bragg, *Joe Brown's Army: The Georgia State Line, 1862–1865* (Macon: Mercer University Press, 1987), 17–22; Joseph E. Brown, January 17, 1863, proclamation in *Athens Southern Banner,* January 28, 1863; C. H. Sutton, "Troubles in North-East Georgia," *Atlanta Southern Confederacy,* February 22, 1863; "From Col. Lee's Expedition," *Atlanta Southern Confederacy,* February 3, 1863. For partial lists of the deserters and Unionists captured and sent to Atlanta by Lee's men, including several of Hennion's band, see "Harnessed Up," *Atlanta Southern Confederacy,* February 1, 1863; "Arrival of Tories, Deserters, &c," *Atlanta Weekly Intelligencer,* February 11, 1863; H. Hennion memoir, 20. For more on George W. Lee's activity in Atlanta and raids on north Georgia, see Dyer, *Secret Yankees,* chap. 4; Jonathan D. Sarris, "'Hellish Deeds in a Christian Land': Southern Mountain Communities at War, 1861–1865" (Ph.D. dissertation, University of Georgia, 1998), chap. 4; and Jonathan D. Sarris, "An Execution in Lumpkin County: Localized Loyalties in North Georgia's Civil War," in *The Civil War in Appalachia,* ed. Noe and Wilson, 139–42.

22. H. Hennion memoir, 20, 22; M. Hennion memoir, 28.

23. Margaret claimed this incident occurred on January 30, 1863, but extracts from Horatio's letters to an uncle, probably written at an earlier date, indicate that it was January 29. H. Hennion memoir, 20; M. Hennion memoir, 29.

24. Such prearranged warning signals between spouses were common in the households of north Georgia Unionists. See Claim of William J. Sawyer, fiche no. 2937, M 1407, Barred and Disallowed Claims, Southern Claims Commission, National Archives, Washington, D.C. See also Fisher, *War at Every Door,* 72.

25. The party that visited Margaret consisted of a local guide and a detachment of the Sixteenth Battalion Georgia Partisan Rangers commanded by Lieutenant Andrew J. Lyle. H. Hennion memoir, 14, 20–21; M. Hennion memoir, 29–30; Janet B. Hewett, Noah A. Trudeau, and Bryce A. Suderow, eds., *Supplement to the Official Records of the Union and Confederate Armies,* pt. 2 (Wilmington, N.C.: Broadfoot, 1995), 5:606.

26. For discussions of the limits of violence directed against white women by Civil War soldiers, see Michael Fellman, *Inside War: The Guerrilla Conflict in Missouri during the American Civil War* (New York: Oxford University Press, 1989), 201; Lee Kennett, *Marching through Georgia: The Story of Soldiers and Civilians during Sherman's Campaign* (New York: HarperCollins, 1995), 305–6; Joseph Glathaar, *The March to the Sea and Beyond: Sherman's Troops in the Savannah and Carolinas Campaigns* (New York: New York University Press, 1985), 72–74. For several examples of mountain women who were victims of violence, see Gordon B. McKinney, "Women's Role in Civil War Western North Carolina," *North Carolina Historical Review* 69 (January 1992): 43–44; and John C. Inscoe and Gordon B. McKinney, *The Heart of Confederate Appalachia: Western North Carolina in the Civil War* (Chapel Hill: University of North Carolina Press, 2000),

118–19, 194–95. For a local study of Appalachia that challenges the notion that the Civil War forced aberrations in prescribed gender roles, see Ralph Mann, "Guerrilla Warfare and Gender Roles: Sandy Basin, Virginia, as a Test Case," *Journal of the Appalachian Studies Association* 5 (1993): 59–65.

27. H. Hennion memoir, 21–22.

28. M. Hennion memoir, 28–30. For other accounts of the ordeals of Appalachian women in the Civil War, see McKinney, "Women's Role," 37–56; Philip S. Paludan, *Victims: A True Story of the Civil War* (Knoxville: University of Tennessee Press, 1981); Mann, "Guerrilla Warfare and Gender Roles," *Journal of the Appalachian Studies Association* 5 (1993): 59–66; John C. Inscoe, "Coping in Confederate Appalachia: Portrait of a Mountain Woman and Her Community at War," *North Carolina Historical Review* 69 (October 1992): 388–413, and "'Moving through Deserter Country': Fugitive Accounts of the Inner Civil War in Southern Appalachia," in *The Civil War in Appalachia*, ed. Noe and Wilson, 158–86; and Inscoe and McKinney, *The Heart of Confederate Appalachia*, chap. 7.

29. James M. Gilmer enlisted in Company K, Forty-third Georgia Infantry on January 5, 1863, in Gainesville, Ga. After his capture at Vicksburg, Miss., on July 4, 1863, James refused to accept a parole and eventually joined the U.S. Navy. "A Brief Account by James M. Gilmer," typescript, Hennion Papers, White County Public Library, Cleveland, Ga.; James M. Gilmer, Confederate Compiled Service Record, National Archives; Service Family Genealogy.

30. H. Hennion memoir, 22; M. Hennion memoir, 30. The Hennions were one of many Unionist families in Georgia that moved northward for the duration of the Civil War. See also Ethelene D. Jones, ed., *Facets of Fannin County, Georgia* (Dallas: Curtis Media, 1989), 257, 302, 421; *The Heritage of Union County, Georgia* (Waynesville, N.C.: Don Mills, 1994), 178; Sarris, "Anatomy of an Atrocity," 679–710; Dyer, *Secret Yankees*, 136.

31. An Athens newspaper editor claimed in June 1863 that although the number of Unionists in White County was small, "from the mischief they have done, they are certainly very active"; "Disturbances in the Up-Country," *Athens Southern Watchman*, June 17, 1863.

32. The White County Home Guards killed at least five of Hennion's associates, including Jake Ferguson and Jake Wofford. The *Southern Watchman* editor predicted that the deaths of Ferguson and Wofford would probably break up the band of tories at Mossy Creek Camp Ground. "Expedition into North Georgia," *Athens Southern Banner*, October 28, 1863; "Another Tory Killed," *Athens Southern Banner*, December 9, 1863; "Jake Ferguson Shot!" *Athens Southern Watchman*, December 9, 1863; "Bryson and his Banditti," *Athens Southern Watchman*, October 14, 1863; "From the Up-Country," *Athens Southern Watchman*, September 30, 1863.

33. M. Hennion memoir, 34.

34. H. Hennion memoir, 22; M. Hennion memoir, 30–31.

35. Returns for the months of November 1864 through May 1865 in "Reports of Persons and Articles Hired at Chattanooga, Tennessee, by Assistant Quartermaster Captain R. W. Wetherall, U.S. Army, January–July 1865," and "Reports of Persons and Articles Hired at Chattanooga, Tennessee, by Assistant Quartermaster Captain E. B. Kirk, U.S. Army," RG 92, National Archives; Quartermaster Personal Narratives, E. B. Kirk, Box 5, vol. 5, RG 92, National Archives.

36. M. Hennion memoir, 31–33.

37. H. Hennion memoir, 11, 14, 15, 16, 20, 21, 22; John Pettegrew, "The Soldier's Faith: Turn-of-the-Century Memory of the Civil War and the Emergence of Modern American Nationalism," *Journal of Contemporary History* 31 (1996): 57–58.

38. It is impossible to determine how many additional household tasks Margaret Hennion assumed during the Civil War; she may have raised livestock and provided foodstuffs for her family before the conflict. For a perceptive examination of women's activities in antebellum western North Carolina, see Mary K. Anglin, "Lives on the Margin: Rediscovering the Women of Antebellum Western North Carolina," in *Appalachia in the Making: The Mountain South in the Nineteenth Century*, ed. Mary B. Pudup, Dwight B. Billings, and Altina L. Waller (Chapel Hill: University of North Carolina Press, 1995), 185–209.

39. U.S. Tenth Census, 1880, Inhabitants of Hanover Township, Morris County, N.J., E.D. 118, sheet 8, line 18; U.S. Eleventh Census, 1900, Inhabitants of Hanover Township, Morris County, N.J., E.D. 57, sheet 10, line 100; Hennion Family Genealogy, typescript, Parsippany Historical and Preservation Society, Parsippany, N.J.; Service Family Genealogy.

40. For north Georgia Unionists referring to a "reign of terror" see Davis, "Memoirs of a Partisan War," 107; Deposition of Booker Graveley in Claim of John S. Johnson, fiche no. 11155, M1407, Barred and Disallowed Claims, Southern Claims Commission, National Archives; Deposition of Lemuel J. Cook in Claim of William Sawyer, fiche no. 2937, M1407, Barred and Disallowed Claims, Southern Claims Commission, National Archives.

Vermont Yankees in King Cotton's Court

Cyrena and Amherst Stone in Confederate Atlanta

THOMAS G. DYER

*I*n 1976 a manuscript dealer sold to the University of Georgia library an eighty-page document written in longhand on legal-size sheets. Its content indicated that it was a diary, although the form and character of the entries suggested that it was a transcription and not the original. The diary spanned the period January 1–July 22, 1864, and was written by an unidentified woman of strong Union sympathies who lived in Atlanta during the months leading up to the cataclysmic battle and siege of Atlanta late that summer. Possibly unique among diaries pertaining to the American Civil War, the document reflects the experience of a Union woman who recorded the frightful, violent tumult that marked the beginning of the death agony of the Confederate States of America. Aware of the danger of keeping such a journal, the diary's author carefully protected her identity (referring to herself only as "Miss Abby"), artfully obscured the identities of others who also belonged to a small community of Unionists living in the Rebel city of Atlanta, and deliberately concealed information that might lead Confederate authorities to her or her allies.[1]

The story continues with a novel. Entitled *Goldie's Inheritance: A Story of the Siege of Atlanta*, written by Louisa Bailey Whitney of Royalton, Vermont, and printed in 1903, the novel hovers between history and fiction as it tells of a young Vermont woman who leaves the state to take a teaching position in Atlanta a few years before the opening of the Civil War. She remains in Georgia after the outbreak of the war, firmly maintains her loyalty to the Union, and secretly gives aid and comfort to Union prisoners held in Atlanta. Embedded in the novel are large unexpurgated chunks of "Miss Abby's" diary and other substantial sections, covering the years 1861–63, which appear to be drawn from missing portions of the original diary. It quickly became evident to this reader that Louisa Whitney based her book on the same document that the University of Georgia acquired in 1976.[2]

The diary and the novel came together only after several years of tedious research in numerous archives and after an intensive effort to identify the author of the diary, using both internal and external evidence. In the end, "Miss Abby" proved to be Cyrena Bailey Stone, half-sister of the novel's author, Louisa Bailey Whitney. The research led ultimately to a reconstruction of the membership and activities of a group of loyal Unionists who remained in the "second capital" of the Confederacy throughout the war. The diary and the novel, together with documents drawn from many other sources, provide a basis for the story of Cyrena Bailey Stone and her husband, Amherst Willoughby Stone, who, once caught up in the Civil War, became members of the Unionist circle in Atlanta.[3]

Cyrena Stone stood at the heart of the Unionist community in Atlanta. A person of courage and resolve, she personified a strict loyalty to the Union exceedingly rare in the Confederate South. Under conditions of constant stress and danger, she wrote her diary and in doing so made a record of a heretofore invisible portion of the Civil War. Amherst Stone, whose loyalty would in time become more problematic, represents a more common type of Unionism, one that was conditional and even opportunistic but that still involved great hazards. The Stones' experiences and those of other members of their family illustrate the complicated character of national loyalty under wartime conditions of physical and psychological peril.

Cyrena Ann Bailey began life in 1830 in the northern Vermont village of East Berkshire, the fifth child of a Congregational minister and Yankee tinkerer, Phinehas Bailey. He had a reputation as a hardworking, strong-minded, and devout pastor, "more Calvinistic than Calvin," one commentator later noted. The area's natural beauty and arcadian setting—a lush valley

Louisa Bailey Whitney, undated. Mount Holyoke College Library and Archives.

only ten miles from the Canadian border—made life pleasant enough for the Baileys, but the minuscule salary Bailey earned as a minister kept his family on the edge of destitution in East Berkshire and later pastorates.[4]

Cyrena spent her childhood and early adult years in East Berkshire and a succession of similar villages in eastern New York. Her mother died in 1839, leaving the nine-year-old Cyrena to carry much of the burden of managing the family while Bailey, now nearly penniless, sought to avoid "breaking up" his family and dispersing the children. He soon found a new wife, added more children to the family, and took the entire brood back to East Berkshire when a call to that pastorate came again in 1845.[5] Cyrena's childhood was filled with the elements of her father's religion—rigorous devotion to prayer, frequent church attendance, regular devotionals, daily Bible reading, and family fasting.[6] Very little else is known about her early years. No doubt she was educated in the common schools of the villages in which she lived. She also seems to have profited from her father's emphasis upon learning in the home and in later years would show a literary flair, writing with a skill that exceeded considerably the level of instruction associated with the common schools.[7]

In her teenage years Cyrena became a handsome woman with dark eyes, dark hair, and a lively personality—if her half-sister's partially fictionalized account of her life is believed and if she bore a resemblance to the same sister. Although Phinehas Bailey's firm hand and well-known aversion to dances and other forms of riotous living likely prevented her from having an extensive social life, she did take part in the round of activities common to the rural youth of northern Vermont, including chaperoned picnics and excursions as well as the more ritualized visits between families.[8]

It was perhaps on one of these visits that Cyrena met young Amherst Stone, four years older than she, the son of a prosperous local farmer, Mitchell Stone. Young Amherst had ambition, and although he apparently did not attend college, he did study or "read" law in St. Albans.[9] Admitted to the bar in 1848, Stone, like many nineteenth-century Vermonters, decided to emigrate from the state, encouraged perhaps by the abundance of lawyers in St. Albans and the abundance of siblings (five brothers and a sister) on his father's farm.[10] Amherst looked to the South for opportunity. Why he chose Georgia is unknown, but by 1850 he had settled in the town of Fayetteville, about twenty-five miles south of Atlanta. Stone practiced law there, and within a short time he became active in civic affairs and participated in the founding of a local academy.[11]

In August 1850 Cyrena Bailey and Amherst Stone married and began

THOMAS G. DYER

their domestic life together in Fayetteville. Two years later, Cyrena gave birth to a little girl whom they took to Vermont to visit family when the child was eleven months old. Sadly, within a few months after the visit, the child died a wracking death from consumption, moving Cyrena to find expression for her grief in a reflective essay that she wrote for an Augusta, Georgia, newspaper.[12] In 1854, soon after their loss, the Stones moved to Atlanta, perhaps because of the greater opportunities awaiting a young lawyer in that new but fast-growing town of five thousand people or perhaps in an attempt to leave behind the scene of their child's death.

In Atlanta the Stones began to walk among the emerging commercial and professional elite. Stone's position as a lawyer did not automatically guarantee that he would be able to move with the powerful; only six years later there were at least forty lawyers in the city.[13] Nevertheless, the ambitious, resourceful Amherst worked his way into the network of business and mercantile leaders who guided the city's most influential commercial enterprises. The Stones met some of these powerful men through church membership and found commonality with others, such as the prominent merchants Sidney Root and E. E. Rawson and the dentist H. L. Huntington, who were also transplanted Vermonters. Less than two years after he and Cyrena had arrived, Stone took part in the founding of a successful bank and in an ambitious but ultimately unsuccessful railroad venture. As his legal practice prospered, the Stones became even more prominent, helping to found the Atlanta Female Institute and the Central Presbyterian Church.[14]

With prosperity came property. Amherst soon acquired extensive real property and built a large home with several outbuildings, including a cotton house and a cottage on the outskirts of the city. He also acquired a substantial amount of cash—precisely how much is not clear, but at least fifteen thousand dollars.[15] In addition, Amherst Stone had other property. By 1860 the Vermont native owned six slaves, or "servants," as he and Cyrena (and much of the rest of the South) called them.[16] Because of their backgrounds, owning other humans likely gave both of the Stones pause, although it appears to have given the greater concern to Cyrena. Her minister father had no truck with slavery, roundly condemning it and imbuing his family with biblical and moral arguments against the "peculiar institution." Slavery had reached into the Baileys' lives in a more direct way. Although a fierce opponent of human bondage in the South, Phinehas Bailey did not embrace the abolitionist arguments calling for immediate emancipation of slaves and refused to condemn those religious organizations that did not subscribe to such tenets. This position cost him his pastorate at East Berkshire when the congregation adopted the more radical posture and found a pretext for firing its aging minister, who "felt the liberation of the oppressed African race was but a part of the work awaiting Christian effort and that it was neither right nor wise, for the sake of this to oppose every other good enterprise."[17]

Amherst Stone's drive toward status and wealth may explain his decision to own slaves. Cyrena's position is more difficult to gauge, but clues to her quandary and to Amherst's views on slavery can be gleaned from *Goldie's Inheritance.* In the novel, the heroine, Goldie Hapgood, draws most of her character from Cyrena, although another persona, Amy Allen, provides a vehicle for dealing with matters like slaveholding, which the author cannot reconcile with the purity of the protagonist.[18] In the early portion of the book, Amy, a teacher and close friend of Goldie's, is about to leave Vermont for Georgia to marry Egbert Fay, a New England lawyer who has emigrated to Georgia and bears an obvious resemblance to Amherst Stone. Both Egbert and Amy had sworn that they would never own slaves, resolving "to keep our hands clean of it forever." Just as Amy is departing, she receives a letter from Egbert explaining that a client, a "religious woman [of] extreme old age," has asked him to arrange her business affairs and to dispose of her property, which consists only of "three slaves for whose welfare she was very solicitous." The old woman could die peacefully, she told the lawyer, if only he would agree to buy the slaves at what Egbert reports is a "remarkably low" price.[19] Egbert leaves the choice to Amy, who seeks the advice of Goldie Hapgood, fearing that a minister or some other "sage advisor" would offer only a "concoction of Northern prejudice, having no element of sympathy." Goldie presents an easy and quick solution. Amy should "do the most natural thing in the world, take a missionary view of it: you could do these slaves a great deal of good." Goldie continues, "It looks right to me, but it's queer, isn't it? I would have said this morning that it was impossible to make you a slave-holder."[20]

The accuracy of the fictive explanation of the transformation of the Stones to slaveholders remains open to conjecture, but it comports perfectly with a hoary and widespread justification for slaveholding advanced by Southerners and transplanted Northerners alike. Moreover, the general faithfulness of the novel to Cyrena's life also lends credence to the account. Like the fictitious Fays, the Stones' slaveholdings were small. They included a married couple, a single female, and three children.[21] Slaveholding was relatively common among the Atlanta Unionists, but, as was true with other local Unionists and those elsewhere in the South, both Amherst and Cyrena saw

THOMAS G. DYER

no conflict of interest in owning slaves while professing strong views on national loyalty and strenuously opposing secession.

The comfortable life that the Stones had built for themselves began to appear threatened as the crisis of disunion intensified in the late 1850s and 1860. During the summer of 1860, several Vermonters living in Atlanta, including Cyrena Stone, went north to visit family and friends and to contemplate whether remaining in the South seemed wise. Old friends and neighbors urged that the visitors remain in the safety of their New England communities rather than return to the South, warning that if war came, Northerners would make quick work of their Southern brethren.[22] Nevertheless, all returned to Atlanta.

Upon their arrival in Georgia, Cyrena and the others found the crisis growing more acute. In rapid succession the election of Abraham Lincoln, the secession of South Carolina, and the call for a secession convention in Georgia gravely worsened the situation. Hysteria seemed to grip the state and the region. With the mounting tensions came sharply increased pressures against Atlantans who held Unionist sentiments and especially against those like Amherst Stone, who had been a frequent speaker at meetings where the issues were debated. Atlanta newspapers favoring secession boosted the tempo of their attacks on those of Unionist views and even on those who merely advocated cooperation with the North in settling the great national dispute. In January 1861, however, as the Georgia secession convention drew near, substantial numbers of Atlantans still favored a nonsecessionist course; when the votes for delegates to the convention were counted, approximately 38 percent of the city's voters chose candidates who favored a moderate course. Nevertheless, an overwhelmingly prosecession vote in the state convention took Georgia out of the Union on January 19, 1861.[23]

Once the state became part of the Confederacy, the ranks of its Unionists and cooperationists were decimated as thousands of moderate Georgians, forced to choose between loyalty to nation and loyalty to state, chose the latter. Radical secessionists now dominated in Atlanta and began a sustained effort to suppress dissent and enforce a single, correct view of the conflict between North and South. Regulators, investigating committees, and vigilance committees rapidly formed and were charged with determining "how every man stood." Those "who expressed Union sentiments [were] ordered to leave the state and a good many were whipped or lynched," one Unionist remembered.[24] In the face of such pressures and within a matter of a few weeks, only a few Atlantans, probably no more than one hundred, maintained a strict allegiance to the United States.

Thus secession effectively caused the Unionist group to go underground and to exercise great care concerning what they said and to whom. Those who had published Unionist arguments now found it nearly impossible to express dissenting views without running great personal risk. As community pressures increased, vocal citizens like Amherst Stone became publicly quiet, although he and a dozen or so friends met secretly to provide mutual support and to plan their futures.[25] To have written or to have spoken in anti-Southern terms ensured a visit from a vigilance committee. Despite the threats, however, Cyrena Stone continued to express Unionist sentiments and, using the pseudonym "Holly," published an essay that could easily have been interpreted as anti-Southern. Written for the *Commonwealth*, a local newspaper whose editor was a Unionist, the essay lamented the passing of the Union and decried the "death-sleep of the fairest, the noblest Republic upon which ever shined the Sun," language certain to have engendered rage among the radical secessionists.[26]

The fall of Fort Sumter in April 1861 created dread and fear in Atlanta's Unionist community. Cyrena Stone's Vermont friend, Mrs. Henry L. Huntington, described the event as "the knell of all our hopes."[27] The fictional Cyrena Stone reacted to the surrender of Sumter with dismay but also with what would become a well-developed survival skill, choosing neutral language or words of ambiguous meaning to respond to the pointed remarks of ardent Confederates. One visitor to the Stone household, probing Cyrena's loyalty, emphatically declared that P. G. T. Beauregard, the Confederate general commanding the assault on Fort Sumter, should have immediately hanged the Federal commander when the fort surrendered. "It seems to me that Beauregard took the wiser course" in sparing Major Robert Anderson, a noncommittal Cyrena replied.[28]

For Atlanta Unionists, unlike the vast majority of Georgians, allegiance to the United States superseded loyalty to the state but clashed with more intimate loyalties. Loyalty to neighbors and neighborhoods became moot issues as Unionists were systematically excluded from society and social relations at the most basic levels. Old friends now became avowed enemies, and once-cordial neighbors became spies who watched every move of the hated Unionists. The same sorts of social exclusion extended even to the churches, where Christian brotherhood dissolved into systematic shunning. And on the streets children joined in the harassment, hurling contemptuous insults.[29]

Some Unionists also had to contend with situations of great difficulty

THOMAS G. DYER

when national loyalty collided with allegiance to family. These heartrending conflicts most often involved a decision by one or more family members to support the Confederate cause. In one instance a strong Atlanta Unionist watched helplessly as his fifteen-year-old son was caught up in war fever and ran away from home to join the Confederate army.[30] Even staunch Unionists like the Stones could not escape this most basic of conflicts. One of Amherst's brothers, Chester A. Stone, had followed his brother to Georgia from Vermont, arriving about 1856. Ten years younger than Amherst, he lived with his brother and sister-in-law, clerked in a general merchandise store, established a sound business reputation, and became a partner in the enterprise in short order. Like his brother, Chester Stone entered the civic life of Atlanta and in 1857 enlisted as a charter member of the Gate City Guard, a local militia unit. During the secession crisis, he leaned toward the South, displaying strong beliefs concerning states' rights. When war broke out and the Gate City Guard was activated to Confederate service, he cast his lot with the new Southern nation and in December 1861 became the guard's elected captain.[31]

In mid-March 1861 orders came for the Gate City Guard to report for active duty, and for two days a cheering Rebel city turned out for sermons and elaborate, enthusiastic ceremonies to send its first company to repel Yankee invaders.[32] Cyrena and Amherst Stone were probably among the cheering crowd that sent the military unit on its way from the Atlanta depot. The Stones were a close-knit family, and both Cyrena and Amherst must have agonized over Chester's departure. Cyrena's anguished response to her brother-in-law's decision and his leave-taking was illustrated in several sections of *Goldie's Inheritance*, which hint at the despair she felt when Chester decided to join in "the gay pageant of treason." At the train station the fictional Cyrena's eyes were "blinded with tears." It would have been hard enough merely to say good-bye to the younger brother going off to war, "bad enough just to see him going to face danger and possible death; but the deeper pain to which neither . . . could be reconciled was to know that he was going to fight against the land of their birth, perhaps their own kindred." A "great shadow had fallen" upon the Stone household.[33]

Chester Stone was soon fighting with his unit in the mountains of Virginia, and in the summer of 1861 Cyrena and Amherst returned to Vermont for what would prove to be their last visit for several years.[34] The Stones, like many Americans, believed that the war would be short; they would never have guessed that within a few months a passport system would be instituted, making exit from the South much more difficult. For now, however, they returned to the familiar confines of northern Vermont and visited with family and friends, including another of Amherst's younger brothers, Charles Birney Stone, who would soon become a Union soldier.

This journey to Vermont ended with an episode that would cast serious doubt upon the character of Amherst Stone's commitment to the Union cause. News of the Confederate victory in the war's first major battle, at Bull Run, reached East Berkshire on the day before Cyrena and Amherst were to take the mail coach for St. Albans to begin the long journey back to the South. The Union loss at Bull Run quickly became the dominant topic of conversation. According to one observer, the effect of the defeat "overspread the faces of all with gloom" that was "everywhere noticeable."[35]

The Stones boarded the coach and were soon joined by another passenger. Introductions revealed that he was William Clapp, the nephew of an old enemy of the Stone family who bore the same name. The elder Clapp had feuded for years with the Stones, probably over business dealings with Amherst's uncle, James Stone. As the coach bounced along, young Clapp listened closely to the conversation between Amherst and Cyrena. Clapp thought Amherst was "in the best of spirits as though he had got rid of some kind of restraint and was running over with desire to give vent to some kind of inward glee." It was the Confederate victory that gave Amherst pleasure, and in an undertone he told Cyrena that "he had a good mind to wave a Confederate flag." According to Clapp, Cyrena showed great distress at Amherst's comments and "tried to check him during the whole journey." The voluble Stone went on to predict the fall of Washington in a matter of days and a full Confederate victory with a hundred days. Cyrena pleaded with him to be silent. He refused. For the remainder of the trip to St. Albans, Cyrena cried softly.

Clapp later reported that he was seized by a "fever of patriotic indignation" at Amherst Stone's "treasonable sentiments" and contemplated swearing out a warrant but decided that it would be a "quixotic" undertaking.[36] Within two years, however, the affair on the mail stage between East Berkshire and St. Albans would come back to haunt Amherst Stone with a vengeance. For now, the Stones continued their return to Atlanta.

Amherst's behavior compounded the clash of loyalties that Cyrena Stone must have felt. Chester Stone's loyalty to the Confederacy and Amherst's alleged sedition on the Vermont stage would have put wrenching emotional pressures on anyone and would have made the maintenance of resolute Unionism extremely difficult especially if, in private, Amherst's loyalist sentiments were as fragile as Clapp's account of the ride on the stage indicated.

But Cyrena Stone persisted in her adherence to the Unionist values she espoused and, as time would show, because even more aggressively Unionist and increasingly less affected by the disloyalty of her brother-in-law and the doubtful behavior of her husband.

In the fall of 1861, after the return to Atlanta, Cyrena, using a pseudonym, published in the *Commonwealth* another essay, which superficially resembled other essays becoming common in Southern newspapers as casualty lists lengthened and early enthusiasm for the war began to waver. Written from the perspective of a soldier dying on the battlefield, the essay differed from archly pro-Southern pieces in the absence of specific references to the South or to the icons of Southern nationalism. Cyrena Stone wrote about all soldiers who were dying on the battlefields of the Civil War, not just Confederates as conventional Southern patriotism would have dictated. Perhaps the artful deception escaped many of the *Commonwealth*'s readers, or perhaps it added to the enmity toward Cyrena Stone among those Confederate Atlantans who suspected that she was the pseudonymic "Holly."[37]

The early Confederate victories gave way in 1862 to several stinging defeats and to the realization that the war would be a protracted, bloody struggle. Concomitantly, there was a steadily increasing emphasis upon enforcing conformity and dealing forcefully with the Unionists and other enemies within. Throughout 1862 Atlanta newspapers constantly warned residents of the city to watch out for a panoply of enemies, including spies, abolitionists, Lincolnites, "neutral Yankees," and, of course, loyal Unionists. Disloyalty to the Confederacy was quickly equated with treason, and the newspapers urged the city authorities to ferret out those who posed a threat to the Confederacy and the orthodoxy of Confederate nationalism. And in the increasingly tense atmosphere of wartime Atlanta, disloyalty, defined and redefined at will by the Confederate authorities, could be something as simple as failing adequately to support the Southern war effort or raising questions about the wisdom of the Confederate cause.[38]

Such disruptive activities as armed resistance or sabotage would have been futile because of the small number of Unionists and because Atlanta was deep in Confederate territory. The Unionists found a mode of resistance to the Confederacy, however, that enraged the authorities and indirectly aided the Union cause. Federal prisoners began to arrive in Atlanta in 1862, soon after the battle of Shiloh. Only a few, housed in the poorest hospitals of the city, came at first, but in time their numbers would swell to thousands. Many were sick and wounded and received very little, if any, medical attention. With minimal rations and squalid living conditions, the prisoners needed help, and they got it from the Unionists.[39]

Cyrena Stone was among the most active of those who aided the prisoners. She, like many Atlanta women, frequently visited the city's numerous military hospitals, where Union and Confederate patients sometimes were housed near each other. On various pretexts she and her Unionist associates would manage visits to the Union prisoners, sometimes by paying small bribes of food or money to guards, or on occasion through the use of feminine wiles to distract them. Throughout the war Cyrena collected money for Union prisoners and then passed it secretly to them during hospital visits. Some used the money to buy food and medicine; others used it to aid in their escapes.[40] These were treasonous acts, filled with danger, and they were among the many times when the actions of the real Cyrena Stone conformed to those of her fictional shadow, when the currents of the novel flowed parallel to the real occurrences in Civil War Atlanta.

Confederate officials eventually decided to crack down on the Unionists and put an end not only to the aiding of Federal prisoners but also to the other disloyal acts ascribed to them. In the late summer of 1862, martial law was declared in Atlanta, and the provost marshal of the city acquired broad powers to arrest and punish criminals and traitors.[41] Colonel George W. Lee, the provost marshal, was an illiterate prewar saloon keeper who managed to become head of a company of several hundred troops charged with the maintenance of civil order in Atlanta. Lee, whose checkered military career included charges of thieving, vowed to rid the city of traitors and in doing so launched a plan that brought about what Amherst Stone described as a "perfect reign of terror" against the Unionists.[42]

Suddenly and without warning, on a Thursday in late August 1862, Lee and his men arrested at least eight and perhaps as many as twelve of the most prominent Unionists. Five men were clapped into one of the many Atlanta jails, and three women were arrested as well. One of the men, Michael Myers, an Irish immigrant dry-goods merchant, died of the effects of a brutal beating on the day after their arrest. The other men spent varying lengths of time in prison, ranging from a few weeks to several months.[43]

Cyrena Stone was almost certainly one of the three women arrested and interrogated. In Louisa Whitney's fictional narrative, rumors circulate through Atlanta that Goldie (the Cyrena character) has been hanged for treason; in fact, she has only been summoned to a local hotel by "Colonel L.," the provost marshal, for a "grand investigation" into the possible existence of a Union organization of three hundred members and a plot to incite

THOMAS G. DYER

a slave rebellion. Goldie, accompanied by an "advisor" (probably meaning Amherst), arrives at the hotel to find other women, weeping and fearful, gathered in the lobby. She is the first to be summoned to a small upstairs room where a court of inquiry is presided over by "Colonel L.," assisted by a tall man "with hatred of the Yankees written on every feature" and by "a man of some sixteen summers who stood leaning against the bed in an artistic attitude." To Goldie "the room was so unlike the typical courtroom, and the court so lacking in real dignity, that fear vanished, and a sense of the ludicrous took its place." Citing religious reasons, Goldie refuses to be sworn, agrees instead to affirm, and then evades the court's questions about the existence of a Unionist organization in the city. After less than probing questions, the court dismisses her and allows her to go free.[44]

Cyrena Stone's treatment at the hands of the court of inquiry appears to have been more benign than that of other Atlanta women summoned by the courts-martial during the "reign of terror," if the version in *Goldie's Inheritance* is to be believed. Mary Hinton, another Unionist woman arrested at the same time, described aggressive and probing questioning about Unionist activities, but the queries put to Cyrena and the general tone of the court took on a somewhat burlesque quality in the novel. Both accounts may be accurate. Mary Hinton did not have the same social standing as Cyrena: Amherst Stone was still an important and wealthy man in Atlanta, despite his Unionist reputation. Colonel Lee, the provost marshal, would have been more careful around the Stones, if only because of their connections with the city's elite. Mary Hinton, on the other hand, had just moved to the city and as a young single woman had few ties of substance that might afford protection. In addition, she had the added burden of being the sister of Martin Hinton, who had been arrested and imprisoned as a Unionist spy only a few weeks before. Thus, it is possible that the novel's account of Goldie/Cyrena's arrest and questioning is faithful to the truth.[45]

The killing of a Unionist and the imprisonment of others badly shook Amherst, who later reported that the "reign of terror" continued for nearly six months. During that time intense harassment, constant fear, anxiety to preserve his wealth, and the ubiquitous threat of conscription in the Confederate army led Stone to make plans to escape from Georgia and return to the North. Ever resourceful, he laid a complicated plan to flee the region, deciding to leave Cyrena behind until he could find a way to bring her out also.[46]

In late 1862 it was still possible for men to leave the Confederacy, even those who were thought to be Unionists, but taking out entire families was largely impossible. In effect, family members became hostages ensuring that the men would return. It was also quite difficult to take wealth out of the region, but Stone decided that as a part of his escape, he would try not only to salvage some of his personal wealth but also to turn a profit. He had learned that substantial amounts of cotton were being shipped out of Union-occupied New Orleans and sent to the North with the permission of Federal authorities. This led Stone and some of his Unionist friends to organize a company to take their cotton out through the Union naval blockade of the Confederate coast. Blockade companies were relatively common in the South, but Stone's would be decidedly different from most. With the knowledge that Union officials supported the exportation of Southern cotton to the North, Stone planned secretly to seek permission from the United States government to bring the cotton out and sell it in a Northern port. He also wanted a guarantee that if the cotton was seized by Federal ships manning the blockade, it would be returned to him and the other Unionists who were party to the plan.[47]

No blockade company could be made up only of Union men; thus, the newly formed company also included a number of loyal Confederates, although the Unionists owned a majority of the stock. The Confederate members of the company were not to be told of the proposed arrangement with the United States government; neither were they told that the company did not contemplate returning any other commodities to the South. "We would not let them know it," Stone wrote. "We were afraid of them. They belonged to the rebel side and I have no doubt they thought it was a regular blockade company." Stone also audaciously sought the permission of the Confederate government to transport the cotton and, with the assistance of the Confederate senator Benjamin H. Hill of Georgia, secured the desired permission, but only after Hill represented that the company would ship its cotton to a neutral port and then return goods to the Confederacy.[48]

Difficulty in securing a Southern steamer to take the cotton out gave Stone the opportunity to persuade the company that it should send him into the North, where he would hire a Northern vessel and also get the desired permission from the United States government. With permissions from both governments, the chances for success would be greatly enhanced, and the venture would be as secure as possible in the chancy blockade-running business.[49] The company agreed, and Stone made ready to leave the city. Waiting until the winter had passed, he said good-bye to Cyrena in early April 1863 and began to make his way to the Union lines north of Richmond. The trip was dangerous—doubly so since Stone carried with him at least fifty thousand dollars in a mixture of financial instruments drawn on Northern banks and Confederate currency. Another man, George Briggs, was sent on a different route and also carried a large sum of the company's money. Stone made it to Richmond safely, stopped over briefly (possibly to confer with Hill), and then sneaked through the Union lines into Washington during the night.[50]

Relieved to be safely out of the South, Stone soon went on to New York City and checked into the opulent St. Nicholas Hotel, a favorite haunt of politicians and expatriate Southerners. He stayed in New York for ten days, making preliminary arrangements for a steamer and paying visits to Cyrena's brother and sister, Keyes and Mary Bailey, and possibly to his cousin Chester A. Arthur, the future president, who was then a prominent New York lawyer. While in New York, Stone deposited the fifty thousand dollars in a bank.[51]

Stone decided that he could complete many of his business arrangements by telegraph and mail, so he went on to Vermont for a visit with family and friends. Nearly two years had passed since he had visited his relatives, and he had had virtually no communication from them since the war began. Apparently preparing to close a deal, Stone left East Berkshire on May 8 to return to New York, passing through St. Albans en route. What he did not know was that his telegrams and mail from East Berkshire had been intercepted by Rolla Gleason, the Union provost marshal in Burlington, who was looking for him in St. Albans.[52]

Gleason had been alerted to Stone's presence in Vermont by William Clapp, whose nephew had overheard Amherst's braggadocio on the stage to St. Albans with Cyrena in 1861. The vengeful Clapp, an old enemy of Stone's, had "instituted inquiries" about Amherst, the results of which he reported to Gleason, who then ordered that his correspondence be intercepted. Convinced that he had a Confederate agent within his grasp, Gleason found Stone in St. Albans, arrested him, and charged him with being a Rebel emissary and smuggler. A surprised Stone readily admitted the blockade-running scheme, expecting perhaps that Rolla Gleason would be understanding, even sympathetic to the complex plan. Decidedly unsympathetic, Gleason turned Stone over to a deputy provost marshal from New York who, alerted to the fifty-thousand-dollar bank deposit, had also been looking for Stone in connection with the proposed blockade-running activity. For good measure Gleason alleged that Stone had also "indulged in conversation of a disloyal character—rejoicing at our defeats & rebel successes," a clear reference to the mail stage incident after the First Battle of Bull Run.[53]

Having successfully escaped from the South, Stone now endured the ironic ignominy of being arrested in his home state in front of old friends and neighbors and being transported, very probably in irons, across eastern New York to the military prison at Fort Lafayette in New York Harbor. Stunned, shocked, perhaps even bewildered, Amherst Stone found himself in the exceedingly dangerous position of having been charged with being an agent of the Confederate government, and at a time when the writ of habeas corpus had been suspended.

Stone was completely unprepared for prison life and for the stark, crowded, dank imprisonment that awaited in a cell full of Confederate officers in Fort Lafayette.[54] But he was resourceful, and he devised a plan for his release, informing Secretary of War Edwin Stanton of the complete details of his background and the blockade-running escapade in the hope that Stanton would order his freedom.[55] Stone stayed at Fort Lafayette for about two months before being transferred to Fort Warren in Boston Harbor, where he appears to have successfully bribed a deputy marshal who brought him before General John Wool at the St. Nicholas Hotel in New York. Released from custody by Wool in July 1863 (he claimed that Stanton was responsible), Stone took up lodging again at the St. Nicholas in the midst of the bloody New York draft riots.[56]

Over the next six months Stone moved between New York, Washington, and Nashville, Tennessee, trying to put the blockade scheme together and also seeking the aid of L. C. Turner, the Federal judge advocate general, in getting Cyrena out of Atlanta. Stone claimed that his wife was "sick & distressed on account of my absence," and Turner gave him permission to return to Atlanta—permission he never used, claiming that Cyrena had gotten word to him in Nashville that his return would bring, at the very least, certain imprisonment. Stone went back to New York, made preparations to go into business (presumably to practice law), and settled in at the St. Nicholas.[57]

On January 30, 1864, he was arrested again and reimprisoned in Fort Lafayette as a result of the energetic vendetta of William Clapp and his enthusiastic collaborator, Rolla Gleason, and in connection with the alleged bribe. During this imprisonment Stone had a great deal more difficulty in getting the attention of civil or military authorities and remained in Fort Lafayette for more than eight months, awaiting trial by a military commission but held without a formal charge for the entire period. Finally, he managed to hire Benjamin Baily, a lawyer from Putnam County, New York, who visited the White House in August 1864 and obtained a note from Abraham Lincoln to an official in the war department regarding the case. The official was probably Assistant Secretary of War Charles A. Dana, who had shown some interest in Stone's case since the late spring. It is possible that Stone had had some connection to Dana, who had lived in Vermont, or that Stone's cousin Chester A. Arthur may have contacted Dana on his behalf, although there is no evidence to support either conclusion. Dana set in motion a chain of events that led to Stone's release from Fort Lafayette in mid-September 1864.[58]

Amherst Stone plunged back into the life of a free man with vigor and characteristic guile, promoting himself and seeking the acquaintance of influential men. He attracted the attention of Henry J. Raymond, editor of the *New York Times* and chairman of the National Union Executive Committee, Abraham Lincoln's re-election campaign organization. Stone volunteered his services to Raymond to aid in Lincoln's campaign. Raymond had evidently heard Stone orate and wrote to Union General John A. Dix asking that Stone's bond money (probably the fifty thousand dollars) be released. "He wants to take the stump for the Union cause," Raymond wrote, "but wants these bonds discharged first." The bond was released, and if Stone did campaign for Lincoln, it is not hard to imagine that in his campaign rhetoric he would have identified himself as an exiled Southerner who, having escaped from the South and having remained true to the Union, could now freely support the re-election of a president who had preserved the Union. That is how he saw himself in later life, and that is how he presented himself to others after the war was over.[59]

While Amherst was in the North, Cyrena remained in Atlanta. And although slaves and white servants kept her company during the nearly two years of his absence, along with a menagerie of pets—cats, a dog, a dove— she sometimes thought of herself as "alone on the hill" where the Stone house stood, "with no husband or brother near," although Chester Stone, then enrolled in the local militia, occasionally spent some time with her.[60] The surviving fragment of the diary that Cyrena Stone kept, however, does not reveal a person who dwelled upon loneliness or isolation. Instead, it shows a woman almost always able to deal effectively and confidently with a situation of great difficulty and peril, and who, in the space of seven months of journal keeping, mentions her husband only two or three times. Cyrena Stone showed great courage and self-reliance in the face of cataclysm.

During these years Cyrena led a life governed by her ardent patriotism and a passionate commitment to the Union. As the war progressed, her life was increasingly filled with risk-taking, an unwavering longing for the appearance of the Union armies, and a daily routine that blended the remnants of a comfortable existence with fast-increasing privation and struggle. She did not attempt to flee the city as the Union armies approached. "This is my home," she wrote on the eve of the battle for Atlanta, "& I wish to protect it if possible. There may be no battle here—If not I am safe; if there is one, where is any safety?"[61] Sometimes she longed for Vermont and the comforting majesty of "those lofty mountains sweeping against the sky." But the nearness of the gargantuan struggle being waged between Confederate and Union armies less than 120 miles from Atlanta and the pressures of being a Unionist in the Rebel city controlled her actions and her mind.[62]

The "disloyal" activities continued throughout the months leading up to the battle of Atlanta in July. Cyrena and the small group of Unionist women still visited the wounded and suffering Union soldiers but had to do so with much more stealth. And as the number of Union prisoners declined, with many transferred to the hellholes of Andersonville and other Confederate prison camps, the women intensified their efforts to care for the few remaining, most of whom were sick or badly wounded and could count on practically no care from Confederate surgeons.[63]

Pressures from the Confederate authorities seemed to ebb and flow during the final months before the battle. One friend told Cyrena that "bitter threats" had been made against her, and another reported that her name remained on a list of twenty to thirty persons in Atlanta who would immediately be arrested if they sought to flee. Still others came to her with the chilling news that she had been branded a spy. One woman, also on the provost marshal's list, urged Cyrena to "burn or bury every scrap of writing, that would excite suspicion. . . . For you know they say you have been corresponding with the enemy ever since they came to Chattanooga and giving them information—& if we are all arrested, your house will certainly be searched." Cyrena confided to her diary, "It was a new idea, my keeping them informed! What next?"[64]

Throughout this period, symbols of national loyalty became even more important to Cyrena and other Unionists. All during the war, Cyrena kept in her possession a small American flag, secreting it in a variety of hiding places, at one time in a jar of preserved fruit, at another in her sugar canister. Atlantans with sympathies for the Union would regularly come to the Stone household and ask to see the flag, the possession of which was illegal in the Confederacy. During these visits, they practiced such patriotic rituals as soft singing of the "Star-Spangled Banner" and "Hail, Columbia" and engaged in whispered discussions about the worthlessness of life without a "true" government. Such contact with other Unionists remained a necessity, as a way

THOMAS G. DYER

both to exchange information and to provide psychological support in a situation where a sense of ubiquitous danger was mixed with passionate hope for early liberation by the Union armies. Caution had always to be exercised, however, especially when someone arrived whose loyalties were unknown and who asked to see the flag or tried to engage Cyrena in political discussions.[65]

During the late winter and early spring of 1864, constant rumors swept through Atlanta concerning the position of the Federal armies and the likelihood that a battle would be fought near the city. Confederate faith that General Joseph E. Johnston would dispatch the Union forces remained unabated, but as the Confederate army constantly fell back toward Atlanta, morale began to drop. Former friends who had become enemies now began to seek Cyrena out, believing that if the unthinkable occurred and Atlanta fell, she and other Unionists would be good friends to have. "I shall look to you for protection," one woman told Cyrena, who wrote in her diary that "others have attempted to make friends with those they have abused & persecuted untiringly for being suspected of Union sentiments & showing kindness to prisoners."[66]

Cyrena had kept informed of the steadily advancing Union armies through the newspapers and by word of mouth. "Oh bid them hasten who have promised to come," she wrote in her diary in the spring. In late June cannon could be heard from her house on the outskirts of Atlanta, signaling the presence of the Federal army within twenty miles of the city. By early July most of Atlanta had grown frantic with fear of imminent catastrophe and terrified at the prospect of Yankee invaders in the streets. While her neighbors sought to leave the city, Cyrena Stone stayed. Earlier in the year, she had written that she had lived so long with "these great hopes" of liberation that "a life without them—of without seeing their inclination—would seem zestless and void." She preferred to remain rather than "to sit in a quiet room, a thousand miles away and read in some morning paper—'On the 1st of——, long line of blue swept through the streets of Atlanta.'"[67]

By mid-July all Cyrena Stone's neighbors had retreated to the city or had left the area altogether. The sounds of musketry and cannon had been growing louder each day, and on July 21 these sounds erupted into a cacophony of explosions as the Union and Confederate forces struggled for the possession of Atlanta. Despite the din and the danger, Cyrena still found time late at night to record in her diary a description of the "red waves of war" that threatened to engulf her. Huge shells, "horrid whizzing screaming thing[s]," now passed over the Stone house and "came flying through the air, and burst with a loud explosion above us." A Confederate colonel who had taken refuge in Cyrena's house counseled her to remain where she was, declaring that it would be more hazardous inside the city, less than a mile away. Unknown to him, a few yards away, Cyrena had provided a hiding place for two free blacks who had been assaulted by Confederate soldiers. Earlier, she had hidden four runaway slaves in the cotton house on her property. At midnight she recorded in her diary aspects of the tumult that swirled around her: "Words cannot picture the scenes that surround me—scenes & sounds which my soul will hold in remembrance forever. Terrific cannonading on every side—continual firing of musketry—men screaming to each other—wagons rumbling by on every street or pouring into the yard—for the few remnants of fences—offers no obstructions now to cavalryman or wagoner,—and from the city comes up wild shouting, as if there is a general melee there."[68]

By the next morning, July 22, it had become obvious that the Stones' house would be destroyed by the fierce battle and that Cyrena would be compelled to retreat. She left reluctantly, however, and only when a friend came from town to take her and the rest of her household to refuge with another Unionist, a mile away, in the city. After the short trip, in the midst of the battle for Atlanta and shortly after her arrival at her friend's home, her diary abruptly ceases in mid-sentence.[69] Her half-sister's novel, *Goldie's Inheritance*, yields up the remainder of Cyrena Stone's experience in Civil War Atlanta.

Surviving the battle, Cyrena—if we may identify her with the fictional Goldie—spent the next six weeks with her Unionist friend, a woman with four children and a husband who, like Amherst, had gone north. Those six weeks coincided with the siege of Atlanta, as Union and Confederate forces fought to a stalemate and bombs and shells fell constantly on the city, whose remaining residents tried to survive by living underground in dug-out "bomb-proofs." Cyrena and her host frequently took refuge in such a small, cramped underground space as the bombs continued throughout the torrid, humid month of August. Food became even scarcer, and the city teetered on the edge of starvation. At least twice, huge shells hit the house where Cyrena was living; one ripped the ceiling apart but failed to explode, and the other exploded, wounding two of the residents.[70]

At last, on September 1, 1864, the Confederate troops evacuated Atlanta, and the next day the city surrendered to General Sherman's officers. Cyrena's home had been destroyed during the battle, and practically all of her possessions were lost as a result of the siege. All that was left was her flag and

Atlantans preparing to leave the city, September 1864. *Harper's New Monthly Magazine*, September 1864.

her Bible. When the Union troops entered the city, Cyrena unfurled the long hidden banner as a sign of welcome.[71]

Cyrena Stone remained in Atlanta for some weeks after the Federal occupation and was among the sizable number of the city's residents sent north by the Federal forces before they burned the city in early November. Before leaving, she had a reunion with a Vermont cousin, a Union officer who sought her out in the wrecked city. He wrote to his mother that Cyrena "was the noblest woman he ever saw" and "had remained true to the flag all this time and amid scoffs and jeers had ministered to the wants of the Union prisoners there most of the time for two years." She had been, he reported, "shunned and excluded from society but had 'endured all for righteousness sake.'" Back in Vermont, other family members, including her half-sister Louisa, were overjoyed to hear that Cyrena was alive after their more than three years of separation.[72] Cyrena reunited with Amherst in Nashville late in 1864, and the two proceeded to Vermont, where she seems to have remained until the fall of 1865.[73]

Meanwhile, the ever ambitious Amherst had capitalized upon political contacts made during the Lincoln presidential campaign. Rumors circulated that he had been appointed United States district attorney for Georgia by President Andrew Johnson after Lincoln's assassination.[74] Although these were untrue, Stone did eventually win appointment as United States commissioner in Savannah, where he moved in the summer of 1865.[75] Over the next eight years, he practiced law, brokered cotton, held a succession of federal and state political appointments in Georgia, and became active and influential in the Republican Party. Both carpetbagger and scalawag, he was reviled for the close political alliances he formed with leading black politicians in the state.[76] By 1873, however, Stone prepared to leave Georgia and accept an appointment from President Ulysses S. Grant as a federal judge in the Colorado territory, where he joined his brothers, the former Confederate captain Chester A. Stone and the former Union lieutenant Charles Birney Stone, who were in business together. Stone died in Leadville, Colorado, in 1900 after a spotty career there, which included some measure of fame (he was kidnapped by outlaws while a federal judge) and notoriety (in his later years, he received unfavorable publicity for amorous adventures with younger women).[77]

The character of the relationship between Cyrena and Amherst Stone after the war is unclear. Although there is no evidence to suggest marital discord, they clearly spent substantial periods apart—Amherst in Georgia and Cyrena in Vermont. Cyrena always returned to Vermont in the summers, but in 1868 she remained into the winter, evidently quite ill and living in Sheldon, near one of her sisters. Even before the war her health had been questionable, and she had made occasional visits to "medical institutions" in New York and perhaps elsewhere. Now, as the darkness and cold of the Vermont winter set in, she lay dying on a Saturday afternoon scarcely five miles from her childhood home in East Berkshire. For a week, she suffered "extreme pain and was partially deranged" before she finally succumbed at three o'clock on the afternoon of December 18, 1868. She was thirty-eight years old.[78]

The Civil War experiences of Cyrena and Amherst Stone help to illuminate the complex nature of national loyalty during that time and the ways in which a single family could reflect divisions over the national future. Cyrena Stone came as close to unconditional loyalty to the Union as was possible in that portion of the Confederate South, remote from significant populations of loyalists. Amherst Stone's Unionism, although seemingly staunch in the prewar period, obviously could be adjusted to circumstance. The fact that he was almost universally regarded by Atlanta Unionists as a "loyal man" both during and after the war shows that the Unionists themselves understood that perhaps no loyalty to the United States could be simon-pure, given the circumstances in Civil War Atlanta. That those same Unionists, however, were largely unaware of his activities casts doubt on the fundamental character of his Unionism. The loyalty of one brother to the Confederacy and one to the Union complete the illustration and indicate how complex the experiences of a single family could be in the vortex of a war when it came to choosing sides.

NOTES

An earlier version of this essay appeared in *Vermont History* 60 (fall 1992): 205–29, and is reproduced here with the permission of the journal.

1. Miss Abby's Diary, Hargrett Rare Book and Manuscript Library, University of Georgia Libraries, Athens.

2. Louisa M. Whitney, *Goldie's Inheritance: A Story of the Siege of Atlanta* (Burlington, Vt.: Free Press Association, 1903). For a full discussion of the novel, see Thomas G. Dyer, "Atlanta's Other Civil War Novel: Fictional Unionists in a Confederate City," *Georgia Historical Quarterly* 59 (Spring 1995): 147–68.

3. This essay is part of a larger study entitled *Secret Yankees: The Unionist Circle in Confederate Atlanta* (Baltimore: Johns Hopkins University Press, 1999), in which the Stones are placed more fully in the context of wartime Unionism and the Civil War.

4. Mrs. L. M. Whitney, "Memoir of Rev. Phinehas Bailey: A Father's Legacy," Vermont Historical Society, Montpelier (hereafter cited as "A Father's Legacy" to distinguish it from Bailey's own autobiographical memoir, cited below). See also Jeffrey D. Marshall, "The Life and Legacy of the Reverend Phinehas Bailey," Occasional Paper No. 9, Center for Research on Vermont (Burlington: University of Vermont Press, 1985), and "The Straightest Path to Heaven: Louisa Bailey Whitney and the Congressional Foreign Missionary Movement in Nineteenth Century Vermont," *Vermont History* 55 (summer 1987): 153–66.

5. Whitney, "A Father's Legacy," 31–42. "Memoirs of Rev. Phinehas Bailey, Written by Himself: Transcription from the Shorthand Notes now in the possession of his daughter Mrs. Louisa M. (Bailey) Whitney, Royalton, Vermont July 1902," 43, Vermont Historical Society (hereafter cited as Bailey, "Memoirs").

6. Whitney, "A Father's Legacy," 34–35.

7. A collection of Cyrena Stone's published writings is found in the Bailey-Hopkins Scrapbook, Francis L. Hopkins Collection, Bailey/Howe Library, University of Vermont (hereafter cited as Hopkins Collection). She always used a pseudonym, but each of her writings is identified in the family scrapbook as her work. Her sister, Mary A. Bailey, as well as her half-sister, Louisa M. Whitney, also published a variety of writings.

Cyrena and her siblings also benefited from her father's inventive turn of mind. He designed and perfected a system of shorthand based on a phonetic design, and he taught it to his children, who soon became adept at using the system in their studies, personal correspondence, and diaries. It is possible that Cyrena kept the original "Miss Abby's" diary in that obscure shorthand. See Marshall, "Life of Bailey."

8. Whitney, *Goldie's Inheritance*, 5–38. See the photograph of Louisa M. Whitney as a young woman on p. 123.

9. U.S. Census, 1860, Franklin County, Vt., 48. *Leadville (Colo.) Herald-Democrat*, May 1, 1900; Lewis Cass Aldrich, ed., *History of Franklin and Grand Isle Counties, Vermont* (Syracuse, N.Y.: D. Mason, 1891), 228–29. There is no record that Amherst Stone attended any college in Vermont or in neighboring states.

10. Abby Maria Hemenway, ed., *The Vermont Historical Gazetteer: A Magazine Embracing a History of Each Town, Civil, Ecclesiastical, Biographical, and Military* (Burlington, Vt.: A. M. Hemenway, 1871), 2:94; obituary of Lydia Samson Stone, Bailey-Hopkins Scrapbook.

11. U.S. Census, 1850, Fayette County, Ga., 21; Carolyn C. Cary, ed., *The History of Fayette County, 1821–1871* (Fayetteville, Ga.: Fayetteville Historical Society, 1977), 21–38.

12. Bailey, "Memoirs," 53; clipping from the *Augusta (Ga.) Chronicle and Sentinel*, August 15, 1854, Bailey-Hopkins Scrapbook.

13. Franklin M. Garrett, *Atlanta and Environs: A Chronicle of Its People and Events* (Athens: University of Georgia Press, 1954), 1:489.

14. Ibid., 408–409, 456; Florence W. Brine, "Central Presbyterian Church," *Atlanta Historical Bulletin* 3 (July 1938): 182.

15. City of Atlanta, Assessors Book, 1861, Atlanta History Center.

16. U.S. Census, 1860, Slave Schedule, Fulton County, Ga.

17. Whitney, "A Father's Legacy," 53.

18. Whitney, *Goldie's Inheritance*, 40.

19. Ibid., 41–42.

20. Ibid.

21. U.S. Census, 1860, Fulton County, Ga. How Vermont relatives might have reacted to the knowledge that the Stones owned slaves is not clear. There is no evidence to suggest that old Phinehas Bailey ever learned that his daughter and son-in-law had become slave owners before he died in 1861.

22. Keyes A. Bailey to Louisa Bailey, August 20, 1860, Hopkins Collection. Many of the letters used from this collection have been transcribed from the Bailey shorthand by Jeffrey D. Marshall of the University of Vermont. On another Atlantan who returned home to Vermont that summer, see Ben Kremenak, ed., "Escape from Atlanta: The Huntington Memoir," *Civil War History* 11 (June 1965): 161.

23. Amherst W. Stone to General John A. Dix, June 28, 1864, in Lafayette C. Baker–Levi C. Turner Papers, 1862–65 (microfilm), case no. 2441, RG 94, Adjutant

General's Records, War Department Division, National Archives, Washington, D.C. (hereinafter cited as Turner-Baker Papers); Garrett, *Atlanta and Its Environs,* 1:494. For a thorough discussion of the secession crisis in Georgia, see Michael P. Johnson, *Toward a Patriarchal Republic: The Secession of Georgia* (Baton Rouge: Louisiana State University Press, 1977). For attacks by Atlanta newspapers on Unionists, see the *Daily Intelligencer* and the *Southern Confederacy,* November 1860–January 1861.

24. Testimony of Julius Hayden, in *Julius A. Hayden* v. *United States of America,* case no. 2543, U.S. Court of Claims, Federal Records Center, Suitland, Md.

25. Testimony of C. T. C. Drake, in *Thomas G. W. Crusselle* v. *United States of America,* case no. 2974, U.S. Court of Claims, Federal Records Center.

26. [Holly], "The Spring of 1861," Bailey-Hopkins Scrapbook. This essay, like most that Cyrena Stone published, includes at the beginning the printed phrase "For the Commonwealth" or other newspaper in which it appeared.

27. "The Huntington Memoir," Special Collections Division, University of Iowa Library, Iowa City. The published edition of the Huntington memoir cited in n. 24 omits sections from the original document. This quotation is drawn from the original manuscript.

28. Whitney, *Goldie's Inheritance,* 143.

29. Miss Abby's Diary, passim. (Citations to page numbers in the diary are to the transcribed version in the University of Georgia Main Library.) Testimony of Sarah Hinton, Claim of Martin Hinton, Records of the Southern Claims Commission (Allowed Claims), Fulton County, Ga., RG 217, National Archives.

30. Testimony of Nedom L. Angier, Claim of Nedom L. Angier, Southern Claims Commission (Allowed Claims), Fulton County, Ga., RG 217, National Archives.

31. U.S. Census, 1860, Fulton County; *Atlanta Daily Intelligencer,* April 17, 1860; Henry Clay Fairman, *Chronicles of the Old Guard of the Gate City Guard, Atlanta, Georgia, 1858–1915* (Atlanta: Byrd, 1915), 8, 33.

32. Fairman, *Chronicles of the Old Guard,* 18–27.

33. Whitney, *Goldie's Inheritance,* 141.

34. Fairman, *Chronicles of the Old Guard,* 28–32.

35. William Clapp to Major John A. Bolles, September 19, 1864, Union Provost Marshal's File of One-Name Papers re Citizens (microcopy no. 345), National Archives.

36. Ibid.

37. "The Dying Soldier," Bailey-Hopkins Scrapbook.

38. See, for example, *Atlanta Daily Intelligencer,* April 13, 1862.

39. Garrett, *Atlanta and Environs,* 1:551.

40. Miss Abby's Diary, 21; Testimony of Robert Webster, in *Robert Webster* v. *United States of America,* case no. 13502, U.S. Court of Claims.

41. Garrett, *Atlanta and Environs,* 1:525–28.

42. *Williams' Atlanta City Directory for 1859–1860* (Atlanta, M. Lynch, 1860); Braxton Bragg to Joseph E. Johnston, March 2, 1863, *Official Records of the War of the Rebellion,* ser. 1 (Washington, D.C.: Government Printing Office, 1880–1902), 32(2):656–57.

43. *Atlanta Southern Confederacy,* August 29, 30, September 3, 1862.

44. Whitney, *Goldie's Inheritance,* 165–67. The novel is the only source providing details about the arrest, probably from the missing portions of Cyrena's diary. In this as in other segments that appear to be from the diary, the narrative bears the marks of Cyrena's literary style.

45. Testimony of Mary Hinton, Claim of Martin Hinton, Southern Claims Commission (Allowed Claims), Fulton County, Ga., RG 217, National Archives.

46. A. W. Stone to E. M. Stanton, June 19, 1863, A. W. Stone to General John A. Dix, June 28, 1864, Turner-Baker Papers. These two letters contain lengthy discussion of the plan.

47. Ibid.

48. Ibid.

49. Ibid.

50. Ibid. Rolla Gleason to Stanton, September 3, 1863, in Register of Letters Received by the Secretary of War, Main Series 1800–70 (microform), reel 106, register no. 116, RG 490, National Archives (hereafter cited as Register, Secretary of War Letters). This is a summary of a letter from Gleason to the secretary of war.

51. Stone to Stanton, June 19, 1863, Stone to Dix, June 28, 1864, Turner-Baker Papers; Gleason to Stanton, September 3, 1863, Register, Secretary of War Letters; Thomas C. Reeves, *Gentleman Boss: The Life of Chester Alan Arthur* (New York: Alfred A. Knopf, 1975), 33–35.

52. *Burlington Free Press,* May 12, 1863.

53. Ibid.; Gleason to Stanton, September 3, 1863, Register, Secretary of War Letters; John Sedgwick to Charles A. Dana, September 14, 1864, Turner-Baker Papers.

54. *"Fort-La-Fayette Life," 1863–64 in extracts from the "right Flanker," a manuscript sheet circulating among the southern prisoners in Fort-Lafayette"* (London: Simpking, Marshall, 1865), Hargrett Rare Book and Manuscript Library, University of Georgia Libraries.

55. Stone to Stanton, June 19, 1863, Turner-Baker Papers.

56. Stone to John A. Dix, June 28, 1864, Turner-Baker Papers.

57. Stone to L. C. Turner, August 24, 21, 1863, Stone to John A. Dix, June 28, 1863, Turner-Baker Papers.

58. Rolla Gleason to Stanton, September 3, 1863, Register, Secretary of War Letters; Benjamin Baily to ———, August 19, 1864, Sedgwick to Dana, September 14, 1864, Turner-Baker Papers.

59. H. J. Raymond to Major General John A. Dix, October 11, 1864, Register, Secretary of War Letters.

60. Miss Abby's Diary, 19–20, 47, 62, 28, 61.

61. Ibid., 62.

62. Ibid., 14–15.

63. Ibid., 23–24.

64. Ibid., 45–46.

65. Ibid., 40–41, 38; Whitney, *Goldie's Inheritance*, 197.

66. Miss Abby's Diary, 39.

67. Ibid., 13.

68. Ibid., 65, 63, 54.

69. Ibid., 71–72.

70. Whitney, *Goldie's Inheritance*, 250–52.

71. Ibid., 253–54.

72. Elizabeth H. Whitney to Louisa M. Bailey, October 12, 1864; Louisa M. Bailey to Joel F. Whitney, October 28, 1864, Hopkins Collection.

73. *Leadville (Colo.) Herald Democrat*, May 1, 1900. While there, she wrote an essay celebrating the autumn colors of the Green Mountains that was soon published in a Savannah newspaper. "Out in the Woods," *Savannah National Republican*, November 10, 1865, Bailey-Hopkins Scrapbook.

74. The rumors had been accepted as fact and were included in several histories. I find no documentation in the National Archives or in standard guides to federal officeholders to support the claim. The source of the rumor appears to have been a Buffalo, N.Y., newspaper. See Walter P. Reed, *History of Atlanta, Georgia* (Syracuse, N.Y.: D. Mason, 1889).

75. *Savannah Daily Herald*, May 12, 1865.

76. Sharon Young, "Amherst Willoughby Stone," biographical sketch, Georgia Historical Society, Savannah.

77. *Leadville (Colo.) Herald Democrat*, May 28, 1882; *History of the Arkansas Valley, Colorado* (Chicago: O. L. Baskin, 1881), 373–74; "Chester Able Stone," *The Trail* 17 (December 1924): 7; "Biography—Hon. A. W. Stone" ("Mrs. Maude Magofflin—Interviewer"), Colorado Historical Society, Denver.

78. Persis Lorette Hopkins to Louisa Bailey, December 22, 1868, Hopkins Collection.

Poor Loving Prisoners of War

Nelly Kinzie Gordon and the Dilemma of Northern-Born Women in the Confederate South

CAROLYN J. STEFANCO

*A*fter spending the summer of 1862 traveling with family members, Nelly Kinzie Gordon returned home to Savannah, Georgia. As she and her cousin Maria Kinzie Steuart reached the Gordon family mansion and "were about to come up the front steps . . . [they] found that buckets of . . . [sewage] from a cesspool had been dashed all over the front door, porch and steps." The two women bypassed the mess by entering a side door to the house and sending a slave "out to clean away the filth." But they could not so easily sidestep the message conveyed by such an action. Local citizens were clearly unhappy about the presence of the two Northern-born women in the city. Nelly called the perpetrators "vulgar brutes" and believed she and her cousin had been targeted merely "as a protest against us—especially Maria—because we were the nieces of General Hunter!!!" (Union General David Hunter had enraged Savannahians by capturing nearby Fort Pulaski and by attempting to abolish slavery in the three states under his command, including Georgia, months before Lincoln issued the Emancipation Proclamation.) Nelly expected that her marriage to William Washington

Gordon II, a Confederate captain, would end any speculation about their loyalty and protect them from such abuse. She stressed that he "had been fighting at the front from the beginning of the war," and "that Maria's husband was a prominent General in the Confederate army, who was just recovering from his desperate wounds."[1]

Marriage alone, however, would not shield the Kinzie cousins or others like them. Many white Northern-born women who remained in the Confederacy found it difficult to avoid criticism on political grounds. It was essential that they reject the beliefs with which they had been brought up and demonstrate unwavering support for the war, a stand that Nelly advocated during the first year of the war. In effect, some Northern-born women were held to higher standards of loyalty than white women from the South. At the same time, they were expected to deny having a political role, in keeping with traditional definitions of womanhood.[2] Yet every word and action suggested political significance. When Northern-born women complained about food shortages or battlefield losses, for example, Confederates saw them as traitors and explained their defection as stemming from their Northern origins, even though their views often reflected commonly held opinions of the time.[3] For women in intersectional marriages, the Civil War became an impossible contradiction.[4] Because Nelly Kinzie Gordon's everyday statements and actions received public scrutiny, her experiences, like those of other Northern women who had married Southern men, reveal both the Confederacy's expectations of white women, and more important, how the personal aspects of their lives were infused with political meaning during the war years.

A complex set of relationships helped to shape Nelly's ideas about gender and politics. Historians who examine the lives of Confederate women often use marriage to explore the impact of the war.[5] In Nelly's case, certainly, the war and its aftermath tested her relationship with her husband and provided opportunities, as scholars have found in other case studies, for greater autonomy and independence.[6] Yet Nelly exchanged as many letters with her mother, who lived in Chicago, as she did with her husband, who was fighting for the Confederacy, between 1861 and 1865, and she spent considerably more time in Savannah—with her mother-in-law, sisters-in-law, cousin, and other women friends and neighbors—than she did with her husband during the war years.[7] The significance of these relationships among women have often been eclipsed by the heterosexist lens of historical inquiry.[8] Yet Nelly's whole circle of family and friends provides the actual context for the development of her ideas about loyalty and patriotism.

Eleanor "Nelly" Kinzie Gordon, ca. 1855. Georgia Historical Society.

Nelly's characterization of Savannahians as "vulgar brutes" over the sewage incident seems plausible if one reads some of her own words about the war.[9] Although she claimed to eschew politics, Nelly argued that her marital obligations required her to side with her husband and to champion his cause. Documents from the Civil War period certainly support this interpretation. Early in 1862, for example, Nelly echoes her husband's sentiments about the Union and its chances for victory: "I am disgusted at the course pursued by the government at the North! Such blindness! Such Folly! But with . . . an inefficient President like Lincoln! and a Mercenary Army. . . .

CAROLYN J. STEFANCO

What in God's name *can* you expect? . . . They will never . . . conquer the South, nor subdue the so-called Rebellion. That Conviction is stronger & stronger every day!"[10]

Even fifty years after the war, when the *Ladies Home Journal* published a story about Savannah's role in the Confederacy, Nelly wrote to the editor to correct what she believed to be inaccuracies in the account. In this letter from 1914 she called herself "a dutiful wife" who "went heart and soul with my husband; and prayed for the success of the Confederacy with all my might."[11]

Familial and scholarly assessments of Nelly's life published over the course of the twentieth century also portray her allegiance to the Confederate war effort. Her youngest son, George Arthur Gordon, in a sketch of Nelly's life published after her death, claims that she "made her choice for her Husband and the Confederacy without hesitation and suffered all the agonies of four long and harrowing years."[12] In *Lady from Savannah*, the story of Nelly's more famous daughter who founded the Girl Scouts, she is portrayed as divorced from politics and cherishing only the role of dutiful, though nevertheless spunky, wife.[13] Mary D. Robertson, who edited Nelly's 1862 journal, called her a "northern rebel."[14] And a host of historians and popular writers who continue to tell the story of Nelly's meeting with Sherman in 1865 reinforce the notion that she "was fervent in her support for the Confederacy."[15]

This interpretation supports what Drew Gilpin Faust calls a "legend of female sacrifice," which began during the war and found expression in works on Confederate women published from the mid–nineteenth through the mid–twentieth centuries.[16] By emphasizing female sacrifice and overlooking women's complaints about the Confederacy, this version of white Southern women's history glorifies both white womanhood and the interests of the Lost Cause.[17] If the Northern wives of Southern men could also be portrayed as Rebels, both the appeal and the image of the Confederacy are further strengthened. Nelly helped to create the impression that she had always sided with her husband, thereby contributing to scholars' assessments of her loyalty to the Confederacy.

The "legend of female sacrifice," however, masks the reality of the war experience for many white Southern women. As both Faust and George Rable have shown, Southern white women, who were at first "fervently patriotic," had by 1862 or 1863 become bitter about the sacrifices they were called upon to make and skeptical about the chances of Confederate victory. To white men, women's expressions of discontent seemed unpatriotic and on a deeper level threatened the male role as patriarch and a man's sense of personal and familial honor. To white women, men had relinquished their responsibilities as family protectors when they made decisions that appeared to put the nation above the family.[18]

Nelly Gordon's ideas about the Confederacy were actually much more complex than some of her own writings and published accounts about her life suggest. Like many white Southern-born women, she initially expressed enthusiasm for the Confederacy, but then renounced her support for the war late in 1862. After that change in her allegiance, Nelly did more than criticize the war effort and beg her husband to come home, however. She continually sought his permission to leave the South, regularly accepted aid from high-placed Union officials, fought with her in-laws over the war, spent more than seven months with her cousin Maria, who readily admitted her support for the Union, and even sent information about Confederate forces to her Northern relatives. No matter how much she later tried to deny her own actions, they, and not simply her familial connection to General David Hunter, explain the defacement of her home in Savannah.

Disagreements during the years of her courtship with William Washington Gordon II foreshadow Nelly's wartime difficulties with family and friends. Although Willie looked forward, in 1854, to the day when a "wee maiden has transferred her allegiance . . . to one Gordon by name," it would take Nelly four years to see the Gordons as her family and Savannah as her home.[19] The couple's religious differences have frequently been mentioned as an issue of contention—she was an Episcopalian, he a Presbyterian—but slavery was actually the greatest source of conflict in their early relationship.[20]

Their arguments stemmed from the fact that Willie had changed his views on the issue. When Nelly and Willie met in 1853, while both were studying in the Northeast, they shared serious doubts about slavery.[21] After spending many years away at school, Willie graduated from Yale in 1854 and returned to Savannah. The subject he had once viewed abstractly he now benefited from practically, given the fact that as many as twenty-five slaves lived in and around the Gordons' urban mansion.[22] When Nelly tried to taunt him by reciting what she called the many "abominations" of slavery depicted in *Uncle Tom's Cabin*, Willie admitted in his letters that despite his doubts about "the *expediency* of the system," he had adopted "the regular Southern 'Hands off' feeling on the subject" and promised that "nothing can make me defend or *believe* in it [more] save an attack on it."[23] As Willie grew more accustomed to life in the South, he made more frequent comments in justification of slavery. Slave Christmas celebrations, for example, reminded him "more of Savage than Civilized life," thereby justifying expressions of benev-

CAROLYN J. STEFANCO

olence toward those whom God had called him to oversee.[24] Willie tried to impress on Nelly his views, which now echoed familiar proslavery ideas of the antebellum period.[25] From loving admonitions in which he asked her to allow him to use his authority—"so please be a good girl and mind what I say"—to self-justifying pronouncements in which he claimed that, for her own good, she should center her "thoughts," "feeling," and "interests" on the South, Willie tried every means to convince Nelly of the superiority of his judgment.[26]

Nelly objected to life in the South because of slavery, but she also made other arguments designed to facilitate a return to her childhood home of Chicago. Her frequent comments about the benefits of Chicago before her wedding to Willie continued afterward. Within weeks of their marriage in 1857, she asked her parents, Juliette Magill and John Kinzie, to seek a military appointment for Willie in the North, and then to promise him business opportunities in Chicago. She also attempted to solicit parental aid in her cause by complaining bitterly about her living situation at the Gordon home. The couple lived with Willie's widowed mother, Sarah Anderson Stiles Gordon, who Nelly believed treated her as a mere boarder. Besides, she had no one with whom to attend the Episcopal church.[27]

To her mother, in particular, Nelly looked for support, but Juliette Kinzie gave her daughter what Nelly may have considered contradictory messages. She worked to create the employment opportunities that would entice Willie to Chicago and sent Nelly money on a regular basis, which enabled her to remain at least financially independent from her husband. Yet, particularly after Nelly and Willie's first child was born, in September 1858, Juliette Kinzie insisted that she and Nelly's father could no longer be her guardians. Nelly must look to Willie as her protector.[28]

If Nelly hoped to escape a less than happy home life with the Gordons by spending the summer and fall of 1859 with her parents, she was sadly disappointed. Nelly set out for Chicago with the hope that she could prove to her family and friends that marriage and motherhood had not changed her a bit.[29] Much to her chagrin, her mother agreed. Juliette Kinzie expected Nelly to be what she had always been—a dutiful daughter. After months of what Nelly considered to be mistreatment, she made a clear decision between the two roles in life offered her.[30] Choosing wife over daughter at least acknowledged her adult status, though it still required her submission. Willie, who had serious misgivings about Nelly's trip, fearing that it would only add to what he saw as her inability to see Savannah as her home, discovered that her time in Chicago had the opposite effect. The couple agreed shortly before her return to Savannah that they would no longer have what Willie called a "divided allegiance."[31]

Nelly's desire for unanimity at home seems to have influenced her political views between 1859 and 1861. The nearly daily letters she exchanged with her mother during these years reveal her rejection of both sections' viewpoints and her opposition to war before the fall of Fort Sumter. She disliked Lincoln enormously and believed that he, like all Northerners, hated slavery and would abolish it as soon as he came to power.[32] Although she still despised slavery as an institution, she now saw abolitionists as "firebrands" who would lead the country to war. But while she disdained this Northern element, she also criticized the secession movement. "I was bitterly opposed to it," she wrote. "When Georgia 'went out' the city [of Savannah] was illuminated. I sneaked upstairs and extinguished every light in my room. . . . Willy however, suspected me, and went up and turned them all on again!!"[33]

When fighting broke out and her husband was commissioned as an officer in a Georgia regiment, Nelly, who blamed Lincoln for causing the war, adopted the Confederate perspective.[34] Her energetic pursuit of this viewpoint during the spring of 1861 is revealed by an incident regarding the mail. When letters from her parents failed to arrive in their usual timely fashion, Nelly dispatched a note to the postmaster in Chicago, charging him with reading her mail in an attempt to gain information about the Confederacy. The postmaster sent the note to her parents who were, not surprisingly, "mortified." In the next letter she wrote, Juliette Kinzie implored Nelly to "exercise a little of your excellent sense." She implied that Nelly's fears bordered on paranoia, and she explained the pains taken by her father to apologize for what they saw as their daughter's aberrant behavior.[35]

The Kinzies failed to understand their daughter's predicament, however. First, the Savannah Daily Morning News, which Nelly read, published articles demanding that "all Northern mails should be stopped even when one thousand miles off," since spies used the mail to get messages to Washington.[36] It is not surprising, then, that Nelly might assume that the Chicago postmaster might have been enlisted in a similar effort to aid the Union war effort. Second, Nelly's husband, Willie, had forced her to take sides. He explained: "You have got to choose between North and South, between your Mother and her kin and me. . . . If you go North and mix with those who are the enemies of this country . . . you must be prepared to remain there for you can never come back to me as my Wife."[37] The Kinzies held out hope that Willie would allow Nelly and their now two grandchildren to find safe haven in Chicago for the duration of the war.[38] Nelly knew that he was not likely to consent to such a plan. For Willie, as for other Confederate men, it was a matter of honor.[39] Like many white Southern men with Northern-born wives, Willie insisted that Nelly remain in the South.

White women in intersectional marriages walked a fine line in their attempt to remain dutiful daughters and wives and to live within the bounds of conventional gender definitions. Each set of relatives, North and South, conveyed different expectations based on feelings of love, notions of family loyalty, and demands for patriotic expression. The resulting tensions often forced them to choose sides. By aligning themselves with either the Union or the Confederacy, these women took a public stand on a political issue. These declarations of loyalty, when accompanied by desires to take on male roles or so-called masculine personality traits, called into question society's definitions of femininity. Such decisions, therefore, not only disappointed one family or the other; they held the potential to invite harsh rebuke from both.

The experiences of other Northern women who had also married Southern men taught Nelly important lessons about her predicament. Abby Days Slocomb, a childhood friend of Nelly's, chose her husband over her parents. She supposedly wrote her Unionist father "insulting, abusive letters" that, according to Juliette Kinzie, abrogated "the terms of God which commanded her to honor her parents." Abby's correspondence reveals that she had become fanatical in her devotion to the Confederate cause. It was reported that she proclaimed, for example, that should her husband "fall and be unable to carry on the warfare, she would seize his bayonet and go forth to supply his place."[40] Confederate women's desire to march into battle served patriotic ends, but as Drew Gilpin Faust explains, it originated from "feelings of purposelessness" and "represented a potential threat to existing gender assumptions."[41]

Nelly's cousin Maria Kinzie Steuart, who was both a niece and the "adopted" daughter of Union general David Hunter and his wife, Maria Kinzie Hunter, aligned with the Hunters instead of her husband. When her husband, George Steuart, went off to fight for the Confederacy, Maria (a Chicago native who had moved with her parents to Kansas) went to stay with her in-laws in Baltimore for a short time. Finding them to be "rank secessionists," however, she declared herself a Republican and returned to the Hunters' home in the North.[42] When describing Maria's actions in June 1861, Juliette Kinzie asked Nelly, "Isn't she great?"[43] Nelly disagreed, arguing that Maria should have stayed with her husband.[44] Juliette Kinzie shortly thereafter joined her daughter's criticism of Maria, on the grounds that she had carried her beliefs too far. Though not objecting to her political views per se, Juliette Kinzie called Maria's willfulness unbecoming and claimed that she had, in fact, "seized upon a slight pretext" for the sole purpose of displeasing her husband.[45] Maria Steuart's and Abby Slocomb's examples reveal the ease with which one might invite spousal disapproval and cross accepted gender boundaries. Nelly hoped, of course, she would do neither.

By adopting the South as her home and proclaiming her anti-Union views, Nelly joined the chorus of born and bred Confederate women who ardently supported the war in its first year.[46] Yet she did not participate in the common patriotic activities of white middle- and upper-class women, such as sewing clothes as part of soldiers' aid societies, writing patriotic songs, and raising money for the troops by holding bazaars and putting on plays.[47] Even though Nelly had married into a prominent local family, her in-laws and Savannah residents saw her as an outsider. One day when shopping, for example, Nelly ran into Ella Howard Waring, the wife of one of her husband's "most intimate friends." Nelly recorded Mrs. Waring's greeting:

> "Well, Nelly—I hear you have got a brother in the Yankee Army!"—(I wonder in what army she expected he would be) I said "Yes, that is true." "Well," she said "All I can say is, I hope the first bullet fired, will kill him dead!" "Thank you, Ella," I replied, "The same to your own brother!" [My] chance for retaliation came very shortly [because] Jett Howard was hit in the nape of his neck by a minie ball. . . . I met Ella Waring walking on Bull Street just afterwards, with a party of friends. I stopped them. "Ella," I said sweetly, "I hear your brother is shot—*in the BACK*. Mine is perfectly well!"[48]

Nelly was perceived, and saw herself, as a Northerner. White Southern women's fears of the "Yankee devil," for example, did not worry her. This is made clear in one of Nelly's accounts of her "escape" from Virginia in March 1862. She had gone to visit Willie when Union troop movements threatened to leave her behind what he called "enemy lines." In her 1862 journal, she explained only how she got home to Savannah.[49] However, on unbound pages in her handwriting found among her papers, she provided a much more complete account of her feelings at the time. While Willie worried that she "should be captured!!!" Nelly explained that "this fate did not appear to me so very terrible. I thought to myself 'why all I have to do would be to report to the Yankee commanding officer, explain who I was, and telegraph to Chicago to my father; or still better, request to be sent to Washington to my Uncle General David Hunter.—Besides, I had Cousins galore within hale on the

CAROLYN J. STEFANCO

other side![']" But I wisely kept all these ideas to myself."[50] Despite her private thoughts, Nelly remained publicly committed to the Confederacy until the spring of 1862, when her devotion began to waver.

She was actually wrong about her uncle's location in March. He had been sent to command the Department of the South, which included the states of South Carolina, Georgia, and Florida, while she was in Virginia. In April, with Nelly's brother Arthur as his aide, Hunter's forces captured Fort Pulaski, outside Savannah.[51] Nelly declared this a "disgraceful surrender" and went on to explain that this and other Confederate defeats resulted in part from laziness and inefficiency. Because of slavery, according to Nelly, "they're so used to being worked for, that they don't know what it means to work—& they won't do it."[52] In these feelings Nelly reflected the opinions of many in the North and South, who blamed slavery for what they saw as a poor work ethic among white Southerners, and echoed the thoughts of Confederate women, who were growing more critical of the performance of the troops.

When General Hunter declared martial law in the states under his command in May, proclaimed the slaves free, and planned to arm them, Nelly could not share white Southerners' sense of utter outrage.[53] When her mother-in-law, Sarah Gordon, became relentless in her criticism of Hunter and insisted that Nelly read his "outrageous Proclamation," a fight ensued in which Nelly insisted that she loved Hunter and confessed that she was glad that he had tried to free the slaves. Sarah "exclaimed . . . passionately, I wish no son of mine had ever married a Northerner!" As a result of this exchange, Nelly sought sympathy from Willie in a letter. But he advised her to "cherish if you choose the *recollection* of your Uncle David but do it as of one dead and buried or in a lunatic asylum."[54]

A month later, in June 1862, devastating news arrived that would prove to be a turning point for Nelly. Her brother John was killed fighting for the Union. Willie took upon himself the unhappy task of informing her. Although he was "very, very sorry" and "sympathized with her. . . with all [his] . . . heart," Nelly could not be consoled.[55] The loss of relatives in battle, along with the inability of the Confederacy to provide for families on the home front and to attain its promised victory, weakened the morale of many Confederate women by the middle of 1862.[56] Given the additional conflicts inherent in Nelly's position, she abandoned all pretense of support for the Confederacy after her brother's death. To her cousin Maria, who, with her young daughter, joined Nelly and her two children at a popular resort in north Georgia in early September, she looked for comfort.[57]

Maria Kinzie Steuart's presence in Georgia exacerbated tensions in the Gordon marriage and between Nelly and her family and neighbors in Savannah. Ironically, George Steuart had encouraged his wife to visit Nelly, believing that Nelly would serve as an appropriate role model—a woman who, despite her Northern birth, understood her responsibilities as a wife and adopted the Confederate cause as her own. Nelly's husband, Willie, however, used the word *calamity* when describing the months from September 1862 to April 1863, which Nelly and Maria spent together in Georgia. From Maria's arrival, he wrote, "I date the commencement of our disagreements, the beginning of my uneasiness, the first suspicion of distrust."[58] Maria had no intention of hiding her pro-Union sympathies and apparently supported Nelly's decision to reveal her true feelings about the war. Savannahians, who heard stories about the women's "speeches upcountry," threw sewage on the front of the Gordon house upon the two women's return to the city in the fall of 1862.

What Willie did not know was that Nelly and Maria had agreed to leave the South in the winter of 1862–63. Maria, who made her intentions known immediately, was delayed until the spring of 1863 by her husband's threats to retain custody of their child.[59] Only when she convinced him that she had had a change of heart—which she seems to have accomplished by resuming a sexual relationship with him—was she able to leave the South with her daughter.[60] David Hunter promised to allow Maria to "borrow as much money as she needs to pay for her expenses to this place [Savannah] & he will refund it." He would then "receive her and send her North." Although Hunter hoped that Nelly would accompany his niece, only Maria and her child made the journey.[61]

Nelly had pleaded with Willie to allow her to leave the South. Recognizing that she had little chance of gaining his approval to join her parents in Chicago, she planned trips to Canada in 1863. Juliette Kinzie thought that Willie might "relent in the spring as to suffer you to go to Quebec, or rather to St. Catherines which is a great resort of southerners, as well as of western people."[62] But despite promising her mother that, "consent or no consent," she and the children would go, Nelly would not defy her husband on this matter. Still hoping, perhaps, that her destination was the issue, she next tried to convince Willie to allow her to travel to Cuba, where she expected to meet her parents.[63] By the summer of 1863, even Sarah Gordon had changed her mind, agreeing now that she should be allowed to leave.[64] Willie, however, would not budge. Confederate losses in 1863 led William Henry Stiles, Willie's brother-in-law, to admit in a letter to Willie that "things look pretty

CAROLYN J. STEFANCO

gloomy now for us."[65] But although Confederate men could not alone control the outcome of battles, they could, seemingly, control their wives. And so while Nelly defied Willie in many smaller matters (she traveled by flag of truce to see her brother Arthur, for example, and continued communicating with her uncle David Hunter), she refused to leave the South without Willie's permission.[66]

Unfortunately, Nelly's presence in Savannah aroused greater suspicion and anger over time. The frequent arrival from the Kinzies in Chicago of money and trunks filled with food and fine clothing enabled Nelly to live a life of ease in comparison to most Confederate women.[67] Her access to goods generally in short supply also enabled her to help Confederate family members. She frequently sent packages to Willie, for example, containing items such as catsup, coffee, sugar, tobacco, and cake.[68] But her bounty also created bitterness among Gordon family members, who looked to Nelly for assistance and resented their dependence. When Nelly sought absolution from her favorite sister-in-law, Eliza Gordon Stiles, after the war for not helping her more, Eliza described a diet consisting of nothing more than "salt pork & rice every single day," prayed that "God will never send such suffering on you & your children," and explained that she didn't expect Nelly to understand how deprived they had been, "coming as you do from the opulence of the North."[69] The Stileses at least had some food. One can only imagine that the situation was even more desperate for the women who participated in the Savannah bread riot of 1864. As in other riots that plagued the urban South beginning in April 1863, the Savannah rioters cried for "bread or blood" and dispersed only "when troops were called out."[70]

By continuing to send letters, as well as goods, back and forth across enemy lines, Nelly also invited hostility from white Southerners. She must have known that any type of communication could lead to charges of consorting with the enemy. A Savannah newspaper, for example, had carried a story about the arrest of a Mrs. Allen, another Northern woman who had married into a Southern family. Allen's guilt, presumably on charges of spying, was established with the "letters written by her, forwarded by blockade runners."[71] Juliette Kinzie's explanation for her inability to get mail to her daughter also provided a warning. "What can have become of all my letters?" she asked. "I greatly suspect the functionaries in your Savannah P.O. They naturally have a spite of you, knowing where your heart is—and they are determined that you shall have no *northern* comfort that they can deprive you of."[72] Juliette and Nelly were both committed to maintaining a close relationship, despite the war, and this led them to attempt to get news and packages to each other by any means available. Early in the war, for example, Nelly had decided to entrust her journal to a man named Hughes, who promised to get it to the Kinzies in Chicago. When it failed to arrive, Hughes explained its disappearance by claiming that he had been robbed. But in January 1864, some two years later, the Kinzies learned that Hughes was a spy, who had been "arrested at Washington, on his way from Richmond" and that Nelly's journal had been found among his possessions. Juliette's attempt to give her daughter advice about who should and should not be trusted inadvertently included Nelly among those defined as untrustworthy. "If a person from this quarter [the North] seems, when in the South to fraternize with the rebels," Juliette instructed her daughter, "be sure he is *a spy* on one side or the other, and distrust him—have nothing to do with him, even to send a letter by him."[73]

Nelly's parents, of course, assumed her innocence. But Confederates were more likely, as Juliette's admonition suggested, to brand white Northerners as traitors. Despite Nelly's experience with Hughes, she again asked someone to carry a package to the North. This time, her actions resulted in her being "reported to Richmond as a suspicious character." Willie explained, in a carefully worded passage, that "Mrs. Lee of Nashville passed the lines with a large package from you to your Mother stating that it was a Diary, but which was subsequently discovered (or suspected I dont understand which) to be reports . . . of all [troop] movements around Savh."[74] Because Willie's letters had provided Nelly with military information, he was asked to explain both their actions at General Johnston's headquarters. The dramatic change in Nelly's views, in comparison to the beginning of the war, are implied in Willie's statements about this situation. Although he assured Nelly that he accepted the goodness of her intentions and admitted that "neither I nor anyone can object to your writing to your mother," he added that even if she were capable of *"being disloyal to the South,"* he refused to believe that she would do "anything which could injure" him personally.[75]

Nelly's departure from Savannah eight months later would prove to be a crushing blow to Willie. She had continually promised her parents that with or without Willie's consent, she would follow Maria's example. But Juliette had long realized that her daughter, who called herself a "poor loving prisoner of war," would never be liberated until "there is no longer an iron will to control her."[76] Only when the forces of the Union became stronger than the power of her husband did Nelly gain her freedom. Shortly after the surrender of Savannah to Sherman, the families of Confederate officers were ordered to leave the city. Sherman, who knew the Kinzies, arranged for

CAROLYN J. STEFANCO

William (Willie)
Washington Gordon II,
ca. 1862. Courtesy of
Juliette Gordon Low
Girl Scout National
Center.

Nelly's and the children's safe passage to Chicago.[77] Willie, who recoiled at "wonderful accounts of . . . [Nelly's] influence with Gen. Sherman," and who insisted that "the glory of a wife—[is] to stand or fall with her husband," confessed that the "anguish I have endured since the 12th of January [the day she left] has been greater than I can express. . . . I have been too proud to let *anyone* know that your conduct hurt or displeased me." Willie claimed that *"the misery of my life"* is the fact that "you do not think as I do, you do not feel what I feel. You have other thoughts and feelings & wishes foreign to me."[78]

Nelly had tried her best to live up to her husband's expectations. But the tensions inherent in that position, given her Northern origins and her own views about the war, forced her to make statements and take actions that defied both her husband and traditional gender expectations. Like her cousin, she took a political stand and advocated the Union's cause. But like those of many Confederate women, her decisions were motivated as much by self-interest as they were by sectional loyalty. Savannahians pointed to Nelly's Northern origins as explanation for her behavior. In reality, Nelly's actions, like the war itself, were not so simple.

Much later than Nelly's mother, cousin, and Northern family members, and his own mother and sisters, Willie would finally recognize what his wife had become—an independent woman who did not share his political views. Every one of her actions offended him. He felt humiliated, for example, by the fact that "the first letter received from you after you were under the Yankee flag . . . [was] signed Nelly *Kinzie* Gordon." And he found the "traveling and visiting" she was doing to be neither "lady like" nor "decorous." Yet he also concocted new tests of her loyalty to him, such as when he threatened to disown her if she had accepted any hospitality or aid from her Uncle Hunter.[79] Learning the next day that Nelly was in Washington with Hunter, he now addressed her as "the niece of so mighty a one of my masters" and realized that "besides country, cause, hope—I seem about to lose (or have already lost) the love, honor and obedience once pledged to me."[80]

Willie's world was turned upside down because the Confederacy had been defeated. Since he equated Nelly with the North, he had come to see both as his conquerors. In reality, of course, Nelly was neither victor nor victim. As late as the spring of 1864, Juliette Kinzie assumed that Nelly may have still believed "that a woman's patriotism should hold place *after* wifely duty."[81] Perhaps she came to this conclusion because of Nelly's reluctance to leave Savannah. But in every other way, Nelly's actions reflected concerns about her own well-being and the welfare of her children and other family members. This explains her willingness to risk public censure in the Confederate South by aiding her outspoken cousin, visiting her brother and uncle, accepting money and supplies from Northern relatives, and twice trusting virtual strangers to carry her journals to her mother in Chicago.

The transformation of Nelly's ideas about the war and a woman's patriotic duty must be examined in the context of these actions and with the recognition that her many relationships helped to shape her opinions. Nelly's love for Willie certainly played a role. But so did her feelings for her mother and brothers. Nelly considered the ideas that many people expressed. The women she communicated with most regularly influenced her, as did those with whom she spent much of her time during the war. Like many white Southern women, she deplored the sacrifices war demanded. But unlike them, she had found her political voice as a Northerner living in the Confederate South.

NOTES

This essay is dedicated to my father, Edward Stefanco, for helping me to remember what is most important in life.

1. Untitled typescript, in the possession of Margaret Gordon Seiler [hereafter cited as Seiler typescript], 118. Maria Kinzie Steuart was both the niece and the "adopted" daughter of David and Maria Hunter. Although Steuart was sometimes called by the nickname Posy, I will refer to her as Maria in the text. Historians have often noted that Confederate civilians, particularly women, treated Unionists in ways similar to the one Nelly described. See, for example, Leonard V. Huber, "The Battle of the Handkerchiefs," *Civil War History* 8 (1962): 48–53; George Rable, "'Missing in Action': Women of the Confederacy," in *Divided Houses: Gender and the Civil War*, ed. Catherine Clinton and Nina Silber (New York: Oxford University Press, 1992), 140; and Drew Gilpin Faust, *Mothers of Invention: Women of the Slaveholding South in the American Civil War* (Chapel Hill: University of North Carolina Press, 1996), 202, 207–14.

2. Eleanor M. Boatwright, "The Political and Civil Status of Women in Georgia, 1783–1860," *Georgia Historical Quarterly* 15 (December 1941): 301–24, explains women's lack of legal rights in Georgia; and Kathleen L. Endres, "The Women's Press in the Civil War: A Portrait of Patriotism, Propaganda, and Prodding," *Civil War History* 30 (1984): 31–53, analyzes the messages found in women's magazines about "the proper conduct expected of [women] . . . during the war" (p. 48).

3. See George C. Rable, *Civil Wars: Women and the Crisis of Southern Nationalism* (Urbana: University of Illinois Press, 1989); and Faust, *Mothers of Invention,* for the transformation in Confederate women's views about the war. For an exploration of white Northern women in the war, see Elizabeth D. Leonard, *Yankee Women: Gender Battles in the Civil War* (New York: W. W. Norton, 1994).

4. Many historians note the difficulties of families with ties to both sides. Catherine Clinton's *Tara Revisited: Women, War, and the Plantation Legend* (New York: Abbeville Press, 1995), 56–57, for example, reminds us of the experiences of Mary Todd Lincoln, Pierce Butler, and other, more ordinary, Americans. But no one, to my knowledge, has written exclusively about intersectional marriages and family relationships among women in the Civil War era. Published primary sources about white Northern women who had married Southern men include a few accounts in Katharine M. Jones, ed., *Heroines of Dixie: Confederate Women Tell Their Story of the War* (1955; reprint, Westport, Conn.: Greenwood Press, 1973); Wilma King, ed., *A Northern Woman in the Plantation South: Letters of Tryphena Blanche Holder Fox, 1856–1876* (Columbia: University of South Carolina Press, 1993); and Christine Jacobson Carter, ed., *The Diary of Dolly Lunt Burge, 1848–1879* (Athens: University of Georgia Press, 1997). These accounts all indicate support for the Confederacy. Charles M. McGee Jr. and Ernest M. Lander Jr., eds., *A Rebel Came Home: The Diary and Letters of Floride Clemson, 1863–1866,* rev. ed. (Columbia: University of South Carolina Press, 1989), discusses a Confederate woman's experiences in the North in 1863. White Southern women who supported the Union are portrayed in Kym S. Rice and Edward D. C. Campbell Jr., "Voices from the Tempest: Southern Women's Wartime Experiences," in *A Woman's War: Southern Women, Civil War, and the Confederate Legacy,* ed. Edward D. C. Campbell Jr. and Kym S. Rice (Richmond: Museum of the Confederacy, 1996), 73–111. Ruth Currie-McDaniel, "Northern Women in the South, 1860–1880," *Georgia Historical Quarterly* 76 (Summer 1992): 284–312, considers the experiences of Northern women who were married to Northern men in primarily the postwar period. Nina Silber, *The Romance of Reunion: Northerners and the South, 1865–1900* (Chapel Hill: University of North Carolina Press, 1993), investigates Northerners' views of, and experiences in, the postwar South.

5. See, for example, essays found in *In Joy and in Sorrow: Women, Family, and Marriage in the Victorian South,* ed. Carol Bleser (New York: Oxford University Press, 1991); and Joan Cashin, "'Since the War Broke Out': The Marriage of Kate and William McLure," in *Divided Houses,* ed. Clinton and Silber, 200–212.

6. For additional information on Nelly and the Gordon marriage, see Carolyn J. Stefanco, "Claiming Our Ancestors: Nelly Kinzie Gordon and the Issue of Loyalty in the Civil War" (paper presented at the annual meeting of the Georgia Historical Society, Savannah, April 1990), "A Matter of Honor: Female Patriotism

in the Confederate South" (paper presented at the Ninth Berkshire Conference on the History of Women, Poughkeepsie, N.Y., 1993), and "Northern-Born Women in the Confederate South: The Construction of White Female Political Identity" (paper presented at the Third Southern Conference on Women's History, Houston, 1994).

A voluminous literature exists on the impact of war on women. Scholars studying the American Revolution, such as Mary Beth Norton, *Liberty's Daughters: The Revolutionary Experience of American Women, 1750–1800* (Boston: Little, Brown, 1980); the Civil War, such as Anne Firor Scott, *The Southern Lady: From Pedestal to Politics, 1830–1930* (Chicago: University of Chicago Press, 1970); and the Second World War, such as William Chafe, "World War II as a Pivotal Experience for American Women," in *Women and War: The Changing Status of American Women from the 1930s to the 1950s*, ed. Maria Diedrich and Dorothea Fischer-Hornung (New York: Berg, 1990), have found that wartime transforms gender roles.

7. In *Mothers of Invention* Faust also notes that "in the new 'world of femininity' on the Confederate homefront, numbers of married as well as unmarried females were without the regular company and comfort of men" (p. 151).

8. Carroll Smith-Rosenberg provides the best description of a homosocial world for women in "The Female World of Love and Ritual: Relations between Women in Nineteenth-Century America," in *Disorderly Conduct: Visions of Gender in Victorian America* (New York: Oxford University Press, 1985), 53–76.

9. Positive views of Savannah by visitors during the war are provided by William Howard Russell, *My Diary North and South*, ed. Eugene H. Berwanger (New York: Alfred A. Knopf, 1988); Mary D. Robertson, ed., *A Confederate Lady Comes of Age: The Journal of Pauline DeCaradeuc Heyward, 1863–1888* (Columbia: University of South Carolina Press, 1992); and Caroline Couper Lovell, *The Light of Other Days* (Macon, Ga.: Mercer University Press, 1995).

10. Eleanor Kinzie Gordon (known as "Nelly" or "Nellie"; hereafter cited as NKG), Civil War diary, January 16, 1862, Gordon Family Papers, Box 12, file folder 125, Georgia Historical Society, Savannah [hereafter cited as GHS].

11. NKG, "To the Editor of the Ladies Home Journal," November 25, 1914, Box 7, file folder 81, GHS.

12. George Arthur Gordon, "Eleanor Kinzie Gordon: A Sketch," *Georgia Historical Quarterly* 1 (September 1917): 186.

13. Gladys Denny Shultz and Daisy Gordon Lawrence, *Lady from Savannah: The Life of Juliette Low* (Philadelphia: J. B. Lippincott, 1958), 69.

14. Mary D. Robertson, ed., "Northern Rebel: The Journal of Nellie Kinzie Gordon, Savannah, 1862," *Georgia Historical Quarterly* 70 (fall 1986): 477–517.

15. For a recent example, see Derek Smith, *Civil War Savannah* (Savannah: Frederic C. Beil, 1997), 226. Juliette Gordon Low's own recollections of this event

do not portray her mother as a Confederate. See Juliette Low, "When I Was a Girl," in *Juliette Low and the Girl Scouts*, ed. Anne Hyde Choate and Helen Ferris (Garden City, N.Y.: Doubleday, Doran, 1928), 3–5.

16. Drew Gilpin Faust, "Altars of Sacrifice: Confederate Women and the Narratives of War," *Journal of American History* 76 (March 1990): 1203. See Jacquelyn Dowd Hall and Anne Firor Scott, "Women in the South," in *Interpreting Southern History: Historiographical Essays in Honor of Sanford W. Higginbotham*, ed. John B. Boles and Evelyn Thomas Nolen (Baton Rouge: Louisiana State University Press, 1987), 454–509, for a historiographical essay on Southern women as a whole. Historians have also studied the meaning of sacrifice during other wars. See, for example, Mark H. Leff, "The Politics of Sacrifice on the American Home Front in World War II," *Journal of American History* 77 (March 1991): 1296–1318.

17. On the Lost Cause see Gaines M. Foster, *Ghosts of the Confederacy: Defeat, the Lost Cause, and the Emergence of the New South* (New York: Oxford University Press, 1987). Nancy T. Kondert supports the Lost Cause interpretation of white women's experiences in "The Romance and Reality of Defeat: Southern Women in 1865," *Journal of Mississippi History* 35 (1973): 141–52. John M. Coski and Amy R. Feely explore "how southern [white] women remembered and commemorated the Confederacy, the war, and their own wartime experiences" in "A Monument to Southern Womanhood: The Founding Generation of the Confederate Museum," in *A Woman's War*, ed. Campbell and Rice, 134.

18. References are to Rable, *Civil Wars*, 47, 74, 54, and 86.

19. William Washington Gordon II [known as "Willie" or "Willy"; hereafter cited as WWG] to NKG, November 21, 1854, Gordon Family Papers, Box 1, file folder 15, Southern Historical Collection, University of North Carolina, Chapel Hill (hereafter cited as SHC).

20. Schultz and Lawrence, *Lady from Savannah*, 54.

21. WWG notes his earlier doubts concerning slavery to NKG in a letter dated December 18, 1854. In a December 26, 1854, letter to NKG, WWG says, "I feel vexed at ever having doubted the system as much as I often did in the past." Box 1, file folder 4, SHC.

22. Sarah Anderson Stites Gordon (Willie's mother, hereafter cited as SG) owned twenty-one slaves, nine of whom were children (below the age of fourteen), according to the U.S. Census, 1860, Savannah, Slave Schedules. Sarah's daughter Eliza Stiles, her son-in-law William H. Stiles Jr., and their infant daughter were also listed as residents of the Gordon home, at the northeast corner of Bull and South Broad Streets in Savannah. The 1860 census reveals that William H. Stiles Jr. owned four slaves (all over the age of fourteen). See "Slave Inhabitants in the City of Savannah 3rd District, 19th of August 1860," U.S. Census, 1860, Savannah, Slave Schedules.

23. WWG to NKG, December 18, 1854, Box 1, file folder 4, SHC.

24. WWG to NKG, December 26, 1854, Box 1, file folder 4, SHC.

25. See Drew Gilpin Faust, ed., *The Ideology of Slavery: Proslavery Thought in the Antebellum South* (Baton Rouge: Louisiana State University Press, 1981), for information on proslavery ideology. Rather than questioning the status quo, Willie was instead consumed with the struggle to adopt an adult male role and to establish himself as family patriarch. (His father died when he was eight and his older brother had left home.) Although he referred to himself in letters to Nelly as "Negro Boss of the Establishment" both at work and at home, Willie was, in fact, an apprentice to a cotton factor and since he initially received no pay, he was financially dependent on a guardian named in his father's will. His mother's correspondence, in addition, reveals that she, not her twenty-one-year-old son, ran the house. See SG to WWG, August 24 and September 13, 1856, Box 1, file folder 4, GHS.

26. WWG to NKG, July 7, 1855, Box 15, file folder 2, SHC; and WWG to NKG, October 24, 1855, Box 1, file folder 4, SHC.

27. Juliette Magill Kinzie [hereafter cited as JK] to NKG, January 30, 1858, Box 1, file folder 4, SHC. Sarah Gordon did wield a great deal of power over her son, her daughter-in-law, and her household. See the chapter entitled "Keeper of the Keys" in my book-length manuscript on Nelly for more information on Sarah's relationship with her daughter-in-law in the 1857–61 time period.

28. JK to NKG, n.d., Box 15, file folder 8, SHC.

29. WWG to NKG, June 29, 1859, Box 15, file folder 9, SHC.

30. Untitled typescript, miscellaneous records, Juliette Gordon Low Girl Scout National Center, Savannah, 83. This typescript contains scattered pages from a larger manuscript that no longer exists.

31. WWG to NKG, August 12, 1859, Box 15, file folder 10, SHC.

32. JK to NKG, April 26, 1861, Box 16, file folder 14, SHC.

33. Seiler typescript, 86.

34. JK to NKG, April 26, 1861, Box 16, file folder 14, SHC.

35. JK to NKG, May 29, 1861, Box 16, file folder 15, SHC.

36. The *Savannah Daily Morning News* carried this story from Richmond on May 10, 1861, p. 1, col. 1.

37. Willie made this point over and over again in letters to Nelly. This statement, which he prefaced with "I thought I had made it plain to you in the beginning of the War," is from WWG to NKG, July 29, 1862, Box 16, file folder 16, SHC.

38. JK to NKG, December 5 and December 10, 1860, Box 15, file folder 13, SHC.

39. Willie certainly embraced the code of honor that, according to Bertram Wyatt-Brown, governed behavior in the slave-owning South. His own difficulties in forging an adult male role and in accepting his wife's ties to the North, combined with the more general challenges to the social order engendered by war, made Willie more sensitive than most to personal insult. When an enlisted man seemed

to threaten his reputation in Savannah, for example, he challenged him to a duel. Willie's own self-doubts help to explain this behavior, as well as his insistence that Nelly remain in Savannah. To him, public appearances took precedence over family well-being. See Bertram Wyatt-Brown, *Southern Honor: Ethics and Behavior in the Old South* (New York: Oxford University Press, 1982). Wyatt-Brown defines honor "as the cluster of ethical rules, most readily found in societies of small communities, by which judgments of behavior are ratified by community consensus" (p. xv). He argues that honor became especially meaningful when crises occurred (p. xv).

40. JK to NKG, June 17, 1861, Box 16, file folder 15, SHC.

41. Faust, "Altars of Sacrifice," 1206, 1207.

42. JK to NKG, June 17, 1861, Box 16, file folder 15, SHC. For additional information about Maria Kinzie Steuart and the Hunters, see Edward A. Miller Jr., *Lincoln's Abolitionist General: The Biography of David Hunter* (Columbia: University of South Carolina Press, 1997). According to Miller (p. 49), Hunter had once lived in Chicago but moved his family to either Independence or Leavenworth, Kans., around 1858.

43. JK to NKG, June 17, 1861, Box 16, file folder 15, SHC.

44. JK to NKG, July 7, 1861. Box 16, file folder 15, SHC.

45. JK to NKG, Jul 29, 1861. Box 16, file folder 15, SHC.

46. Rable, *Civil Wars*, 47.

47. Smith, *Civil War Savannah*, 27 and 97, discusses the specific activities in which Savannah women engaged. Rable, *Civil Wars*, 138–44, and Faust, *Mothers of Invention*, 23–29, summarize the efforts of Confederate women's voluntary associations. For a recent discussion of white Northern women's war work, see Lori D. Ginzberg, "A Passion for Efficiency," chap. 5 of *Women and the Work of Benevolence* (New Haven: Yale University Press, 1990).

48. Seiler typescript, 87. Nelly reports that this incident occurred right after the fall of Fort Sumter. Nelly had two brothers, Arthur and John, who fought for the Union.

49. Civil War diary, April 6, 1862.

50. Handwritten, unbound journal pages offer a different interpretation of these events. See Box 13, file folder 131, GHS. This suggests that Nelly, like the South's most famous diarist, Mary Boykin Chesnut, may have rewritten her wartime journal. See Michael P. Johnson, "Mary Boykin Chesnut's Autobiography and Biography: A Review Essay," *Journal of Southern History* 67 (November 1981): 585–92.

51. Robertson, "Northern Rebel," 481.

52. Civil War diary, May 4, 1862.

53. Lincoln revoked Hunter's edict abolishing slavery. See Miller, *Lincoln's Abolitionist General*.

54. Seiler typescript, 108; and WWG to NKG, May 30, 1862, Box 16, file folder 16, SHC. Nelly also argued with her sister-in-law, Gulie. But since sectionalism was only one of many sources of contention in their relationship, I have chosen not to include information about Nelly and Gulie in this paper.

55. WWG to NKG, June 29, 1862, Box 16, file folder 16, SHC.

56. Rable, *Civil Wars*, 75, 86, 211–12. Faust, "Altars of Sacrifice," extends this argument by stating that "we must not ignore gender as a factor in explaining Confederate defeat" (1203). Victoria E. Bynum, *Unruly Women: The Politics of Social and Sexual Control in the Old South* (Chapel Hill: University of North Carolina Press, 1992), esp. chap. 6, contends that white Southern women played an instrumental role in North Carolina Unionist activity.

57. Nelly and assorted Gordon female relatives traveled to Madison Springs in May 1862. In July she and her children went to Athens, twenty miles away from Madison Springs, which is where Maria and her daughter joined them in September.

58. WWG to NKG, June 5, 1865, Box 16, file folder 20, SHC.

59. Juliette Kinzie wrote that "Gen. Stuart threatens to take Minnie from her [Maria]." See JK to Arthur Kinzie [herafter cited as AK], February 5, 1863, Box 16, file folder 18, SHC.

60. Maria's second daughter, Mary, was born in early February 1864, nine months after her departure from the South, according to JK to NKG, April 3, 1864, Box 16, file folder 19, SHC.

61. AK to NKG, May 10, 1863, Box 16, file folder 18, SHC. See JK to NKG, June 22, 1863, Box 16, file folder 18, SHC, for news of Maria's arrival in Washington.

62. JK to NKG, January 19, 1863, Box 16, file folder 18, SHC.

63. JK to AK, January 19 and February 25, 1863, Box 16, file folder 18, SHC.

64. Juliette Kinzie wrote, in response to a letter from Nelly, "I am glad Mrs. G. takes a different view of the subject from what she once did." See JK to NKG, June 22, 1863, Box 16, file folder 18, SHC.

65. William Henry Stiles Jr. to WWG, July 12, 1863, Box 1, file folder 7, GHS.

66. AK to General Mercer, February 14, 1862, Box 1, file folder 6, GHS; WWG to NKG, July 29, 1862, Box 16, file folder 16, SHC; and JK to NKG, March 12, 1863, Box 16, file folder 18, SHC.

67. In early October 1863, for example, the Kinzies sent Nelly "a hundred dollars in gold." See JK to NKG, October 2, 1863, Box 16, file folder 18, SHC. Christmas presents sent from the Kinzies to Nelly that year included a purple silk dress for Nelly; two cloaks and a cap; material; a gold thimble for Nelly; combs, brushes, and paper; candy; and shirts, stockings, silver thimbles, and handkerchiefs for the children. See JK to NKG, January 12, 1864, Box 16, file folder 19, SHC. In mid-April of 1864, Juliette Kinzie discussed items that were in transit to Nelly,

including food such as "tea, coffee, sugar and chocolate," clothing, such as a silk dress, corsets, and shoes, and candles. See JK to NKG, April 18, 1864, Box 16, file folder 19, SHC. And in late 1864 a box containing linen sheets, cotton sheets, black stockings, oil paints, coffee, sugar, tea, knickknacks, fabric, and mincemeat was in transit. See JK to NKG, November 1864, Box 1, file folder 9, GHS.

68. See, for example, WWG to NKG, August 13, [1864], and August 20, 1864, Box 1, file folder 9, GHS.

69. Eliza Gordon Stiles to NKG, September 14, [ca. 1866], Box 1, file folder 10, GHS.

70. For information on wartime shortages in the Confederacy, see Mary Elizabeth Massey, *Ersatz in the Confederacy* (1952; reprint, Columbia: University of South Carolina Press, 1993). Massey discusses Confederate bread riots on p. 166. Also see Paul D. Escott, "'The Cry of the Sufferers': The Problem of Welfare in the Confederacy," *Civil War History* 23 (September 1977): 228–40.

71. *Savannah Daily Morning News,* July 20, 1863, p. 2, col. 1.

72. JK to NKG, December 15, 1864, Box 16, file folder 18, SHC.

73. JK to NKG, January 12, 1864, Box 16, file folder 19, SHC.

74. JK to NKG, January 12, 1864, Box 16, file folder 19, SHC; WWG to NKG, May 5, 1864, Box 1, file folder 8, GHS. It seems that small pieces of information shared by women did dramatically affect the outcome of Civil War contests. See, for example, Sylvia G. L. Dannet, "Rebecca Wright—Traitor or Patriot?" *Lincoln Herald* 65 (1963): 103–12.

75. WWG to NKG, May 5, 1864, Box 1, file folder 8, GHS (emphasis added). Willie explained in this letter that a bout of diarrhea delayed this "interview." He continued, however, to provide Nelly with detailed descriptions of battles and troop movements. But he now marked such sections of his letters "Private." See, for example, WWG to NKG, July 29, 1864, Box 1, file folder 8, GHS. Willie's decision to share battle news with Nelly was not unusual. James M. McPherson explains that "in contrast with twentieth-century wars, Civil War armies did not subject soldiers' letters to censorship. . . . Soldiers' letters were therefore uniquely blunt and detailed about important matters that probably would not pass a censor . . . [such as] details of marches and battles." See *For Cause and Comrades: Why Men Fought in the Civil War* (New York: Oxford University Press, 1997), 12.

76. JK to AK, February 25, 1863, Box 16, file folder 18, SHC. This quote, recast in the plural, was used as the title of this essay.

77. Eleanor Kinzie Gordon, "The Maid Announced General Sherman," in *When Sherman Came: Women and the "Great March!"* ed. Katharine M. Jones (Indianapolis: Bobbs-Merrill, 1964), 97–100.

78. WWG to NKG, June 5, 1865, Box 16, file folder 20, SHC.

79. Willie wrote that he trusted that "in your recent visit . . . [to Washington that you had] respect enough for me & my sentiments towards . . . [Hunter]

CAROLYN J. STEFANCO

to have nothing to do with him. If you have slept under his roof, if you have eaten at his table, if you have availed yourself of his protection or used his name or influence . . . to procure any other favor from the Yankee Govt. . . . I shall never forgive you, so help me God." WWG to NKG, June 5, 1865, Box 16, file folder 20, SHC.

80. WWG to NKG, June 6, 1865, Box 16, file folder 20, SHC.

81. JK to NKG, April 18, 1864, Box 16, file folder 19, SHC.

Safety Lies Only in Silence

Secrecy and Subversion in
Montgomery's Unionist Community

WILLIAM WARREN ROGERS JR.

*I*n the spring of 1864, Federal forces attempted an invasion of Texas. The Red River campaign failed miserably. The overdue good war news was celebrated throughout the Confederacy. Yet in Montgomery, Alabama, birthplace of the Confederacy, Unionists received the report with "great mortification." The previous year, when Major General John C. Pemberton surrendered the symbolically and strategically crucial garrison at Vicksburg, Unionists in Montgomery had celebrated clandestinely at a local party. As the war turned against the South, one Montgomerian loyal to the Lincoln administration took pleasure in the declining fortunes of the "so-called Confederate States." By late 1864, another Unionist in the Alabama capital was confidently mapping the progress of Grant's forces as the Army of the Potomac moved toward Richmond. The amateur cartographer predicted within thirty days the fall of the Confederate capital and Robert E. Lee's surrender. The loyalties of these Montgomerians were hardly representative of the general population. In the small city of some ten thousand people, no more than thirty were Unionists. Even so, they maintained loyalties under adverse circumstances and ardently opposed the Confederate States of America.[1]

Unionists varied in numbers and strength throughout the South. In the northern and western edges of the Confederacy, where the secessionist spirit had never run as rapidly or deep, Unionists were well established. In parts of the mountain South, particularly East Tennessee, loyalty to the United States was evident from the outset. Southerners favoring the Lincoln government also fared well in cities occupied by Northern troops. Memphis, Nashville, and New Orleans offer examples. In some of these and other areas, allegiance to the United States did not carry as great a stigma of disloyalty. But in the vast majority of the deep South, where passion for the Confederacy was stronger and enmity towards the Union fiercer, Unionists faced extreme hostility and even danger. Montgomery was such a place.[2]

Montgomery had been the capital of Alabama since 1846. Located near the headwaters of the Alabama River, the state capital was also a center of cotton trade in the Black Belt. One of every two residents was a slave. Montgomery evolved in the 1850s from a river town to a small city. By 1860 brick buildings were replacing wood structures, and an impressive theater crowned its new status. Fine homes and an undulating landscape made for an appealing setting. With some reason, a visitor in 1860 described Montgomery as "far above the average of Southern cities."[3]

Montgomery's central location in the lower South had much to do with its selection as the capital of the Confederate States of America. Between February and May 1861, before the capital was moved to Richmond, Montgomery took on a special significance. The city was also the home of William Lowndes Yancey, preeminent fire-eater and idol of many residents. On February 16, when Jefferson Davis arrived in Montgomery, the local lawyer had dramatically announced, "The man and the hour have met."[4] Montgomerians eagerly embraced the Confederacy, and Southern nationalism resonated widely and brightly throughout the city. As the war began, one local woman wrote a public letter to Abraham Lincoln demanding that he acknowledge Southern independence and avowing, "I feel strong in my resolves." Despite losing native sons in battle and suffering the deprivations endemic to the Confederate home front, Montgomerians generally supported a war they considered righteous. The maligned enemy drew condemnation in the neoclassical capitol at the summit of Market Street and were equally reviled several hundred yards away at Commerce Street drinking establishments. Residents stood foursquare, and the calling of patriotism and duty remained clear.[5]

Even so, a small number of Montgomerians resisted uncritical loyalty. A community of Unionists existed from the outset. Almost all of them had Northern backgrounds. David H. Carter, born in New York, moved to Montgomery during the 1830s and married locally. Other New York natives included Milton and James Caldwell, brothers. Several natives of Maine, including Israel W. Roberts, Lewis Owen, and James P. Stow, had relocated to Montgomery at various times in the 1840s and 1850s. More recently, in 1859, Samuel D. Seelye had arrived from Connecticut. The economic and social position of Unionists varied widely. Lewis Owen was the president of the Montgomery and Eufaula Railroad. David Carter, the owner of a stable and a boardinghouse, was anything but financially secure. With his property mortgaged, Carter could not even meet his doctor bills during the war. William J. Bibb was a planter whose affluence equaled that of Owen. George Cowles prospered as a dry goods proprietor. Benjamin Hardy, who ran an oyster cellar and a bakery, did not own a home, boarding at the Exchange Hotel. In Alabama's capital allegiance to the Union transcended class lines.

Most of those who remained Unionists in wartime Montgomery had supported John Bell in the 1860 presidential election. They agreed with the Constitutional Union Party's commitment to avoiding secession and maintaining the nation's ties and saw it as the one moderate choice among the extremist stances represented by other candidates on the ballot. William Bibb, the city's most outspoken Unionist, campaigned actively for the Bell ticket. After Lincoln's election the secessionist convention met in January 1861 in Montgomery. Bibb arranged a caucus room for the delegates who opposed secession. Lewis Owen was in fundamental agreement, even though he had endorsed the states' rights candidacy of the Southern Democrat John C. Breckinridge. In some respects, David Carter ranked as the most militant of local Unionists. The ex-Whig also favored the Constitutional Union Party.

It is impossible to infer significant philosophical or moral opposition to slavery among Unionists. Outside the city limits William Bibb worked about fifty slaves on his twelve-hundred-acre cotton plantation. He pronounced secession "criminal and destructive" and compared the sacredness of the Union to the Bible. Bibb added to his workforce by purchasing twenty-five more slaves during the war.[6] Nor could one connect Lewis Owen with the abolitionist school of thought. He was a man of wealth, slaves, and a deep attachment to the United States. As president of the Montgomery and Eufaula Railroad, Owen depended on slave labor to lay railroad track and saw nothing incompatible between owning slaves and favoring the Union cause. Montgomery residents who remained loyal citizens of the United

WILLIAM WARREN ROGERS JR.

Confederate troops in Montgomery, 1861. *Harper's Weekly,* February 9, 1861.

States did not do so from any aversion to the "peculiar institution" at the center of the conflict that brought on the war.[7]

Alabama's capital was a place of considerable wealth and sophistication. On the war's eve, John Wilkes Booth appeared in several theatrical productions in the newly constructed brick theater. Lecturers and performers appeared regularly at the Montgomery and Concert Halls on Market Street. Unionists would secretly gather in far less public venues. One such place was Israel Roberts's hardware store on Commerce Street. The nondescript edifice barely differed in appearance from two other local hardware stores, but the conversations there—praising the Union, condemning the Confederacy— made it unique. Roberts accepted Confederate currency, but the Maine native rejected everything else about the new Southern nation. The Market Street dry goods store owned by George Cowles offered another subversionary forum. At both places Unionists found a haven where they could speak openly and without fear.

Milton and James Caldwell might be present. James P. Stow, hardware store owner and fire department chief, also sometimes joined the informal gatherings. Samuel Seelye, the Connecticut-born doctor, was another kindred spirit. Taking leave of responsibilities at his stables and boardinghouse, David Carter found philosophical comfort with these men. Meetings were not weekly or scheduled, there was no call to order or protocol, and no passwords or secret handshakes were exchanged. Conversation invariably concerned the war's progress. The Confederacy was condemned in general, and some of its local champions were vilified in particular. The comrades shared Northern newspapers, rare in Montgomery, and greatly appreciated the different slant from the news that appeared in the *Montgomery Advertiser* and the *Montgomery Mail*. Even at the darkest of times, Israel Roberts remained confident of ultimate Federal victory. Mutual identification made their minority status more bearable. A shared sense of commiseration was evident.[8]

Nobody was as outspoken at Israel Roberts's store as William Bibb. When the war began, he was forty-one years old, married, and the father of a young daughter. He was an anomaly in the group in that he was the only Southern-born Unionist among them. The strong Confederate credentials of his family made his position even more extraordinary. His parents, Benajah and Sophia Bibb, were leading citizens and strong Southern patriots, and the extended Bibb family was one of the best connected in the city. Sophia was the president of the Ladies Aid Association, an organization that gathered food and clothes for soldiers. Yet their son categorically rejected the Confederacy in theory and in fact. When the Reverend Johnson C. Davis delivered a politicized Rebel sermon at the Episcopal Methodist Church, William Bibb emphatically informed him that he would not return if mixing God and the Confederacy continued. Bibb was a strong-willed and obdurate man, largely unfazed by public opinion. For him the Confederacy was an illegal monstrosity, born out of tortured constitutional logic and carried out by extremists who exploited passions and ungrounded fears. The consequence was the tragic loss of life. In the friendly confines of Roberts's store, Bibb found a receptive audience and, given the opportunity, often launched into "tirades."[9] He considered Confederate victories a "curse" that prolonged the war and rejoiced at Northern victories.[10]

Bibb's activities did not stop with anti-Confederate fulminations. Rather than have his carriage horses impressed by the Confederacy, Bibb sold them. To a cousin who urged him to subscribe cotton for the Confederacy, Bibb replied in no uncertain terms that he would contribute nothing to the wrong-headed cause. He informed another, "I would not give the one Union for a thousand of your Confederacies."[11] Walter Coleman, the mayor of Montgomery during the war, described Bibb's attitude as "very bitter."[12]

Coleman offered this judgment to the Southern Claims Commission. That commission was established by Congress in 1871 to evaluate claims for compensation made by southerners. During the war Federal troops confiscated

WILLIAM WARREN ROGERS JR.

supplies, stock, and a vast array of private possessions from Southerners. Maintaining they had never ceased to be United States citizens, Unionists applied for financial restitution after the conflict. Gaining compensation from the government required proving their past loyalty and Unionist status. Witnesses who knew the petitioners provided testimony that lent credence or belied the protestations of loyalty. William Bibb and David Carter applied for compensation early in the 1870s. Called upon for corroboration, various Montgomerians confirmed both men's Unionist stance. Twenty-four well-placed citizens recalled Bibb's loyalties. The Reverend Johnson Davis was among them. "If ever the Confederate government had an enemy in the midst of its friends, or the Union a friend in the midst of its enemies," Johnson told committee members, "I think Mr. Bibb was that person."[13]

William Bibb's apostasy caused some to demand his appearance before the Vigilante Committee, which had formed within weeks of the firing on Fort Sumter to deal with those whose loyalties were questionable or openly at odds with the Confederacy. Given that Judge Abram Martin chaired the Vigilante Committee, it exercised full legal powers, including the power to order banishment. First the eye of suspicion and then the Vigilante Committee's blunting force fell on numerous unfortunates. A Philadelphia hairdresser was among the first forced to leave the city. Others followed her—some voluntarily and some involuntarily. William Bibb was spared the ordeal, the scrutiny, and quite possibly, the disciplinary action of a Vigilante Committee hearing. Both his prominent family connections and the sympathy others extended Bibb because he was lame and had very poor eyesight saved the outspoken Unionist. As Milton J. Saffold testified, Bibb would "say and do things that other men would not have been allowed to say or do."[14]

Whether Edmond Fowler was forced from Montgomery by the Vigilante Committee is not known. That he felt extreme pressure to depart is certain. Fowler practiced medicine. In spite of that respected occupation, and in fact because of it, the Massachusetts-born doctor attracted severe scorn in 1862. A personal crisis was precipitated by the arrival of several hundred prisoners captured at the Battle of Shiloh. After that engagement the Federal captives were brought up the Alabama River and incarcerated in Montgomery in the spring of 1862. A three-story warehouse served as their quarters for over a month. As a doctor with humanitarian instincts, Fowler felt compelled to attend to the prisoners' considerable medical needs. As a Unionist, he was favorably disposed toward the soldiers. He and his wife, Martha, formed part of a chain that supplied the soldiers with various comforts. The Fowlers acted in collusion with David and Martha Carter. Montgomerians did not know the extent of this operation. Some, however, did conclude that Fowler was too solicitous of the enemy, and he was prohibited from visiting the prisoners. Exposed to virulent criticism locally, Fowler soon departed. He, his wife, and their son, George, moved to New York City. In October 1862, when Fowler met the noted New York diarist George Templeton Strong, he recounted to him his recent travails. That evening, in his diary, Strong wrote empathetically of the "refugee from Montgomery, Alabama." He considered Fowler an "intelligent" and "well-mannered" gentleman who had been "cast out."[15]

William Hedges understood the prevailing mentality and acted accordingly. Seeking economic opportunity, Hedges, a Northern mechanic, had moved to Montgomery in 1858. By 1860 he was a foreman of the Florida and Alabama Railroad and shared a home with four other Northern men. In contrast to the prevailing joyous mood, Hedges and his roommates watched with gloom and a sense of foreboding as Jefferson Davis was inaugurated. They quickly came to realize just how much the war had altered their lives, noting with some trepidation the "barrell-headed inquisitions." Hedges soon learned who shared his loyalties within the community. "The rebellion was not a month old before I had a perfect understanding with them all," he wrote.[16] Fully aware of the Vigilante Committee and what could befall him, Hedges noted that "safety lies only in silence." He trod carefully, voicing his opinions only among known fellow Unionists.

Hedges left Montgomery in 1864 and soon described for *Harper's Magazine* the life of a Unionist in wartime Montgomery. Hedges depicted a camaraderie among Unionists that made for "the closest fellowship."[17] Theirs was an arrangement, underground by nature, based on a shared bond to the United States. Unionists were also bound by the fear of reprisal, fully aware that questioning Confederate orthodoxy risked severe consequences. In an evangelical city where ministers consecrated the Cause from pulpits, the line between church and state blurred. Punishment for those perceived as traitors might be administered by the state or, more draconically, by overzealous vigilantes. Unionists endured epithets and ostracism, and, with reason, they feared violence. As a small group of dissidents, they faced the task of functioning in a hostile, unforgiving, and emotion-charged society.

This reality tempered their words and actions. Lewis Owen, David Carter, and George Cowles were especially close confidants. "I hardly think," Owen later reflected, "we even talked in the presence of other persons about the war."[18] If William Bibb could excoriate the Confederacy, others did not enjoy that privilege. It was the quietly spoken word, more frequently than the deed, that constituted their opposition to the Jefferson Davis government. Samuel Seelye possessed the will but not the chance to translate Unionist sentiments into action. Reflecting on what he and his friends actually accomplished, Seelye admitted, "We had very little opportunity to do anything."[19]

Actions undertaken on behalf of the United States government were few, but they were carried out. In the spring of 1862, when the Shiloh prisoners arrived in Montgomery, they languished in a warehouse very near David Carter's boardinghouse. Captain J. J. Geer, one of the prisoners, recalled, "We often suffered for water in this cotton-shed prison."[20] At times, Geer and other prisoners were allowed to fill buckets of water at Carter's home. When they did so, David and Martha Carter slipped various supplies into their buckets. Martha Fowler, the wife of Edmond Fowler, helped prepare what Carter described as "delicacies." Aware of the prisoners' condition, Fowler apprised his fellow Unionists of the soldiers' needs. The system provided the Federal prisoners with chicken, other sustaining food, and, in hot, insect-ridden Montgomery, much-appreciated mosquito nets. The scale of operations could be large. On one occasion Carter provided the malnourished prisoners with meat from five slaughtered sheep. As the defiant Unionist later declared, "We were never found out."[21]

David Carter's audacity matched his loathing for the Confederacy. In his forties, the stablekeeper was too old to be conscripted into military service. Even so, he sympathized with those who were forced against their principles into the military ranks and on at least one occasion even risked his life to help a conscript. By 1864 Benjamin Hardy, a Northern-born baker, faced conscription in the Confederate army. In Carter he found a man who would help him escape Montgomery and that obligation. Using a travel pass Carter had procured ostensibly for personal reasons, Hardy planned to flee to Florida. There he hoped to make connections with the Federal blockading fleet off the coast at St. Andrews Bay, near Pensacola. The pass would have been essential if Hardy were ever stopped and questioned. Dr. Seelye also cooperated: he hid Hardy in his office on the evening of his flight. Hardy was soon safely in Union-occupied New Orleans.

Abetting a conscript's escape was an offense that carried with it a prison sentence. Yet Carter went well beyond helping this single fugitive. Hardy carried with him a map (drawn by Carter) suggesting the best direction for Federal troops to advance on Montgomery. Well aware that vital supplies were conveyed through the city on the Montgomery and West Point (Georgia) line, Carter envisioned a Federal raid that would originate from the Pensacola area. Deploying quickly northeastward, a force could move on

Montgomery and destroy the railroad. Transportation would be delayed and frustrated, and dependent Confederate forces in Georgia would be weakened. Such were Carter's thoughts and recommendations. "More supplies were waiting shipment," he later informed the Southern Claims Commission, "than could be transported." The strike's success, the resolute Unionist realized, depended on the Federal troops' achieving surprise and approaching the city rapidly. Carter urged cutting telegraph lines. He provided an estimate of troops in Montgomery and maintained that "an army marching fast could get plenty of supplies, and their approach not be detected." He instructed Hardy to give the map and other information to Federal authorities. The plan was feasible but never executed. Perhaps Hardy never gave the map to Union officials, or even if he did, military authorities may have considered civilian advice of limited value.[22]

Other acts of Unionists, although not envisioning the city's fall, provided anti-Confederates vicarious satisfaction. William Bibb contended that "secession was treason and secessionists were traitors."[23] Accepting that logic, the loyalists considered any effort against the Confederate government an act of patriotism. Bibb was instrumental in efforts to raise money for Charles C. Sheats, a north Alabama Unionist imprisoned in Montgomery between 1863 and 1864 for aiding the enemy and helping raise Federal troops. When Sheats was released, Bibb presented him money pooled by local Unionists. He also entertained Sheats at his home. Small but symbolic acts were carried out when possible. As William Hedges observed, comforts were extended to "each in every strait and emergency where help could be given." Something else also provided encouragement. As Federal armies posted victories, Montgomery Unionists realized the inevitability of eventual triumph.[24]

Unionists fully understood the price they might pay for their convictions. Not only did William Bibb's partisan views gain him the disfavor of most of Montgomery; he also fell into disrepute with his family. Benajah Bibb referred to his son as a "traitor."[25] When Bibb visited the Federal prisoners, Montgomerians took extreme exception. Some wanted to hang him or, at the very least, send the defiant Unionist beyond the lines. Samuel Seelye fully appreciated the dangers for those considered "not sound on the Confederate question." Although he "talked freely" with David Carter, the physician was otherwise careful. As Seelye later assured the Southern Claims Commission, if local citizens had known the substance of their private conversations, they "would have put our necks in the halter before night."[26] The situation was sometimes uncomfortable for James Stow as well. Stow, a hardware store owner and fire chief, was well aware of threats to whip or even hang him. With reason, Hedges wrote of the Unionists' collective jeopardy and "the perils that might arise."[27]

Hedges, Seelye, Stow, and most Unionists avoided any major confrontations. David Carter was less fortunate, because of the help he provided to Benjamin Hardy. After his flight from Montgomery, Hardy settled at least temporarily in New Orleans. He talked of his escape, and through Confederate spies in New Orleans, news of Carter's complicity filtered back to Montgomery. Although he denied the allegations, Carter faced mounting resentment. Henry Lee encountered him reading a Boston newspaper and threatened to notify the Vigilante Committee. Augustus Underwood, a city clerk, belligerently told Carter he had "no business" living in the South. His was an embattled position. The view of General James H. Clanton was clear. At a chance post office meeting, the Montgomery officer threatened Carter, who remembered that he "came toward me in a very strange, furious manner." Another Carter critic was inspired by the city's artesian well. A Montgomery landmark, the well provided a water source and also the backdrop for slave auctions. The citizen proposed attaching weights to Carter and dropping the Yankee sympathizer into the well.[28] Carter assured James Stow "they were after him."[29]

Having anticipated problems before the war, Carter had considered leaving Montgomery. By this point departure became a more appealing option. Huntsville, Alabama, two hundred miles north of Montgomery, was in Federal hands, and Carter considered moving there. Continued poor health, a lack of funds, and the reality of having to leave his family behind prevented him from doing so. The Carters were bringing up six children. James Berney, his physician, recalled that Carter was considered a "bad man" and one "who had to be watched."[30] "My family," Carter reflected before the Southern Claims Commission, "was socially discarded."[31] A sporadic surveillance of his home was maintained. As James Stow testified, Carter was afraid he would be "hung for his loyalty."[32]

Stow understood Carter's anxiety. Although he personally maintained a devotion to the United States, and conversely a disdain for the Confederacy, Stow made his way without event. He recalled that Carter "talked more than I did." Paying taxes to the government, although resented by Stow, nevertheless remained a necessity. James Berney also dissented quietly, and as a result his life remained uncomplicated. The physician had opposed secession and resisted the government it brought to life, but he dared not do so brazenly. Although his four sons fought for the Confederacy, Berney maintained, "I had no sympathy with the cause for which my sons and neighbors fought." Berney took strong ideological exception to the Confederacy. Yet, on a practical level, living in Montgomery, he compromised that position. His relationship with Carter is revealing. As Carter's doctor, Berney recommended that he walk for therapy and sometimes accompanied him as he did so. On these occasions, because he was so upset about the war, Carter often began crying. Berney warned him against the histrionics. He feared too close contact with the unstable Unionist and threatened to quit walking with him. Recalling his concern that citizens would associate him with the unpopular Carter, Berney recalled, "I wasn't going to have my head taken off on his account."[33]

Both Stow and Berney were perceptive and accommodating men who recognized reality and acted on it. Daniel S. E. Starr pursued a different course. A native of Connecticut, the brickmason lived on the city's edge with his wife, Sophronia, and their two children. Starr was apparently an iconoclastic man, or at least the journal he kept reflected a committed defiance. The exact contents of that journal, which the *Montgomery Mail* termed an "abolition manuscript," are not known. That Starr's observations reflected poorly on the Confederacy and some local men is certain. He apparently drank too much sometimes, and one acquaintance speculated that on one such occasion Starr revealed the manuscript's existence. Whatever the case, authorities apprehended him at his Mobile Road home on March 10, 1863. A struggle took place, guns were fired, and Starr was arrested. Authorities seized the manuscript or journal.

Starr spent several hours over the next few days testifying before the Vigilante Committee. Word of the circumstances spread in the small city. The *Montgomery Mail* declined to prejudge but noted the consensus among citizens that Starr was guilty. Those unaware of Starr's reputation were advised to ask, "and any [one] of them can tell the reader what that opinion is." Whatever failings he may or may not have had, Starr was viewed as an advocate of black equality and a Yankee traitor. One of the worst war-related crimes on the Southern home front took place in Montgomery sometime on the night of March 14. A group of men forcefully removed Starr from the Monroe Street jail. The next morning's light revealed a grisly scene: Starr's corpse suspended from a tree near the edge of town. Those responsible were never apprehended. The search for his murderers was hardly comprehensive, and although some citizens faulted the method, most believed justice had been served. The logic was elementary, cold, and definitive. Daniel Starr would have turned fifty-three years old within the week.[34]

WILLIAM WARREN ROGERS JR.

The lynching confirmed the worst fears of Unionists. Starr had not associated with those who congregated at Israel Roberts's or George Cowles's stores. Even so, the murdered man was a kindred spirit because he rejected conventional and accepted thinking. In the immediate aftermath David Carter and Samuel Seelye worried that Starr's death might incite others violently indisposed toward Unionists. Seelye informed Carter that he owned several rifles and "could shoot from a distance," and he promised to defend himself.[35]

That was not necessary. The hanging was an aberration that was not repeated. Even David Carter weathered the situation and remained in Montgomery. William Hedges and his Northern roommates, who worked on the railroad, fled to the free states in 1864 after their railroad-labor exemptions were lifted and they faced conscription. That year Hedges wrote in *Harper's Magazine* of the "impalpable oppression" that Unionists faced. By then the war was nearing a close. Montgomery and Richmond fell within ten days of each other in 1865. It was supremely ironic that two Unionists, William Bibb and Lewis Owen, belonged to the committee of ten that surrendered the city. Mayor Walter Coleman thought their presence might provide the committee some leverage in making favorable surrender terms with the enemy. Union General James Harrison Wilson peacefully occupied Montgomery on April 12.[36]

The reaction of citizens to the war's end was one more of relief than of continued defiance. To state that most residents had blindly supported the Confederacy is to generalize. Montgomerians criticized, sometimes passionately, the Richmond government. As elsewhere, the harsh realities of impressment and conscription policies provoked much unrest. Yet that did not provide a window of toleration for Unionists, who based their opposition on the very existence of that government. It was one thing to question the functioning process of a sometimes overbearing Confederate government. It was quite another to deny the Confederate States of America's right to exist.

One Montgomerian who had been loyal to the South reasoned hypothetically to the Southern Claims Commission that if the Confederacy had prevailed, William Bibb "would have been ranked as the biggest tory among us."[37] Another believed the Southern native had "disgraced himself." As it was, he was one of the few Montgomerians who could take the iron-clad oath, and President Andrew Johnson appointed him postmaster. David Carter took the same oath, and in 1865 he was appointed assistant assessor of United States Internal Revenue. Some evidence indicates that Carter opposed the institution of slavery. His appointment under the First Reconstruction

Act as a voting registrar was appropriate, and Carter registered some of Montgomery's first black voters. Lewis Owen took some solace in the loss of his slaves. The railroad president considered the price of keeping his chattel, the permanent establishment of the Confederate States of America, far too high.

After the war James Berney became the collector of internal revenue. Israel Roberts and George Cowles, as successful merchants, continued to supply the public with goods.[38] Samuel Seelye provided medical care almost until the turn of the century. His efforts fighting a yellow fever epidemic in 1897 were nothing less than heroic. When he died the next year, Seelye was eulogized as "beloved and distinguished." In contrast, the services of Dr. Edmund Fowler were lost permanently to the city. Sophronia Starr, the widow of Daniel Starr, continued to live in Montgomery (not without some bitter memories) until her death in 1903.[39]

William Bibb lived for thirty-two years after the war. A harsh foe of the Confederacy during its life, he favored extending lenient peace terms to Southerners after that government fell. He wrote President Lincoln as the conflict ended. "Let me entreat you to be careful of the feelings of the people of the South," Bibb advised. During the uncertain Reconstruction period ahead, Bibb believed Lincoln could gain Southern goodwill by acting magnanimously and avoiding a punitive policy. He confided to the president: "We who have borne the heat and burthen of the day are deeply interested in the quiet settlement of this matter."[40]

William Bibb and others during the war raised the ire of those who branded Unionism as untenable and as indefensible treason. Montgomerians viewed its practitioners with an antipathy approaching that which Christians in the Middle Ages had reserved for heretics. As a much maligned and small minority, Unionists drew comfort from their philosophical kinship and a sense of community among themselves. They met, cooperated, and took sustenance from one another. The gravitation together of the mutually oppressed has a long history. Still, Unionism in Montgomery during the Civil War was a dramatic and specific example of that kind of brotherhood. That some citizens dissented on ideological grounds was both important and revealing. Honoring their convictions but living in Montgomery, the men performed a delicate balancing act. Such was the burden of what one termed "loyal men of the city."[41]

1. Testimony of David Carter, claim no. 5616, in Case Files of Southern Claims Commission, RG 217, National Archives, Washington, D.C. (hereafter cited as SCC 5615). Eighth U.S. Census, Population Schedule (1860), 3–10. On the Red River campaign, see Richard N. Current, ed., *Encyclopedia of the Confederacy* (New York: Simon and Schuster, 1993), 3:1315–17.

2. On Unionism in the South and the experience of Southerners living under Federal occupation, see Stephen V. Ash, *When the Yankees Came: Conflict and Chaos in the Occupied South, 1861–1865* (Chapel Hill: University of North Carolina Press, 1998); Gerald M. Capers, *Occupied City: New Orleans under the Federals, 1862–1865* (Lexington: University of Kentucky Press, 1965), 48, 70, 78, 90–92, 110–11; Walter T. Durham, *Nashville the Occupied City: The First Seventeen Months—February 16, 1862 to June 30, 1863* (Nashville: Tennessee Historical Society, 1985), 6, 90–91; Richard H. Abbott, "Civil War Origins of the Southern Republican Press," *Civil War History* 53 (March 1997): 47–58.

3. *DeBow's Review* 28 (January 1860): 113. For *Times* (London) journalist William Howard Russell's description of Montgomery in 1861, see William Howard Russell, *My Diary, North and South*, vol. 1 (London: Bradbury and Evans, 1863).

4. *Montgomery Weekly Advertiser*, February 20, 1861. On Montgomery during the Confederacy, see William C. Davis, *"A Government of Our Own": The Making of the Confederacy* (New York: Free Press, 1994); on Yancey see Eric H. Walther, *The Fire-Eaters* (Baton Rouge: Louisiana State University Press, 1992), 48–72.

5. *Montgomery Weekly Confederation*, May 10, 1861; on Montgomery see William Warren Rogers Jr., *Confederate Homefront: Montgomery during the War* (Tuscaloosa: University of Alabama Press, 1999).

6. Testimony of William Bibb, David Carter, SCC 21355; Testimony of Samuel Seelye, SCC 5616; Alabama State Census, Slave Population (1860), 226, 235; Alabama State Census, Free Population (1860), 66, 78; on Owens see Thomas Bankhead Owen, *Dictionary of Alabama Biography* (Chicago: S. J. Clarke, 1921), 3:1309; for Seelye see *Montgomery Advertiser*, February 24, 1898; Leonard Mears and James Turnbull, *The Montgomery Directory for 1859–60, Containing the Names of the Inhabitants: A Business Directory* (Montgomery: Montgomery Advertiser Book and Printing Office, 1859), 4, 45.

7. Testimony of Lewis Owen, SCC 5616.

8. Testimony of William Bibb, Benajah Bibb, SCC 21355; Testimony of David Carter, Lewis Owen, SCC 5616; Alabama State Census, Free Population (1860), 62; *Montgomery Directory*, 32, 59, 90, 102; *Montgomery Mail*, October 30, 1860.

9. Testimony of Johnson Davis, David Carter, Israel Roberts, SCC 21355;

Alabama State Census, Free Population (1860), 98; for Benajah Bibb see Owen, *Dictionary of Alabama Biography*, 3:142; for Sophia Bibb see Owen, *Dictionary of Alabama Biography*, 144, 147.

10. Testimony of David Carter, SCC 21355.

11. Testimony of Johnson Davis, David Carter, SCC 21355.

12. Testimony of Walter Coleman, William J. Bibb, William C. Bibb; SCC 21355.

13. Testimony of Johnson Davis, SCC 21355; for establishment and operations of the Southern Claims Commission see Frank W. Klingberg, *The Southern Claims Commission* (Berkley and Los Angeles: University of California Press, 1955), 1–19; for description of records see Gary B. Mills, *Southern Loyalists in the Civil War: The Southern Claims Commission* (Baltimore: Genealogical Publishing Co., 1994).

14. Testimony of Milton J. Saffold; Walter Coleman, Josiah Morris, SCC 21355; Testimony of David Carter, James Berney, SCC 5616; *Montgomery Weekly Advertiser*, August 7, 1861; *Montgomery Post*, August 9, 1861; *Montgomery Advertiser*, April 16, 1862.

15. George Pendleton Strong, *The Diary of George Templeton Strong*, ed. Allan Nevins and Milton Halsey Thomas (Seattle: University of Washington Press, 1988), 215; Alabama State Census, Free Population (1860), 12; for an account of one of the Federal prisoners captured at Shiloh and incarcerated in Montgomery, see J. J. Geer, *Beyond The Lines; or, A Yankee Prisoner Loose in Dixie* (Philadelphia: J. W. Daughaday, 1863), 75–88; Testimony of David Carter, SCC 5616.

16. William Hedges, "Three Years in Montgomery," *Harpers New Monthly Magazine* 29 (July 1864): 196–97.

17. Ibid.

18. Testimony of Lewis Owen, David Carter, SCC 5616; for sentiment of Montgomery clergy toward the Confederacy see J. S. Dill, *Isaac Taylor Tichenor: The Home Mission Statesman* (Nashville: Sunday School Board, Southern Baptist Convention, 1908), 88–108; William Warren Rogers Jr., "'In Defense of Our Sacred Cause': Rabbi James K. Gutheim in Confederate Montgomery," *Journal of Confederate History* 7 (spring 1992): 115–22.

19. Testimony of Samuel Seelye, SCC 5616.

20. Geer, *Beyond the Lines*, 75–88; *Montgomery Advertiser*, April 16, 1862.

21. Testimony of David Carter, SCC 5616.

22. Testimony of David Carter, Samuel Seelye, SCC 5616. For an example of the pass enforcement system in Montgomery see Arthur James Lyon Fremantle, *Three Months in the Southern States, April–June 1863* (Edinburgh: William Blackwood and Sons, 1863), 134–36.

23. Testimony of Shepard A. Darby, SCC 21355.

24. Hedges, "Three Years in Montgomery," 196–97; Testimony of Charles

Sheats, William Bibb, SCC 21355. On Sheats see Sarah Woolfolk Wiggins, *The Scalawag in Alabama Politics, 1865–1881* (Tuscaloosa: University of Alabama Press, 1977).

25. Testimony of Benajah Bibb, Walter Coleman, SCC 21355.

26. Testimony of Samuel Seeyle, James Stow, SCC 5616.

27. Hedges, "Three Years in Montgomery," 196–97.

28. Testimony of David Carter, SCC 5616.

29. Testimony of James Stow, SCC 5616.

30. Testimony of James Berney, David Carter, Samuel Seeyle, SCC 5616; Alabama State Census, Free Population (1860), 78.

31. Testimony of David Carter, SCC 5616.

32. Testimony of James Stow, SCC 5616.

33. Ibid.; testimony of James Berney, SCC 5616.

34. *Montgomery Mail*, March 13, 17, 1863; Testimony of David Carter, SCC 5616; Alabama State Census, Free Population (1860); *Montgomery Advertiser,* April 22, 1903.

35. Testimony of David Carter, SCC 5616.

36. Hedges, "Three Years in Montgomery," 197–201; for surrender of Montgomery see James P. Jones, *Wilson's Raid through Alabama and Georgia* (Athens: University of Georgia Press, 1976),103–25.

37. Testimony of Israel Roberts, SCC 21355.

38. Testimony of Job Weatherly, Israel Roberts, SCC 21355.

39. *Montgomery Advertiser,* February 24, 1898; Testimony of William Bibb, SCC 21355; David Carter, James Berney, SCC 5616.

40. William Bibb to Abraham Lincoln, April 12, 1865, Surname File, Reel 542, Alabama Department of Archives and History, Montgomery.

41. Hedges, "Three Years in Montgomery," 197.

The Williams Clan's Civil War

How an Arkansas Farm Family
Became a Guerrilla Band

KENNETH C. BARNES

*B*efore 1861 Thomas Jefferson Williams appeared an unlikely warrior. He was a grandfather, well into middle age, who worked a small farm and even preached for a congregation of the Disciples of Christ Church. Williams's support for the Union in the Civil War would transform his life and that of his extended family. The War between the States brought a true localized civil war to the hill country of north central Arkansas. Neighbors turned against neighbors as sentiments divided sharply between Union and Confederate loyalties. The Williams family most wanted security for homes and property when war came. Instead, the conflict took away adult male members of the household, brought physical deprivation, and caused the women and children to flee as refugees. The collapse of civilian authority and military discipline in the area brought on a brutal guerrilla conflict in the last years of the war. The blood feud between the Unionist Williams family and Rebel neighbors surrounded them with a web of violence they could have never before imagined. After the war a bitter acrimony between Democratic and Republican families led to a cycle of political violence in Conway County that lasted well into the twentieth century.

The Williams family epitomizes a type about whom we know little from the historiography of Civil War Arkansas. During the war Union officers who commanded Arkansas troops, such as Albert Webb Bishop and James Demby, tried to publicize the plight of Unionists in the state to a Northern audience.[1] However, contrary to the old adage, the losers, not the victors, wrote the history of the war in Arkansas for almost a century afterward. Most of the men of substance and education supported the Confederacy. After the war these former Rebels chronicled the conflict from the Confederate point of view.[2] The more objective historical scholarship of the last thirty years has indeed taken seriously the Union dissent within the state. With more than eight thousand white Arkansans volunteering for service with the Union army, only Tennessee surpassed Arkansas among Confederate states in numbers of native troops in blue. For the most part poorly educated subsistence farmers from the Ozarks, these Unionists left few memoirs or letters to tell their own story. We know little about individual Unionists and their families. They were indeed, as Richard Current has called them, the unknown soldiers of the Civil War.[3]

The extended Williams family, headed by Thomas Jefferson ("Jeff") Williams, probably typified in many ways those in north central Arkansas who supported the Union. Williams and his family came to Arkansas from the hill country of Franklin County, Tennessee, in 1844. Jeff Williams, and his brothers John and Leroy, had first seen Arkansas in the spring of 1838, when, as members of the Tennessee militia, they "escorted" a party of Cherokees west through Arkansas to Indian territory. This task must have brought anguish and a sense of irony, for their mother, Rebecca, was the daughter of a full-blooded Cherokee. Six years after their return to Tennessee, the entire clan of five Williams brothers and three sisters, with spouses and children, packed their belongings and moved in a wagon train, probably with other Tennessee neighbors, to the near-wilderness that was Arkansas.

Clearing land in the hills along the southern edge of the Ozarks, these settlers were among the first white inhabitants in the area. Jeff Williams built a log house on 160 acres in Conway County, near the present community of Center Ridge. His siblings and their families spread out through the northern part of Conway County, with two brothers settling in southern Van Buren County. Jeff Williams became relatively prosperous in the years before the Civil War. In 1860 he was one of only two slaveholders in the township, owning a female slave, age twenty, who apparently helped out with household chores for a large family.[4]

Though a slave owner, Jeff Williams apparently remained devoted to the Union throughout the sectional crisis preceding the Civil War. He named two of his sons, born in the 1850s, Henry Clay Williams and Daniel Webster Williams, for the Whig senators from Kentucky and Massachusetts who symbolized antisectionalist loyalty to the Union after the Compromise of 1850. Immediately after Lincoln's election in 1860, Jeff Williams served as a leader in a public meeting held at the county courthouse at Springfield to discuss the secession crisis. The meeting condemned the inflammatory speeches of both Northern and Southern fanatics. The group resolved their loyalty to the Union and their rights under the Constitution. One of these rights, the meeting concluded, was the right to own slaves.[5]

Five days after this meeting, South Carolina seceded from the Union. In early January a second meeting to discuss secession was held at the county seat. In the southern part of Conway County, the Arkansas River valley widened to an arc of flat, fertile land, and a cotton economy thrived there through slave labor. Planters from the bottomlands dominated this second county meeting, and they took a different view from the hill farmers, like Jeff Williams, who had written the earlier resolutions. William Menifee, who owned thirty-five hundred acres alongside the Arkansas River, gave an eloquent address against Northern aggression. While he spoke, an elected committee prepared a written statement, which the meeting adopted and sent on to Little Rock's secessionist newspaper, the *True Democrat*. Declaring Lincoln's election an outrage to the South, the meeting resolved to support the sovereignty of the state and its right to secede from the Union and called for a state convention to elect delegates to a general convention of Southern states. Should this effort fail to secure Southern rights, the resolutions concluded, Arkansas should follow the other Southern states in seceding from the Union.[6] The public meetings of December 15 and January 7, with two completely different sets of leaders, producing two contradictory sets of resolutions, indicate the division that had taken place in the wake of the 1860 election. As in the South in general, upland and lowland geography had politically fractured Conway County.

Most of the hill people of northern Arkansas, apparently like Jeff Williams, did not oppose slavery. These mountain farmers simply did not see slavery as a significant enough cause for secession from the Union. At Arkansas's secession convention in March 1861, Unionists acted upon these sentiments and defeated the ordinance for secession. However, the convention agreed the state should secede if Lincoln waged war against the six Southern states that had already left the Union. After the firing began at Fort Sumter, a second convention in May took Arkansas out of the Union and into the Confederate States of America.

In the Williamses' neighborhood, Rebel troops began organizing immediately after Arkansas's secession. In May one unit formed at Lewisburg, on the Arkansas River near the present town of Morrilton. The largest settlement in the county, Lewisburg was a commercial outpost where planters from the bottomlands alongside the river sold their cotton. In June and July the Tenth Arkansas Cavalry formed at Springfield with nine companies drawn from Conway and neighboring counties.[7]

But clearly, from its very beginning, the war divided the loyalties of the hill folk of northern Arkansas. The earliest known organized resistance to secession came when Unionists in Conway, Van Buren, and several other counties of northern Arkansas formed underground peace societies in the fall of 1861. According to surviving oaths and constitutions, the purpose of the secret societies was to protect members, their families, and their property from their "enemies." Whether these enemies were Confederate authorities, soldiers, or merely unsympathetic neighbors is unclear. Local authorities in these counties apprehended members of the society, tried some for treason, but impressed most of them in units of the Confederate army. Local authorities took no Unionists into custody in Conway County. It is reasonable to expect that the Williams family, however, became involved with the peace society, for their friends in neighboring Van Buren County were among those arrested and impressed into Confederate service.[8]

What they wanted most was to be left alone. That became impossible in 1862. After the Federal victory in northwest Arkansas at the Battle of Pea Ridge in early March, Arkansas Confederate troops were sent to Corinth, in northern Mississippi, to halt Grant's advance south through western Tennessee. Some of those troops arrived just in time for the costly defeat at Shiloh. That battle was a great blow to the Confederacy, and the effect on Arkansas was no less dramatic. With the shift of Arkansas troops to Corinth, the state stood defenseless in the face of an advancing Union army.

In the meantime, a Federal force with nearly twelve thousand men under General Samuel R. Curtis moved through the Ozarks from Missouri into Arkansas. On May 4 his troops halted near Batesville, on the White River in north central Arkansas. The presence of a large Union army in that area had an electrifying effect. In fact, instead of making the region safe, the arrival of the Union army may have disrupted life even more. It did not conquer and occupy; it merely passed through. The governor fled Little Rock, courts suspended their functions, and civil authorities virtually stopped exercising their powers. Many Arkansans refused to accept Confederate money; consequently, it so depreciated that it became practically worthless. Extortion and price gouging in necessities of life, according to one observer, "menaced the poor with actual starvation."[9]

Adding to the chaos in May 1862 was the threat of conscription of sons and husbands into the Confederate army. The Confederate Conscription Act of April 16, 1862, made military service compulsory for men aged eighteen to thirty-five. By the end of May, Rebel agents were scouring the countryside raising two forces: a Confederate army unit and an Arkansas militia. Union reports from northern Arkansas in May described the country as "in a state of terror" from the impressments into service.[10]

In Jeff Williams's home territory the pressure to enlist was intense. That spring a local planter, Anderson Gordon, raised a new Confederate company in the area. Rebels held township meetings in northern Arkansas to raise troops. When someone failed to participate, one contemporary said, "personal notice was given." Any tardiness to enroll brought surveillance, abuse, and insult from one's neighbors. Jeff Williams, at age fifty-one, was not a likely candidate for the Rebel army. But he had three sons and three sons-in-law of conscription age. His son Leroy, aged nineteen, at one point went to a Confederate camp at Grand Glaize on the White River and enlisted, he said, just to keep the Rebels from killing his father. But the next day he slipped away and came back home to Conway County.[11]

By early June, Jeff Williams and about forty others from Van Buren and northern Conway Counties had banded together and made their way through Rebel territory to join General Curtis in Batesville. Another group from Conway County arrived a few days later. Jeff Williams's band included his four sons, three sons-in-law, two brothers, a brother-in-law, and four nephews. Leroy later wrote: "All of us were pretty well kin folks. . . . We ran away from Conway Co., to prevent being conscripted by the rebel army." According to the official report of Arkansas Union troops presented to the United States Congress after the war, the men from Conway County "were compelled to flee to the army, be killed, or go into rebel service." Just one day after they arrived in Batesville these volunteers were in Federal uniforms, drawing equipment and rations. Enlisted for six months of service, the men became the nucleus of Company B of the First Arkansas Infantry Battalion. They elected Jeff Williams as captain, and his son Nathan as second lieutenant.[12]

KENNETH C. BARNES

Thomas Jefferson Williams, 1862. Courtesy of Polly Church.

Evidently these Arkansas volunteers expected that their service in Curtis's
army would help protect their home territory for the Union. In other words,
they wished to become the home guard companies envisioned by the peace
societies the year before. One native Arkansan, Captain James W. Demby of
the Second Arkansas Cavalry, served with Jeff Williams's company that fall
and described the men as refugees who had come to Batesville for safety.
They faced a choice between conscription into the Rebel army or hiding
out in the woods for the months to come. The men had become soldiers,

Demby explained, so that they could "assist in chastising those who forced them to seek that refuge." No evidence suggests that the Williams men and their neighbors had joined the Union army intending to fight away from their homes. Like other Union supporters in northern Arkansas, they must have been dismayed when Curtis's army moved out of the area as speedily as it came. Curtis had promised the Arkansas volunteers that they would remain in the Batesville area, and they felt surprised and deceived when the march from Batesville began.[13]

After camping almost two months in Batesville, Curtis had run low on supplies. Jeff Williams and the other raw Arkansas recruits marched with Curtis's army in late June southeast along the White River out of the Ozarks into the hot plains and malarial swamps of eastern Arkansas. They stopped in Helena on the Mississippi River, where they remained for three months. Stuck there, immobile in the hot summer months, morale suffered as men worried about their families left behind. One officer in Helena, First Lieutenant Calvin Bliss, reported that the men received little news from their loved ones and feared that they were suffering under the hands of brigands and Rebel neighbors back home. Federal authorities would not allow the Arkansas men to forage their horses in the countryside or draw forage from the quartermaster. As a result, most of their horses died of starvation, were given away, or were stolen. The paymaster at the Helena camp even refused to pay the First Battalion on the grounds that General Curtis lacked the authority to raise such a unit.[14]

Besides morale problems, the men faced devastating illnesses. Packed with thousands of Federal soldiers and former slaves who had fled neighboring plantations, the Union garrison in Helena in the later summer months quickly became malignant with typhoid fever, measles, pneumonia, dysentery, and other camp diseases. Many of the Arkansas recruits died there in Helena before the commanding general, Frederick Steele, finally ordered the entire battalion to St. Louis, a more healthful location upriver. But diseases traveled with the soldiers; dozens continued to battle ill health in the army hospital there. By the time of the company's discharge in St. Louis in December 1862, thirty-four of the original seventy-five men had died, five others had mustered out early because of poor health, and thirteen went to a hospital. Thus two-thirds of the company had died or were hospitalized during the six months of inglorious military service. Jeff Williams's brother John died in Helena of "nervous disease," and another brother, Riley, died of pneumonia in St. Louis. Another brother-in-law and a nephew also died. None were killed in battle.[15]

KENNETH C. BARNES

Stranded in St. Louis, Jeff Williams and the remnant of his company dared not return to their homes in Rebel territory. Instead they made their way toward Springfield, Missouri, where a large Union force under General James G. Blunt had headquarters. There they joined a considerable throng of Unionist refugees from Arkansas pouring into southwestern Missouri in early 1863. Somehow the Williams men communicated with their family back home. Jeff's wife, Margaret, and their younger children, perhaps with others in the clan, made the dangerous journey through the Ozarks to Missouri. For the next eight to ten months, they stayed in Douglas County, just southeast of Springfield.[16]

The Williams men worked as scouts with a Missouri cavalry regiment. Bands of these Union scouts swept down into northern Arkansas from Missouri regularly in 1863, raiding Rebel families and strongholds. Whenever a scouting party went south to the Arkansas line, Leroy Williams claimed, he volunteered to go along. Leroy described how he captured a horse in a skirmish with Confederates while traveling south from Springfield with a cavalry unit. When he arrived in Fayetteville, the First Arkansas Cavalry took his horse, Leroy said, but the soldiers stole another one for him.[17]

While Williams's group scouted in Missouri, Union troops began an offensive aimed toward central Arkansas. The Federal force at Helena repelled a Rebel attack on July 4, 1863, the same day that Vicksburg fell. With new confidence General Frederick Steele moved toward Little Rock in August, as General Blunt's men moved south from Missouri toward Fort Smith. By early September the Arkansas River valley lay for the first time in Union hands.

As the Federal armies moved into central Arkansas, Jeff Williams's family and most of his company returned to their home territory. On September 15, five days after he took Little Rock, General Steele issued special orders authorizing the Union men of Conway County to form a company for the purpose of protecting themselves, their families, and their homes against Rebel violence and depredations. By these orders Jeff Williams organized an independent company, sometimes called Williams's Raiders, of which he became captain and commander. A United States mustering officer swore the men into service at the Union garrison near Lewisburg, on the Arkansas River, about twenty miles south of their homes. Captain Williams's son Nathan was first lieutenant. One year before the commanding officer of the First Arkansas Infantry Battalion, John Bundy, had discharged Nathan Williams early, stating that he was "physically and mentally incapacitated for the duties of an officer and ought never to have been commissioned."

Nathan Williams would take over command of the independent company at his father's death in 1865. The company included Williams's other sons, Leroy, John, and Henry, several sons-in-law, and some other survivors of Company B. Still suffering from chronic camp ailments and hardly able to fight, they feared they would be killed by Rebel bushwhackers if they lived at home. With General Steele's orders, the men finally had authorization to form the home guard company envisioned earlier by the peace societies. As one of the members later wrote, "The only way we could stay near home was by being in that company."[18]

With the Federal push into central Arkansas and the Arkansas River valley, the Rebel command retreated south of the Arkansas River. The Confederate state government fled Little Rock for a temporary outpost in southwestern Arkansas. Meanwhile, the Union army established posts along the Arkansas River at Pine Bluff, Little Rock, Lewisburg, Dardanelle, and Fort Smith. Many Rebel soldiers north of the Arkansas River deserted rather than retreat south with the Confederate army. By September 1863 the Rebel army in north central Arkansas had broken up into small bands of guerrillas and marauders operating in the vicinity of their homes. With this situation and the return to northern Arkansas of Union sympathizers who had hidden out in Missouri, a more vicious stage of guerrilla war set in, which would last until the Confederate surrender in 1865.

The men of Captain Williams's ragtag independent company tried to protect their families and property against the deserters and guerrillas that ravaged north central Arkansas. They also exacted vengeance against their Rebel neighbors. By 1864 law and order had collapsed in Conway County outside the Union post in Lewisburg. The fear of raiders and guerrillas drove citizens in northern Arkansas from their homes. Many took their bed clothing, by one account, to the hollows and thickets and slept outdoors in the coldest weather for fear of being murdered in their beds. When Colonel Robert R. Livingston reoccupied Batesville for the Federal army in December 1863, he found the area "so fearfully lawless, and murders so common" that he refused to organize home guard companies of loyal citizens there. He felt certain that if he formed such groups, Confederate guerrillas would murder many of them and take their arms. "When a man commits himself to the Union now," Livingston observed, "he must stay with the Federal troops for safety, and dare not go home."[19]

These conditions brought the Williams band into close association again with the Union army. Federal officers recruited a regiment of native troops in central Arkansas, the Third Arkansas Cavalry, and mustered them into duty at Little Rock in February 1864. Led by an Iowan, Colonel Abraham Ryan, the unit was sent up the Arkansas River to Lewisburg to hold territory "infested by numerous guerrilla bands who were robbing and murdering Union families." Finding it too dangerous to live in their own homes, Jeff Williams's independent company spent their time in the bush or at the Federal garrison at Lewisburg. The Williams company obeyed the orders of Colonel Ryan and drew rations, ammunition, and clothing. On occasion, Williams's men traveled and fought with the Third Arkansas. They did not have to answer to roll call and received no pay. The primary role for Jeff Williams and his men was to scout their home territory and provide intelligence for Colonel Ryan. As Williams's son put it, "We stayed around home most of the time and scouted about after bushwhackers."[20]

The nemesis for the Williams company in north central Arkansas was a band of Confederate guerrillas led by Colonel Allen R. Witt. In the summer of 1861 Witt had organized men from Conway and Van Buren Counties into a Rebel company called the Quitman Rifles, which became part of the Tenth Arkansas Regiment. After fighting at Shiloh, the unit was captured at Port Hudson, Louisiana. The enlisted men were paroled, and Witt escaped from the USS *Maple Leaf*, which was taking him and other Rebel officers up the Mississippi River to a Federal prison. By fall 1863 Witt and most of his men had returned to central Arkansas, just as the Williams band returned to the area from Missouri.[21]

From their home base in Quitman, about twenty miles east of Jeff Williams's farm, Witt's guerrillas, like Williams's Raiders, lived in the bush and operated semi-independently. Cut off from the Confederate military and political leaders south of the Arkansas River, Witt's troops apparently received no pay and lived off the countryside. Colonel Ryan considered Witt's men to be bushwhackers, while in a letter of 1865, Witt referred to Williams's independent company as a group of jayhawkers and marauders. Although both Witt's men and Williams's raiders were authorized units, they operated in a no-man's-land that lacked both civil law and military discipline.[22]

Throughout the last eighteen months of the war, Witt's men scoured the countryside of north central Arkansas, harassing Union expeditions and scouting operations. In return, detachments from the Third Arkansas at Lewisburg chased Witt's men back to Quitman, where they evaporated into the landscape. On one occasion, Jeff Williams's son, Leroy, accompanied a detachment of the Third Arkansas, led by Captain Archibald Napier, which killed seven of Witt's men and captured seven more. Leroy Williams boasted that he had saved Captain Napier's life and had wounded and taken the prize catch, the Rebel Captain Livingston. Witt, however, eluded the Union grasp.[23]

With Federal offensives in Arkansas during spring 1864, both Williams's and Witt's bands worked closely with their respective commands in several pitched battles in southern Arkansas. Shortly thereafter, in mid-May, the Confederate General Joseph Shelby crossed the Arkansas River with twenty-five hundred men and marched into Conway County, sending the Federal garrisons in Lewisburg into a quick evacuation. Jeff Williams and his company accompanied the five hundred Union troops as they fell back to Cadron Creek.[24]

As Shelby's men marched on the road north to Clinton, they camped just a few miles from Jeff Williams's homestead. Williams's younger brother, William Day Williams, had stayed home with his family while his kin served in the First Infantry Battalion and then the independent company. Nonetheless he fell victim to Rebel violence. A short way down the road from Shelby's camp, William had gone out to work in his cornfield with his son Frank and John McGinty, a Union soldier home on furlough and still in uniform. During a lunchtime break from their labor, the two boys slipped off their clothes for a dip in Point Remove Creek, which ran alongside the Dover–Clinton Road. While swimming they saw the Rebel army coming down the road. Jumping out of the creek, they put on their clothing, grabbed their guns, and started running away, shooting as they went. The Confederates chased them and captured the Williams men. They shot John McGinty, left him for dead, and marched William and Frank off to Batesville. Separated when they arrived, young Frank Williams never saw his father again. Rebels told him his father was killed and his body thrown in the White River. They then released Frank with a message to return to his Uncle Jeff: "Quit killing men, or we're going to come get him."[25]

Jeff Williams and his men sought safety during the summer of 1864 inside the Union camp in Lewisburg, as the Ozarks remained an extremely dangerous place for native Federals. Even families of Union men flocked to the garrison for protection. In July 1864 orders were issued for all soldiers' wives and children in the Lewisburg post to move to a secure camp on the south side of the Arkansas River. From their headquarters near Batesville, Shelby's force swept clean the countryside in north central Arkansas of forage, food, and men. Finding deserters and lawless men roaming the area, Shelby raised several thousand troops over the summer.[26] Another eight thousand Confederate troops, led by General Sterling Price, passed through the area

KENNETH C. BARNES

again in September, linking up with Shelby on their way to Missouri. Ryan once more began the evacuation of Lewisburg. Leroy Williams volunteered for a mission to travel downriver to meet and destroy a Federal boat laden with supplies to keep it from falling into Rebel hands. Leroy met the steamer at the Fourche la Fave River and assisted in burning it. Ryan paid him forty dollars for his service, the only cash money Leroy claimed he ever received from the Third Arkansas Cavalry.[27]

Surviving oral testimony among the descendants of Confederate and Union families in the area testifies to the anarchy of this time. One family of Rebel descent recounted how in July 1864 the Williams band approached on horseback the farm of James Bradley, then called him to the porch and shot him in front of his whole family. They ransacked the house and rode off into the night. Sometime that same summer, Rebels tried to do the same to Jeff Williams's son Leroy. According to family lore, Leroy had come home to visit his mother. As he slept that night he was alerted to the Rebel approach when his horse began pawing and neighing. Leroy vaulted out of bed, wrapped a cloak over his shoulders, and jumped on his horse. As his horse cleared the paling fence surrounding the yard, shots rang out. Leroy escaped unharmed, although his cloak was shot through with several bullet holes.[28]

A few months later, on the night of February 12, 1865, Rebel guerrillas were more successful. Colonel Witt, with nearly sixty men, surrounded Jeff Williams's log house near Center Ridge, shortly after he and his sons had come home to visit their family. Foreseeing his fate, Williams turned to his wife, Margaret, and announced, "My time has come." As he opened the front door, guns in hand, a volley of buckshot struck him from twenty-five yards away. He was killed standing in his own doorway. Williams family tradition has it that the killing fire had come from Ant Bradley, a relative of the man slain the previous summer by the Williams men. Margaret picked up her husband's guns and put them in the fireplace, apparently to keep the Rebels from taking them. Two or three younger children were asleep in the back room when the gunshots awakened them. They rolled out of their beds and under them for cover. Family stories suggest that the Rebels beat the Williams women before they left. Leroy's wife, Sarah Jane, was pregnant and in one account almost lost her child after the guerrillas punched her in the belly with their gun stocks.[29]

Enraged and vengeful, Leroy Williams pursued Witt's men on horseback as they moved west toward Dover. He chased one unlucky Rebel to the edge of a bluff on the mountain just south of the Williams farm. There the man shinnied down a chinquapin tree and eluded Leroy, who could not follow on horseback. Peering over the edge of the bluff, Leroy saw below the form of a man looking down at the palms of his hands. He tracked the man later to the house of a woman who had taken him in and dressed his wounded hands. Leroy had the woman cut off the bandages to see the wounds and then shot the Rebel dead on the spot.[30]

Leroy caught up with Witt's band late on the night of his father's death and killed three men as they watered their horses at the Point Remove Creek. He reportedly came on the rest again after they camped at Sucker Creek, near the community of Cleveland. Riding through the camp, he shot four more. Williams descendants still speak of Leroy's ability to ride with a gun in each hand, holding the reins of his horse with his teeth.[31] The next day Leroy and the Williams men joined with a party of seventy soldiers from the Third Arkansas Cavalry sent by Colonel Ryan to pursue Witt. Over the next three days they chased the Rebels to Clinton and then to Quitman, where Witt's men dispersed. Although Witt again eluded the Federal grasp, they brought five of his men back to Lewisburg as prisoners.[32]

Both Williams descendants and the descendants of the Rebels they were chasing tell the story of how the Williams men tracked their father's killers to Clinton, about twenty miles to the north. The Williams men followed one of the Rebels into a store in town. As the clerk behind the counter, a Pate man, went for his gun, Leroy Williams shot him in the hip. Meanwhile the man Leroy had pursued slipped out the back door. Descendants of Clinton Rebels who tell this story add that after the Williams men shot the Pate man, they poured out the blood from his boots, and one of them put them on and wore them away. Family tradition holds that Leroy Williams alone killed as many as sixteen members of the Rebel posse that had shot his father.[33]

Ryan sent word to Union headquarters in Little Rock about the killing of Jeff Williams, "the noted scout." James Demby, who had known Williams at Helena, eulogized him as a true patriot and esteemed friend. The death of Jeff Williams, however, did not mean the end of his independent company. On February 22 special orders came from Little Rock promoting First Lieutenant Nathan Williams to captain of Williams's Company of Scouts and Spies.[34]

After Robert E. Lee surrendered at Appomattox, Colonel Witt and other Rebel guerrillas in Arkansas still held out. Witt wrote to the Union commanders in Little Rock in May and June requesting that they disarm the independent companies such as that headed by Leroy and Nathan Williams, "who say what they do is under the direction of the U.S. authorities." Surely, Witt declared, Federal officers in Little Rock must not be aware "of the

                                              KENNETH C. BARNES

many murderous crimes and outrageous depredations" they have committed. Witt claimed he had brought this to Ryan's attention earlier in the winter, but Ryan took no action. Fearing retribution, Witt refused to surrender until the independent squads were disarmed. He asked further that Federal authorities restore order by using soldiers from other states to occupy Arkansas, "not to send men of this State, who have personal grudges."[35]

In Conway County the bitter feelings between Confederates and Union supporters lasted for years after the Civil War. When the Radical Republican Powell Clayton became governor of Arkansas during Reconstruction in 1868, he immediately organized state militia companies drawn largely from the Unionist areas of the state. In Conway County the Republican militia virtually waged war during the fall against Democrats and Ku Klux Klansmen. The veterans of the Williams independent company volunteered for militia service and renewed their past battles with Rebel neighbors.[36] In August, Clayton called for the Williams militia to march south to Lewisburg to settle a violent standoff between freedmen and white citizens. Before they arrived, however, Clayton traveled by steamer to Lewisburg and defused the crisis himself. He sent a courier north toward Springfield to stop the militia. The men at first refused to disband, according to one account, because they had taken orders before leaving Springfield for coffee and dry goods they were to bring back from the looting of Lewisburg.[37]

The conflict climaxed in December, when several stores and homes in Lewisburg were burned and both freedmen and Klansmen were killed. On December 8 Governor Clayton declared martial law in Conway County and put it under the control of four Republican militia companies, three white and one black. One of the white companies was led by a Williams man. The *Arkansas Gazette* charged that the militia had caused, not quelled, the violence in Conway County. According to the *Gazette*, the militia had lynched several Klansmen, then murdered a Democratic merchant, looted his possessions, and set fire to his shop. The commander of the militia vigorously denied the accusations. By March 1869 civil authority was restored and the militia companies disbanded.[38]

When Reconstruction in Arkansas ended in 1874, these former Unionists lost political power and became an isolated minority. Two former Confederate officers, Colonel W. S. Hanna and Colonel Allen Witt, represented Conway and Van Buren Counties in the constitutional convention that formally ended Reconstruction. Southern Democrats again ran local government. But the Williams clan would long remember their loyalties affirmed during the war. In 1890 they formed chapters of the Grand Army of the Republic and Sons of Veterans, and they remained staunchly Republican in their loyalties well into the twentieth century. Until his death in 1927, Frank Stobaugh, the drummer for the Williams independent company, led a ritual parade every Memorial Day in Center Ridge. Wearing his Union uniform and beating his old drum, he headed a small procession of gray-headed Union veterans to the local cemetery. He continued the tradition even when he was the only survivor, with his grandson following behind him carrying the United States flag.[39]

This account of the Williams family does not explain Unionism as a whole in Arkansas. It tells the story of one group of kinfolk and some neighbors who struck their ties to the Union cause. The Williams family fit the classic pattern of subsistence hill farmers who supported the Union in opposition to the pro-Southern advocates from the commercial plantation region just a few miles downhill, along the Arkansas River.[40] However, this class model does not explain why a good number of their mountain neighbors supported the Confederacy and thus became the enemy. Ideological factors partly explain the Union loyalties of the Williams family, for Jeff Williams had demonstrated a prewar commitment to the Union, although he apparently did not oppose slavery. But as much as anything, the Williams clan simply wanted to be left alone to protect their farm and homes. Siding with the Union initially was the way they thought they could achieve this goal. They were wrong. But even during the most locally violent phase of the war, 1864–65, their organization into an independent company afforded them an opportunity to stay near home and protect property and family. The experience of the Williams clan shows to what extent kinship and local leadership influenced allegiance and actions in wartime.[41] Last, their experiences also indicate that these allegiances and adversarial relationships, struck in war, lasted for decades.

The Williams family and their like do not figure in the standard histories of the politics and battles of the Civil War South. But yet the survival of such a substantial body of oral history among Williams descendants indicates the traumatic and personally significant nature of their Civil War experiences. For the Williams family and their neighbors of Conway County, the war meant disruption of their family life, tragic violence that took life on both sides of the conflict, and a cycle of retributive feuding which continued for generations. The extended family became a fighting unit. The transformation of Jeff Williams from a Disciples of Christ preacher into a guerrilla fighter, his cruel death, and the brutal retribution his sons exacted well reveals the moral chaos the Civil War brought to northern Arkansas.

The author wishes to thank Polly Church and Gregory J. W. Urwin, who shared information about the Williams family that provided the beginning of this project. An earlier version of this essay appeared in the *Arkansas Historical Quarterly* 52 (Autumn 1993): 286–317 and is reproduced here with the permission of the journal.

1. See Albert Webb Bishop, *Loyalty on the Frontier; or, Sketches of Union Men of the Southwest* (St. Louis: R. P. Studley, 1863); James W. Demby, *Mysteries and Miseries of Arkansas; or, a Defence of the Loyalty of the State* (St. Louis: n.p., 1863).

2. Note the two earliest surveys of the war in Arkansas: John Harrell, *Arkansas*, vol. 10 of *Confederate Military History*, 12 vols. (Atlanta: Confederate Publishing Co., 1899); and David Y. Thomas, *Arkansas in War and Reconstruction* (Little Rock: Daughters of the American Confederacy, Arkansas Division, 1926).

3. For additional material on Arkansas Unionists, see Ted Worley, "The Arkansas Peace Society of 1861: A Study in Mountain Unionism," *Journal of Southern History* 24 (1958): 445–56; and Joseph R. Bellas, "The Forgotten Loyalists: Unionism in Arkansas, 1861–1865" (M.A. thesis, Ohio State University, 1991). See also the section on Arkansas in Richard Nelson Current, *Lincoln's Loyalists: Union Soldiers from the Confederacy* (Boston: Northeastern University Press, 1991). See also the excellent discussions of Unionist views in James M. Woods, *Rebellion and Realignment: Arkansas's Road to Secession* (Fayetteville: University of Arkansas Press, 1987); and Michael B. Dougan, *Confederate Arkansas: The People and Policies of a Frontier State in Wartime* (University: University of Alabama Press, 1976).

4. Seventh and Eighth U.S. Manuscript Censuses, 1850 and 1860. The other slave owner in Lick Mountain Township, Henson Scroggins, owned a female slave and her two children. Two sons of Henson Scroggins married daughters of Jeff Williams. Information about Williams and his family has been collected in Polly Church, *Our Williams Family: A History of One Williams Family in America* (North Little Rock, Ark.: n.p., 1992).

5. *Little Rock Arkansas Gazette*, January 19, 1861.

6. *Little Rock True Democrat*, January 19, 1861.

7. *Historical Reminiscences and Biographical Memoirs of Conway County, Arkansas* (Little Rock: Arkansas Publishing Co., 1890), 16–17; Harrell, *Arkansas*, 306.

8. For information on the Peace Society see Worley, "Arkansas Peace Society"; and Diane Neal, "Treason or Patriotism? Union Peace Societies in Arkansas during the Civil War," *Journal of Confederate History* 1 (1988): 339–49. Several members of the Peace Society in Van Buren County were friends of the Williams family. Some Stobaugh men arrested and impressed into Rebel

service for their association with the society deserted and later joined the Williamses' Unionist band.

9. U.S. War Department, *The War of Rebellion: A Compilation of the Official Records of the Union and Confederate Armies*, ser. 1 (Washington, D.C.: Government Printing Office, 1880–1901), 13:66 (hereafter referred to as OR); see Confederate General Thomas Hindman's report of conditions in Arkansas when he assumed command there in May 1862, in OR, ser. 1, 13:30.

10. Harrell, *Arkansas*, 100–101; OR, ser. 1, 13:30, 66.

11. *Historical Reminiscences of Conway County*, 15–16; OR, ser. 1, 13:418, 436; Bishop, *Loyalty on the Frontier,* 11; Leroy Williams Pension File, National Archives, Washington, D.C.

12. Leroy Williams Pension File; Albert Webb Bishop, *Report of the Adjutant General*, 39th Congress, 2d Session, Senate Miscellaneous Documents, no. 53, p. 245.

13. Demby, *Mysteries and Miseries of Arkansas*, 11–12, 44; Bishop, *Report of the Adjutant General*, 245.

14. Bishop, *Report of the Adjutant General*, 236–45; Demby, *Mysteries and Miseries of Arkansas*, 22, 37; *Home Aegis and Monthly Review*, July 1864, 97.

15. Leroy Williams Pension File; OR, ser. 1, 13:738, 752; Demby, *Mysteries and Miseries of Arkansas*, 45; Union Service Documents, Arkansas, 1st Battalion, Infantry, microfilm at the Arkansas History Commission; Bishop, *Report of the Adjutant General*, 245; Morton W. Williams Pension File, National Archives.

16. Depositions by Daniel Webster Williams and Henry Clay Williams, September 1899, Morton W. Williams Pension File.

17. Harrell, *Arkansas*, 167; Leroy Williams Pension File.

18. OR, ser. 1, 22(2):533; Union Service Documents, Arkansas, 1st Battalion, Infantry; Daniel Webster Williams and Thomas Wells depositions, Morton W. Williams Pension File; Alexander McCuin Pension File, National Archives.

19. Thomas, *Arkansas in War and Reconstruction*, 249; OR, ser. 1, 22(2):699, 756. For the most insightful study of guerrilla war in neighboring Missouri, see Michael Fellman, *Inside War: The Guerrilla Conflict in Missouri during the American Civil War* (New York: Oxford University Press, 1989).

20. Bishop, *Report of the Adjutant General*, 134; Leroy Williams Pension File; Thomas Jefferson Williams Pension File, National Archives; Henry Clay Williams deposition, Morton W. Williams Pension File.

21. OR, ser. 1, 24(3):703, 26(2):3–5, 27(2):786, 34(1):91–92, 96; OR, ser. 2, 5:732; *Confederate Veteran* 6 (1898): 529; *Historical Reminiscences of Conway County*, 15.

22. OR, ser. 1, 48(1):885, 920, 48(2):844; Confederate Service Records, 10th Arkansas, microfilm. For a discussion of the terms *guerrilla, jayhawker,*

and *bushwhacker,* see Leo E. Huff, "Guerrillas, Jayhawkers, and Bushwhackers in Northern Arkansas during the Civil War," *Arkansas Historical Quarterly* 24 (1965): 127–48.

23. OR, Ser. 1, Vol. 34, pt. 3, 717; pt. 4, 31–32; Ser. 1, Vol. 41, pt. 3, 69; Leroy Williams Pension File.

24. OR, ser. 1, 34(1):924–28, 34(3):635, 670–71, 930–32.

25. Johnny Mason, interview with Polly Church, April 29, 1978. Mason was the adopted grandson of Frank Williams. One piece of written evidence that corroborates Mason's account is an intestate record filed by William Day Williams's heirs after the war, which stated that he died in June 1864. Intestate Record Book, 1859–85, p. 102, Conway County Courthouse, Morrilton, Ark.

26. Regimental Order no. 31, July 18, 1864, Regimental Letters and Orders, 3d Arkansas Cavalry, National Archives; OR, ser. 1, 34(3):258, 41(2):665. See John Edwards's account of Shelby's activities in *Shelby and His Men* (Cincinnati: Miami Printing, 1867), 298–360; Edwards's account must be taken with a degree of skepticism. See also Albert Castel, *Sterling Price and the Civil War in the West* (Baton Rouge: Louisiana State University Press, 1968), 197, 203.

27. Castel, *Sterling Price,* 203–4; OR, ser. 1, 41(3):116–17, 139, 223; Leroy Williams Pension File.

28. Joe Bradley, "Murdered by Federals," *Van Buren County Historical Journal* 16 (spring 1995): 21–23. Leroy's story is told by Joe Stobaugh, interview of February 2, 1992, Arlie Williams, interview of February 7, 1992, and Thelma Hensley, interview of February 8, 1992. Small details in each of their tellings differ; e.g., one version has seven bullet holes, another thirteen; Stobaugh has Williams sleeping on the front porch of the Williamses' log house, Hensley has him in a bedroom inside.

29. OR, ser. 1, 48(1):111; Lonnie Maxwell, interview with Polly Church, summer 1963; Ruth Cupit interview; Arlie Williams interview. Information in Jeff Williams's Widows Pension application, made in 1891, corroborates the descendants' oral history of the event.

30. Lonnie Maxwell interview, Arlie Williams interview, Thelma Hensley interview, and Martha Nell Smith, interview of February 1992. These Williams descendants all recounted this story although their tellings differed slightly on details.

31. Arlie Williams and Ruth Cupit interviews. For a comparison of these oral history accounts to other Civil War folklore, see James L. Johnston, "Jawhawker Stories: Historical Lore in the Arkansas Ozarks," *Midsouth Folklore* 4 (Spring 1976): 3–9.

32. OR, ser. 1, 48(1):111, 885; Ted Worley, ed., "Diary of Lieutenant Orville Gillet, U.S.A., 1864–1865," *Arkansas Historical Quarterly* 17 (1958): 189. Gillet was a member of Ryan's detachment, which chased Witt's men after the killing of

Jeff Williams. His account and the OR confirm the outline, if not the details, of family oral history of these events.

33. Arlie Williams and Ruth Cupit interviews. Descendants of Clinton Confederates tell the same story; Emma Sue Beavers, interview of May 8, 1992, and Maxine Kelly, interview of April 12, 1992. Emma Sue Beavers is the descendant of Ant Bradley. John Mason also recounts this story and cites the Pate family as his source; John Mason to Ernie Dean, February 26, 1980, Individual File, John Madison [*sic*] Clayton, Arkansas History Commission.

34. *Home Aegis and Monthly Review*, February 1865, 209; Bishop, *Report of the Adjutant General*, 272.

35. OR, ser. 1, 48(2):494–95, 844–45.

36. A listing of the members of the militia can be found in the Conway County Court Record Book, July 1868–May 1871, Conway County Courthouse. Leroy Williams, four other Williams men, and several other veterans of the old company served in the militia. With Republicans now controlling county offices, they each were paid two dollars and eighty-six cents for their militia service from the county coffers. In his pension application years later, Leroy Williams recalled that Governor Powell Clayton asked him to form a company to go to Bradley County, in his words, "to keep the Night Riders from killing niggers." Leroy got the men together, but they never made it all the way to south Arkansas.

37. John Mortimer Harrell, *The Brooks and Baxter War: A History of the Reconstruction Period in Arkansas* (St. Louis: Slawson, 1893), 72. See also accounts of the race war in the *Arkansas Gazette*, August 28–September 15, 1868; and Powell Clayton, *The Aftermath of the Civil War in Arkansas* (New York: Neale, 1915), 144–51.

38. Clayton, *Aftermath in Arkansas*, 151–63; *Arkansas Gazette*, December 10, 1868–January 5, 1869. See also Otis Singletary, "Militia Disturbances in Arkansas during Reconstruction," *Arkansas Historical Quarterly* 15 (summer 1956): 140–50.

39. Mrs. Grant Reddig, interview of October 23, 1992; Marvin Barnes, interview of October 17, 1992; Beva Winningham, interview of October 23, 1992; Robert Morrow, interview of October 22, 1992. For more information about the longstanding political tensions in Conway County, see Kenneth C. Barnes, *Who Killed John Clayton? Political Violence and the Emergence of the New South, 1861–1893* (Durham, N.C.: Duke University Press, 1998).

40. For more on this view, see Current, *Lincoln's Loyalists*, 133–38; and Philip Shaw Paludan, *Victims: A True Story of the Civil War* (Knoxville: University of Tennessee Press, 1981). See also the studies of Civil War Unionists in East Tennessee by Robert Tracy McKenzie and Peter Wallenstein in *The Civil War in Appalachia: Collected Essays*, ed. Kenneth W. Noe and Shannon H. Wilson (Knoxville: University of Tennessee Press, 1997); and Noel C. Fisher, *War at Every*

Door: Partisan Politics and Guerrilla Violence in East Tennessee, 1860–1869 (Chapel Hill: University of North Carolina Press, 1997).

41. For similar arguments about the role of kinship, neighborhood, and local leadership, see Martin Crawford's essay on Ashe County, North Carolina, and Ralph Mann's essay on the Sandy Basin in Virginia in *The Civil War in Appalachia*, ed. Noe and Wilson.

Defiant Unionists

Militant Germans in Confederate Texas

ANNE J. BAILEY

I can anticipate no greater calamity for the country than a dissolution of the Union," Lieutenant Colonel Robert E. Lee wrote from Fort Mason, Texas, on January 23, 1861. As commander of the Second United States Cavalry, his job was to protect the scattered settlements northwest of San Antonio from hostile Kiowas and Comanches, but as the spirit of Southern independence spread, his ranks thinned. "Secession is nothing but revolution," Lee pronounced as many officers in his regiment resigned and declared their allegiance to the South. From this lonely outpost on the Indian frontier, Lee watched as radicals guided Southerners closer to rebellion. Just over a week after Lee sent this letter home to Virginia, delegates to the Texas secession convention met in Austin to consider severing ties with the North. On the day of the vote, seventy men shouted in the affirmative before the first delegate cried out in opposition. The assembled gallery clearly sympathized with the radicals, for boos and hisses greeted each subsequent negative voice. One of those to cast a dissenting vote, James W. Throckmorton, violated the rule that prohibited discussion on the proposal when he declared that he was "unawed by the wild spirit of revolution." Although spectators showered him with insults, Throckmorton turned to the convention's president and defiantly proclaimed, "When the rabble hiss, well may patriots tremble."[1]

Few in attendance agreed with Throckmorton's nationalistic stand, and the final tally revealed 166 in favor of the measure with only 8 against. Still, the Unionists were unwilling to yield without a fight. Some influential Texans, including Governor Sam Houston, hoped to prevent secession through a provision in the ordinance that required a general election to ratify or reject the convention's work. To ensure that all citizens understood what was at stake when they went to the polls, the delegates ordered ten thousand copies of the document printed in English, two thousand in Spanish, and two thousand in German.[2]

The four thousand copies printed in foreign languages meant that lawmakers wanted to reach the 10 percent of the state's inhabitants who were foreign-born. Texas was a blend of many cultures, dating back to the days when it was part of the Spanish empire and later a possession of Mexico. The number who spoke Spanish was significant, but German-speaking immigrants constituted the majority of the foreign-born. Although they recognized the importance of the referendum on secession, most foreigners avoided voicing political opinions, and those who did were not always in agreement. In the general election in February, 24 percent of the state's population rejected the ordinance of secession. Although there was no united opposition, geographically it was concentrated most heavily in the counties along the Red River in north Texas, where many families from the Midwest and border states had settled, and in the largely German counties of central Texas. Still, it would be incorrect to assume that all Germans opposed secession, for many foreigners loyally embraced the Confederate government. Comal County, in the heart of the German settlements, voted 239 to 86 in favor of secession; Gillespie County, on the Indian frontier, voted 398 to 16 against. Nonetheless, it was impossible for state officials to overlook the fact that a number of dissenting counties had a high concentration of Germans. It was clear that Unionist sentiment was strong among a large number of German Texans.[3]

For decades Texas had attracted the attention of Europeans searching for a place that could offer the economic advantages and political freedom denied them at home. Even in the 1820s enterprising entrepreneurs in the German-speaking regions of Europe saw a chance to establish a new Germanic nation in the Mexican Southwest. Although this never happened, through the efforts of German colonizers large numbers of immigrants settled in Texas before the Civil War. They came from Europe with a vision and a desire for a new start in a land that seemed to brim with opportunity. They brought traditions and values that differed from those of other recent arrivals, particularly settlers from the American South. Yet the various ethnic groups coexisted without any serious problems until the secession crisis forced individuals to examine their ideals and stand up for their principles.[4]

European immigrants were divided over what those principles meant, and those differences affected the German settlements in particular. Although more than 30,000 Germans were dispersed in a white population of slightly over 421,000, they were not spread throughout the state; the majority congregated in central Texas, around San Antonio, Seguin, and Austin. By concentrating together they retained their European lifestyle, language, and cultural values. The Europeans fell into two groups: people who arrived before the revolutions of 1848 and those who came after. The early arrivals were labeled the "grays," and the late arrivals were designated the "greens" or, more commonly, the "Forty-eighters."[5]

Regardless of political persuasion, Texas Germans were very successful in maintaining an old world lifestyle. Although this was a positive step in preserving their heritage, it also meant that the settlements attracted the attention of non-Europeans. Some German immigrants readily assimilated and accepted the existing state government without question; some even overcame their objections to the institution of slavery and purchased slaves. In addition, a few became strong proponents of states' rights. On the other hand, there were those who saw many of the customs in the American South as backward, even dangerous. Their objections to slavery were more pronounced, and their ideas about nationalism were more strident. Many Germans, having left Europe because of political oppression, did not want to condone the institution of slavery in their new land. However, Frederick Law Olmsted, who visited Texas in 1854, was basically correct when he observed that few Germans concerned themselves with "the theoretical right or wrong of the institution," and when it did not "interfere with their own liberty or progress," they were "careless of its existence." Still, some Germans, already antislavery upon arrival in America, became abolitionist in sentiment if not in practice.[6]

There were other issues that divided the German communities. The early arrivals had founded towns on land purchased by developers, but those who came later had to move farther west, pushing their line of settlements into the windswept hills and prairies claimed by Kiowas and Comanches.

ANNE J. BAILEY

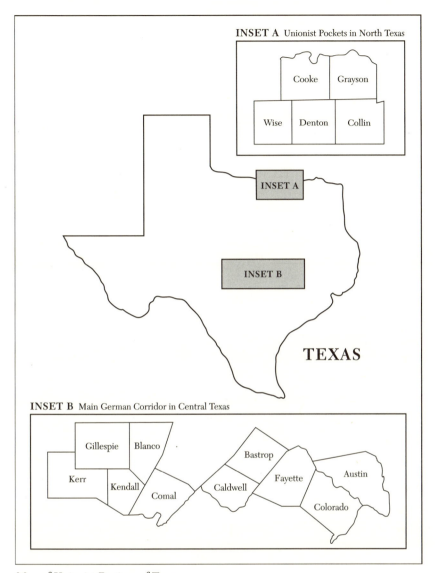

INSET A Unionist Pockets in North Texas

Cooke Grayson

Wise Denton Collin

INSET A

INSET B

TEXAS

INSET B Main German Corridor in Central Texas

Gillespie Blanco

Kerr

Kendall

Comal

Bastrop

Caldwell

Fayette

Austin

Colorado

Map of Unionist Regions of Texas.

Although the United States Army had established a line of forts to protect the scattered towns and farms, the soldiers could not offer total security from hostile natives. In the mid-1850s the national government authorized a new military regiment, the Second United States Cavalry, for service on the Texas frontier. As the secession crisis intensified, concerned Germans worried about their future if the army departed. This reluctance to see Federal troops withdraw, based on genuine uneasiness about their own safety, meant that Germans along the frontier tended to favor the Union when talk of secession spread. If the army left the local military posts, the Germans would lose not only the protection the soldiers afforded, but also a major market for their agricultural goods. These practical considerations probably influenced many German Texans more than the longstanding political divisions between the grays and greens.[7]

Even before secession became an issue, native Texans questioned the loyalty of non-English-speaking residents. Although some Germans steadfastly supported Southern rights, just as many did not, and the majority of Germans preferred to remain neutral in the controversy. Some pro-Union German newspaper editors took a stand. They emphasized the need to protect frontier settlements from hostile Indians and maintained that the Federal government was much better equipped to do so than a fledgling Southern nation. The editors did not reflect the attitude of all German communities, but they did much to influence the way Southerners felt about the immigrants. Until the crisis in 1861, the closed German communities had been nothing more than curiosities to most Texans. Afterward they became objects of suspicion and distrust. This distrust was reinforced when only a handful of counties with a significant number of Germans voted for secession.[8]

Until Texas left the Union, most German Texans had tried to avoid controversial political issues that might call into question their loyalty, but once the state became part of the Confederacy, that proved impossible. When the Confederate Congress passed a banishment act in August 1861, Germans had to declare their allegiance or leave. In a presidential proclamation on August 14, Jefferson Davis declared that any foreigners who remained after that period expired would be treated as alien enemies. The safest path for German Texans, and that of least resistance, was to support the Confederacy. The alternative, departing from the state within forty days, meant they would lose everything they had worked for since arriving in America. It is true that some Germans wholeheartedly embraced the Confederate government, but others only feigned allegiance to the new flag. A few, mainly those in the settlements nestled in the Texas hill country, passively resisted.[9]

Although the budding disaffection did not go unnoticed, it was not a major concern of the state government until the spring of 1862, when the passage of the Conscription Act forced foreigners to declare their loyalties. State officials already knew there was resentment within the alien population, for some agents of the Confederate government had suffered harassment in several predominantly German counties early in the year. But the resistance, typically unorganized, was localized and did not pose a serious threat to the state government. Many of foreign birth voiced legal objections on the grounds that an alien owed no military service to the Confederacy. Although it was a complicated issue, the Confederate government generally avoided controversy by requiring home defense, rather than regular military service, from most foreigners. In Texas, however, Governor Francis R. Lubbock, a staunch secessionist who had won office in a heated election in August 1861, believed that any foreigner who refused to serve should be required to leave the state. Tension increased as Germans fled, some heading for Unionist communities-in-exile in Mexico.

At the same time the state government kept a close eye on the activities of known Unionists. One man the state closely monitored was Andrew Jackson Hamilton, a former Austin attorney, acting attorney general, and member of the United States Congress. He was also a political ally of Sam Houston and during 1861 had worked to find a compromise that would avoid conflict. When this failed, the Alabama-born Hamilton resumed his Unionist activities, and he soon won the support of German Unionists. Brigadier General Hamilton P. Bee, who commanded the Sub-Military District of the Rio Grande, reported, "Information was received establishing the fact that Jack Hamilton and other traitors were unquestionably in arms against the Government and had assembled in the counties designated, their force being variously estimated at from 100 to 500." Bee also claimed that he had evidence that the "traitors were moving their goods and families, with large supplies of provisions, into the mountain districts, and were carrying off the property in some instances of loyal citizens, and at last, to set beyond a doubt their objects and intentions, positive intelligence was received of their having waylaid and murdered one or two well-known secession or loyal citizens." Hamilton fled to Mexico with a small band of supporters in the spring of 1862, leaving behind growing concern about the loyalty of settlers in southwest Texas. In particular, his activities focused the state's attention on Unionist activities in central Texas.[10]

Hamilton was not the only prominent Southerner to defect in the spring. Edmund J. Davis, a Florida native, was a district judge in the Rio Grande Valley when the trouble began in 1860. He had opposed secession, although he did not challenge the decision of the people when they voted to secede. Like Sam Houston, however, he refused to take the oath of allegiance to the Confederacy and in May 1862 boarded a ship at the mouth of the Rio Grande bound for Washington, D.C. Once there, he convinced Abraham Lincoln it was possible to reclaim Texas by rallying the Unionists in the state. Both Hamilton and Jack Smith received commissions in the Union army, both rose to the rank of brigadier general, and both returned to the Southwest to rally Texas Unionists.[11]

The flight of prominent men like Hamilton and Smith drew attention to the growing discontent in the Texas hill country. Suspicion fell heavily on Germans when several hundred men in Gillespie, Kerr, and Kendall counties formed an organization called the Union Loyal League. Members claimed they had no political agenda and maintained that the league's purpose was to patrol the frontier in search of hostile Indians and roving bands of guerrillas. Their avowed aim was "to prevent strife between Union and Confederate partisans; to take such peaceable action as would prevent the forced enlistment of Union sympathizers in the Confederate army; and to protect the homes and families within the area embraced in the limits of the 'Union Loyal League' against marauding bands of Indians." State officials were skeptical of the last point since the Indians had been unusually quiet; most believed that the Germans devoted more energy to avoiding draft agents than tracking hostile natives and outlaws. General Bee pointed to Jack Hamilton's defection as just one example of the growing treachery. Moreover, he claimed that the trouble originated with men, "chiefly foreigners by birth," who were "greatly disaffected and were organizing and arming to resist the law known as the conscript act." Responding to growing concerns, the government ordered a detachment of Confederate cavalry to the Texas hill country. Authorities made sure the small force comprised only American-born soldiers.[12]

For the first time the state decided to take military action against dissenters. Confederate leaders were determined to extinguish the growing Unionist rebellion before it spread through other counties and Texas had to deal with a full-scale revolution. The principal target of the Confederates was Fredericksburg, a small settlement on the Indian frontier that served as the seat of Gillespie County. The residents of Fredericksburg, founded in 1846, had never disguised their lack of enthusiasm for the Confederacy. The general feeling was that the old army had provided protection from the Indians that the state had been unable to match.[13]

By sending in troopers, the authorities had abandoned words for action. General Bee declared martial law in late April, thus placing the inhabitants of his district under military control. Men were required to take the oath of allegiance to both the Confederate and the state government, with anyone who refused subject to arrest. To facilitate the implementation of the law, the state established camps of conscription. Soldiers assigned to these camps

ANNE J. BAILEY

were "to hunt out persons liable to military duty that did not volunteer, and send them into some regiment." The commander of the Rebel detachment found the locals "shy and timid" when he arrived at Fredericksburg in late May 1862. The few townspeople "who were friendly to the Government did not possess moral courage enough to give information to the provost-marshal of the sayings and doings of those who are unfriendly," he complained.[14]

But opposition to conscription continued to spread, and Brigadier General Paul O. Hébert, in command of the Military District of Texas and Louisiana, extended martial law statewide on May 30. He even put Unionist communities on notice that they were expected to comply. To make that point clear in the immigrant counties, the declaration appeared in both English and German in local newspapers, and there was a five-dollar fine for any male of draft age who failed to appear before the provost marshal. A German paper in New Braunfels cautioned, "Those who refuse to comply will be vigorously dealt with." Colonel Arthur Fremantle, an Englishman visiting San Antonio in the spring of 1863, observed that the Germans "objected much to the conscription, and some even resisted by force of arms." It was clear, however, that men subject to conscription had to take an oath of allegiance or suffer the consequences.[15]

Throughout the late spring and early summer of 1862, Confederate soldiers patrolled the hills around Fredericksburg looking for men evading the draft. Two parties of twenty-five soldiers each took wagons to the outlying farms inhabited by families of men suspected of hiding in the hills and brought the women and children to town. "It was a pitiable sight to see all these poor folks stripped of their property, such as it was, earned by hard toil and exposure on a dangerous frontier," observed one sympathetic Rebel soldier. To avoid both the arrest and persecution of their families, many Germans followed other dissenters to Mexico, and a large community of Texas Unionists had evolved at Matamoras, just across the Rio Grande from Brownsville. Since state officials suspected that those who headed south joined one of the Union regiments operating in the river valley, there was a general feeling that the flood should be stopped.[16]

The state responded to the growing crisis by buttressing its previous military initiatives with legal action. Rumors abounded that German bushwhackers had attacked loyal Rebels, and as the threat of violence escalated, the authorities began to hear cases involving men arrested for violating martial law. At the same time, the murder of a farmer prompted the authorities to declare Gillespie, Kendall, and Kerr Counties in open rebellion, and a substantial Rebel force of about four hundred men headed to Gillespie

County in late July. One soldier described Fredericksburg as a town of around eight hundred people, "almost all of them Germans, and Unionists to a man." The government intended, he added, to compel the Germans to take the oath of allegiance to the Confederacy and, once that was done, to "overawe, or convert into Southerners, more Germans of Northern proclivities." The soldiers had permission to take all the measures necessary to prevent the growing dissension from erupting into full-scale warfare.[17]

Unfortunately, extremists on both sides seemed ready for the violence to escalate. When local Confederates did not think the government acted quickly enough, vigilance committees composed of members of the secret Knights of the Golden Circle took matters into their own hands. One German claimed it was "the duty of this committee to watch people whose loyalty to the South was under suspicion and to demand of them that they leave the country." A San Antonio newspaper alleged in July that the bones of Germans were "bleaching on the soil of every county from Red River to the Rio Grande and in the counties of Wise and Denton their bodies [were] suspended by scores from the 'Black Jacks.'" A Confederate soldier recorded in his diary on August 5, "As our regular scouts came in today they found a man hanging right over the trail with his throat cut from ear to ear."[18]

Any gatherings in the hill country attracted the attention of Confederate bureaucrats. When several hundred people from Gillespie, Kerr, Kendall, Edwards, and Kimble Counties congregated outside Fredericksburg on July 4, state officials took notice. Upon learning that the Germans had formed into military companies, the government let it be known that any move to evade military service would not be tolerated. The men claimed that their actions were only part of the Union League's attempt to control the Indian problems, but the government saw it as the start of a budding uprising. Fearing reprisals, the group disbanded to await further developments, but not before some men made plans to head south.

Although Germans had been fleeing to Mexico since the beginning of the war, the state had not taken any significant action to prevent the exodus. There had been no attempt to stop the small groups. The banishment act had sanctioned emigration and allowed Unionists several weeks to depart. Even Governor Lubbock had encouraged emigration. Therefore most of the Germans who planned to leave for Mexico in the summer of 1862 believed that they could go unmolested. Approximately eighty men gathered west of Kerrville on August 1, and sixty-one hardy souls actually rode south.

But the situation had reached a point where the government could no longer disregard such open defiance of the laws, and Confederate troops

ANNE J. BAILEY

were dispatched to stop the group. The man called upon to prevent the Germans from reaching Mexico was James M. Duff. He had been in the region for weeks and understood the difficulties associated with tracking the party through the barren landscape between the hill country and the Rio Grande. Like the Unionists he now hunted, Duff was foreign-born, but unlike the Germans, he had served the Confederacy well. He also had military experience. Upon his arrival in the United States from Scotland in 1849, Duff had joined the army, and he served until 1854. When discharged in Texas, he had made the state his home, eventually becoming a successful businessman in San Antonio and an ardent secessionist. Duff had served the state of Texas during the first year of the war, but in May 1862 he received an appointment as a captain in the Confederate army. His Confederate duties coincided with the heightening tension in Texas.[19]

In this charged atmosphere, the sixty-one Germans rode south. They expected no pursuit and did not anticipate any trouble. Duff, however, had learned their route from the locals and ordered First Lieutenant Colin D. McRae to take a detachment of around one hundred men to arrest the draft evaders and bring them back to justice. For a week under the hot August sun, the Confederates tracked the unsuspecting Germans through the uninviting hills and barren prairies. The Rebels finally caught up with their prey on August 9 at the Nueces River in Kinney County, about a day's march from the Mexican border, and made plans to attack the camp the following morning. What actually happened as the sun peeked over the horizon on August 10 is unclear. What is known is that the Germans were taken by surprise, and when the fighting ended, over twenty Germans were dead or wounded. The Rebels lost only two killed and fewer than twenty wounded. Because of the intensity of feeling on both sides, it was impossible to determine an accurate number; both sides exaggerated the casualties. In his official report McRae stated that the Germans "offered the most determined resistance and fought with desperation, asking no quarter whatever." He had no prisoners to report. A Rebel who talked with the returning Confederate troopers told his diary, "A number of prisoners were taken; but all got away, so the boys said; and I know they would not lie about a little thing like that." The truth was, however, that before the Texans broke camp that day, they had executed the wounded prisoners, leaving the bodies to rot where they fell. More than thirty Germans escaped, although six were killed by Confederate troops in October while trying to cross the Rio Grande. One of the Germans to survive, August Hoffman, made it home safely, but some of his party were later arrested and shot.[20]

Accounts of this event differ so much that it is difficult to distinguish fact from hyperbole. The number of killed and wounded on both sides varies from source to source. In any case, not all the Confederates took part in the massacre. Even Lieutenant McRae had been wounded and probably did not know what occurred. An Englishman named R. H. Williams, who belonged to the Rebel regiment involved, later called August 10 a "shameful day." Still, because both sides embellished the facts, tension increased substantially in the counties where the Germans had lived. A Confederate cavalryman noted: "There is now a daily guard around Fredericksburg. The 'bushwhackers' or traitors are plentiful in this country but keep themselves hid, and they have selected a good country for the business. When *one* chances to fall into the hands of the C.S. soldiers he is dealt pretty roughly with and generally makes his last speech with a rope around his neck. Hanging is getting to be as common as hunting." Another soldier agreed and recorded in his diary, "We are having tough times in this neck of the woods these times. I counted seven men hung on one limb; cut down and thrown over the bluff into Spring Creek."[21]

The incident also had enormous propaganda value. The Confederates claimed a victory over dangerous traitors, while the Germans labeled the incident a bloodbath. To the residents of the hill country, it became the "Nueces Massacre." Nonetheless, even some Germans were skeptical about the accuracy of reports. One German who served in the Confederate army confided to his father, "I cannot give that report any credence though, because the man said, after the fight was over, the soldiers dragged the wounded away from the camping ground and had them shot dead one by one, and that," he insisted, "seems very improbable to me."[22]

While most Rebel soldiers condemned Unionists for rejecting the Confederacy, many also criticized the government for allowing the violence to degenerate into guerrilla warfare. "The *creeks* in this vicinity are said to be full of dead men!" wrote one soldier on August 27. "I witnessed yesterday a sight which I never wish again to see in a civilized & enlightened country. In a water hole in Spring Creek (about 2 miles from camp) there are 4 *human bodies* lying on top of the water, thrown in and left to rot, and that too after they were hanged by neck and dead." The eighteen-year-old soldier was appalled. "If they are traitors no doubt they deserved their reward," he added, but they "should have at least gave them a burial." Moreover, the military cordon did not stop the Germans from fleeing to Mexico throughout the summer and early fall.[23]

In any case, Texas officials could not ignore the threat that Unionists

ANNE J. BAILEY

posed to the state's security, a concern not confined to the Germans in the hill country. In northern Texas, where the population included a large number of midwestern and border-state farmers, Union sympathizers just south of the Red River had formed a secret Peace Party or Loyal League soon after the war began. In the autumn of 1862, as violence continued in the German counties of central Texas, local authorities along the Red River rounded up Unionists they suspected of fomenting insurrection. After more than one hundred arrests had been made in Cooke County, thirty men were executed, some fourteen lynched, and several murdered. Five more were hanged in Wise County and one in Denton County. Rebels apprehended another forty men in Grayson County, but James Throckmorton, who had become a respected "Confederate unionist," prevented any killings.[24]

The unrest in Texas, compounded by the Union navy's capture of Galveston, had not gone unnoticed in Richmond, and in late 1862 the Confederate government decided to replace Hébert as district commander with Major General John Bankhead Magruder. The change was popular with Texans, for Magruder had a distinguished reputation as a fighter that dated back to the Indian campaigns, and, as an added bonus, he was related to some prominent Texans. When he assumed command in November, Magruder urged caution in dealing with the hostile German population. But he wanted the troublemakers removed from the state, and instructed the enrolling officer in Austin to send men who were arrested for evading the law to regiments elsewhere. However, he did not want his action to seem malevolent and asked that it be "done quietly and without show if such a thing be practicable, in order that all odious distinctions between the good and loyal citizens of foreign birth and those who are refractory may be obviated, and that no difficulties from this cause also may arise between our native-born citizens and those of foreign birth."[25]

Magruder's conciliatory attitude did not reap immediate rewards, for it was reported that between a thousand and fifteen hundred Germans had gathered at Fredericksburg to resist local draft agents. One Texan added fuel to the crisis when he told the authorities, "They say the negroes are to be free, and that Jack Hamilton is in the country." He predicted trouble and warned that "the sooner the rebellion be crushed the better for them and the country." Brigadier General William G. Webb, commander of the Second Brigade of Texas State Troops, warned that an internal civil war might erupt if the hotheads in the German communities were not controlled; they intended to "stir up insurrection with all of its horrors."[26]

Open resistance continued as the number of disaffected rose. To complicate matters, opponents of the Confederacy were no longer limited to the foreign-born. Lieutenant Colonel H. L. Webb told Governor Lubbock that at Fredericksburg on January 3, 1863, men made "inflammatory speeches" in which they advised opposition to the draft. The radicals had complete charge, and "the moderates, or conservative portion of the persons composing the meeting, were not allowed to speak." Most importantly, around "one-third of the persons present were Americans. I am of opinion that there is serious danger, that they will give us much trouble, and from all I could learn, they are determined to keep up their organizations set at defiance the Laws of the State, and if practicable join any Yankee force that may land on our soil."[27]

Guerrilla warfare generates its own dark rules, and hill country Unionists knew exactly what those rules were. Germans called the guerrillas *Haengerbande*, but they were simply gangs of Confederates who made war on the families of men who evaded the draft. One Rebel wrote home that "the tories in this part of the country is getting somewhat scarce." The reason, he noted, was that they were "lying and hanging all over the woods." Many Confederates believed that the Union League was only a front for an organization that murdered and pillaged loyal Rebels, and that the Germans were "bloodthirsty bushwhackers and villains disgracing the North and the Union flag by calling themselves Union men." A woman in Fredericksburg who was a child during the war later recounted the terror felt by residents. The Confederates, she claimed, were "mostly hard, bad characters, called guerrillas," and they "murdered many people." The Rebels often waited for men who had been hiding in the hills to come home to visit their families, captured them, and hanged them on the spot. Another German related that as a child his job had been to watch the road for the approach of "soldiers sent out to round up slackers" and to warn the Unionists at his father's house. When anyone rode into sight who looked like a conscription officer, the Germans "fled up the ravine and hid in the dense brush and among the boulders."[28]

Magruder finally agreed that something had to be done before the trouble spread, and he acted promptly. He ordered several cavalry companies, armed with artillery, to LaGrange, with instructions "to disarm the disloyal Germans and enforce the conscript and draft act." He also declared martial law in Colorado, Fayette, and Austin Counties, directly west of Houston. Moreover, Magruder decided to visit the region personally to assess the situation. These three counties, far from the hill country and the Indian frontier, had become the new center of discontent. Although Magruder could not persuade everyone to submit to the draft, he did ease some tensions between the American-born and foreign-born residents. The Germans abandoned their protest meetings (which had drawn as many as six hundred angry Unionists) and stopped harassing the enrolling officers. By February Magruder wrote the governor that "a better state of feeling" existed in the "disaffected regions." He announced that martial law did not extend outside the three counties and he hoped "soon to see the normal tribunals again in operation. The ringleaders, who had been apprehended, were by order turned over to the civil authorities, as these acts were committed prior to my declaration of martial law."[29]

Although the trouble continued in the German communities until the end of the war, and Germans persisted in their objections to the draft, Magruder had done much to quell the threat of a bloody guerrilla war. Arthur Fremantle observed in San Antonio a few months later that although Germans had been "at first by no means loyal to the Confederate cause," they had become "reconciled to the new regime." Although that was not exactly true, there was no longer open resistance. The German Unionists and Confederate Texans learned to coexist. Some Germans joined companies formed by the state to defend the frontier; others simply came to an understanding with the authorities that amounted to a truce. One common practice was to employ the Germans as teamsters to carry freight for the Confederacy in lieu of military service. Local German leaders often obtained exemptions that allowed farmers to harvest their crops. In return, they agreed to abide by state and Confederate laws. Although sporadic violent actions against Germans continued as late as 1865, most of the trouble ended after Magruder arrived.[30]

The war put a unique strain on the Texas Germans. Communities had split over whether to support the Confederacy, but those that had indicated loyalty to the Southern cause fared better that those that did not. Throughout the war German Unionists suffered persecution for their refusal to swear allegiance to the Southern nation and their reluctance to fight for Southern independence. Many German Unionists did not elect their course based on the political issues or slavery, but were motivated by the fear of leaving their families along the Indian frontier unprotected. Yet to Rebel Texans any disaffection with the Confederate cause bordered on treason. As a result, persecution became inevitable. The German communities continued to prosper and grow after the war ended, but the bitterness left by four years of civil strife continued into the twentieth century.[31]

1. Robert E. Lee, who commanded the Second U.S. Cavalry in the absence of Colonel Albert Sidney Johnston, left Texas in late February. Douglas Southall Freeman, *R. E. Lee: A Biography* (New York: Charles Scribner's Sons, 1934), 1:421; J. William Jones, *Life and Letters of Robert Edward Lee: Soldier and Man* (New York: Neale, 1906), 121. Throckmorton addressed his comments to O. M. Roberts, who had been elected president of the convention. Like many Unionists, after Texas seceded Throckmorton declared his allegiance to the Confederacy and fought for the South. He used his powerful political influence to protect other Unionists whenever possible. Ralph A. Wooster, *Texas and Texans in the Civil War* (Austin: Eakin Press, 1995), 11–13.

2. The vote was taken alphabetically, and the first delegate to declare opposition was Houston's political ally Thomas Hughes of Williamson County. Besides Hughes and Throckmorton, the other six to vote against the ordinance were W. H. Johnson, L. H. Williams, and George Wright from Lamar County; J. D. Rains and A. P. Shuford from Wood County, and Joshua Johnson from Titus County. Wooster, *Texas and Texans*, 13.

3. The people approved the ordinance by a vote of 46,129 to 14,697 on February 23. The total number of voters was 60,950, down from the 63,423 that had voted in the 1860 presidential election. However, the number of Texans who voted for John C. Breckinridge (47,548) was almost exactly the same as the number who condoned secession (46,153). Wooster, *Texas and Texans*, 13. Texas had a rich cultural diversity that included not only Spanish, Mexican, and German settlements, but French, Irish, English, Italian, Bohemian, Hungarian, Swedish, and Norwegian towns. While the number of Mexicans was certainly significant, they were not generally regarded well in the state. Although Europeans could also be looked on with disfavor, that feeling did not usually involve the prejudices aimed at most Mexicans. There were some Mexican Americans who took part in the Civil War and served with distinction on the Confederate side, but the majority of Mexican descent remained passive and unaffected. For more on the various ethnic groups, see Ella Lonn, *Foreigners in the Confederacy* (Gloucester, Mass.: Peter Smith, 1965), 13–23, 425. Also see Walter L. Buenger, *Secession and the Union in Texas* (Austin: University of Texas Press, 1984), "Secession and the Texas German Community: Editor Lindheimer vs. Editor Flake," *Southwestern Historical Quarterly* 82 (April 1979): 379–402, and "Unionism on the Texas Frontier, 1859–1861," *Arizona and the West* 22 (autumn 1980): 237–54; Frank H. Smyrl, "Unionism in Texas, 1856–1861," *Southwestern Historical Quarterly* 68 (October 1964): 172–95; and Dale Baum, *The Shattering of Texas Unionism: Politics in the Lone Star State during the Civil War Era* (Baton Rouge: Louisiana State University Press, 1998).

4. The earliest significant German settlement came under Mexican rule and was

financed by Baron von Bastrop in 1823. There is a wealth of information on early German settlements in America. For a sampling, see Franz Löher, *Geschichte und Zustände der Deutschen in Amerika* (Cincinnati: Eggers and Wulkop, 1847); *Der Auswanderer nach Texas: Ein Handbuch und Rathgeber für Die, welche sich in Texas ansiedeln wollen, unter besonderer Berücksichtigung Derer, welche sich dem Mainzer oder Antwerpener Verein anvertrauen* (Bremen: C. Schünemann, 1846); Ottomar von Behr, *Guter Rath für Auswanderer nach den Vereinigten Staaten von Nord America mit besonderer Berücksichtigung von Texas* (Leipzig: Robert Friese, 1847); Gilbert Giddings Benjamin, *The Germans in Texas* (New York: D. Appleton, 1910); Moritz Beyer, *Das Auswanderungsbuch oder Führer und Rathgeber bei der Auswanderung nach Nord Amerika und Texas* (Leipzig: Baumgartner, 1846); L. Constant, *Texas: Das Verderben deutscher Auswanderer in Texas unter dem Schutze des Mainzer Vereins* (Berlin: Reimer, 1847); Detlef Dunt, *Reise nach Texas, nebst Nachrichten von diesem Lande; für Deutsche, welche nach Amerika zu gehen beabsichtigen* (Bremen: Carl W. Wiehe, 1834); Francis Joseph Grund, *Handbuch und Wegweiser für Auswanderer nach den Vereinigten Staaten von Nordamerika und Texas*, 2d ed. (Stuttgart: J. G. Cotta, 1846); Caroline von Hinueber, "Life of German Pioneers of Early Texas," *Texas State Historical Association Quarterly* 2 (1899): 227–32; Friedrich Höhne, *Wahn und Ueberzeugung: Reise des Kupferschmiede-Meisters Friedrich Höhne in Weimar über Bremen nach Nordamerika und Texas in den Jahren 1839, 1840 und 1841* (Weimar: Wilhelm Hoffmann, 1844); Heinrich Ostermayer, *Tagebuch einer Reise nach Texas im Jahr 1848–1849* (Biberach, Germany: Verfassers, 1850); J. E. Rabe, *Eine Erholungsfahrt nach Texas und Mexico* (Hamburg: Leopold Voss, 1893); Friedrich Schlecht, *Mein Ausflug nach Texas* (Bunzlau, Germany: Appun, 1851); C. Stählen, *Neueste Nachrichten, Erklärungen und Briefe der Auswanderer von Texas* (Heilbronn: n.p., 1846); Adolf P. Weber, *Deutsche Pioniere: Zur Geschichte des Deutschthums in Texas* (San Antonio: Selbstverlag, 1894); Moritz Tiling, *History of the German Element in Texas from 1820–1850* (Houston: Rein and Sons, 1913).

5. With the exception of small groups around Dallas and some counties west of Houston, most of the Germans settled to the northwest and southeast of a line running from Austin to San Antonio. For more on the late arrivals, see A. E. Zucker, ed., *The Forty-Eighters: Political Refugees of the German Revolution of 1848* (New York: Columbia University Press, 1950). Some historians argue that the grays were basically conservative while the greens were more liberal and intellectual. Other historians do not believe that there was any significant political difference between the Germans who came before the revolutions and those who came after. Terry G. Jordan warns that it can be misleading to classify the two groups by using the uprisings in 1848; see *German Seed in Texas Soil: Immigrant Farmers in Nineteenth-Century Texas* (Austin: University of Texas Press, 1966), 182–85. Ella Lonn, in her work on foreigners in the Confederacy, gives the number of Germans

in Texas in 1860 as 20,555. Other historians have estimated more than 30,000; see *Foreigners in the Confederacy*, 31. Jason H. Silverman estimates that there were roughly 53,000 Germans in Texas, Louisiana, and Virginia, and only around 20,000 in the remaining eight Confederate states; "Germans" and "Irish," in *Encyclopedia of the Confederacy*, ed. Richard N. Current (New York: Simon and Schuster, 1993), 2:675–76, 822–23. The total population of Texas in 1860 was about 604,000, with 183,000 of that number black. Only Florida and Arkansas had fewer African Americans.

6. Frederick Law Olmsted, *A Journey through Texas; or, A Saddle-Trip on the Southwestern Frontier* (New York: Dix, Edwards, 1857), 432. For more on the German communities, see Rudolph L. Biesele, *The History of the German Settlements in Texas, 1831–1861* (Austin: n.p., 1930). For information on German Texas women, see Judith Dykes-Hoffman, "'Treue Der Union': German Texas Women on the Civil War Homefront" (M.A. thesis, Southwest Texas State University, 1996). On German women and their slaves, see Lauren Ann Kattner, "The Diversity of Old South White Women: The Peculiar Worlds of German American Women," in *Discovering the Women in Slavery: Emancipating Perspectives on the American Past*, ed. Patricia Morton (Athens: University of Georgia Press, 1996), 299–311.

7. The Second U.S. Cavalry was organized in 1855 with men handpicked by then Secretary of War Jefferson Davis, and ten companies, 710 men, left for Texas in October. See Richard W. Johnson, *A Soldier's Reminiscences in Peace and War* (Philadelphia: J. B. Lippincott, 1886), for a personal account of the regiment. See also Harold B. Simpson, *Cry Comanche: The Second U.S. Cavalry in Texas, 1855–1861* (Hillsboro, Tex.: Hill Junior College Press, 1979) for the most complete history and a discussion of fighting Indians on the frontier. Although the Second U.S. Cavalry was organized for service in Texas, it was not the only regiment in the state in 1861. Soldiers frequently visited the German communities along the frontier. At Fredericksburg the register of the Nimitz Hotel carries the signatures of James Longstreet and Philip Sheridan, and after the turn of the century the proprietor proudly displayed the bed where Robert E. Lee had slept. See Rena Mazyck Andrews, "German Pioneers in Texas: Civil War Period" (M.A. thesis, University of Chicago, 1929), 21. For an account of the Indian problems, see J. W. Wilbarger, *Indian Depredations in Texas* (Austin: Hutchings Printing House, 1889); John Henry Brown, *Indian Wars and Pioneers in Texas* (Austin: L. E. Daniell, 1880); and Floyd Ewing, "Origins of Unionist Sentiment on the West Texas Frontier," *West Texas Historical Association Yearbook* 32 (October 1956): 21–29.

8. The only predominantly German counties to approve secession were Austin, Comal, and Colorado. None of these were along the Indian frontier. Austin and Colorado were on the eastern end of the Texas cotton-growing belt.

ANNE J. BAILEY

For how Texas handled the Indian problems, see David Paul Smith, *Frontier Defense in the Civil War: Texas' Rangers and Rebels* (College Station: Texas A&M University Press, 1992).

9. The law allowed state officials to arrest, remove, or confine aliens "against whom complaints may be made" by district attorneys, marshals, and other Confederate officers. "Regulations Respecting Alien Enemies" was passed on August 8, 1861. "A Proclamation by the President of the Confederate States," August 15, 1861. *A Compilation of the Messages and Papers of the Confederacy* (Nashville: United States Publishing Co., 1905), 1:131–32.

10. Report of Hamilton P. Bee, October 21, 1862, U.S. War Department, *The War of the Rebellion: A Compilation of the Official Records of the Union and Confederate Armies* (Washington, D.C.: Government Printing Office, 1880–1920), ser. 1, 53:454–55 (hereafter cited as OR).

11. Many of the Germans joined Union units. The 1st Texas Cavalry (U.S.), which organized at New Orleans late in 1862, consisted almost entirely of Germans. The 2nd Texas Cavalry (U.S.), raised at Brownsville in December 1863, also had a significant number of Texas Germans. Hamilton was appointed a brigadier general and military governor of Texas; he returned to the state in 1863 when Union forces attacked the Gulf coast. Ezra J. Warner, *Generals in Blue: Lives of Union Commanders* (Baton Rouge: Louisiana State University Press, 1964), 114–15, 198. See also Allan Ashcraft, "The Union Occupation of the Lower Rio Grande in the Civil War," *Texas Military History* 8 (1970): 13–26; and Frank H. Smyrl, "Texans in the Union Army, 1861–1865," *Southwestern Historical Quarterly* 65 (October 1961): 234–50.

12. Andrews, "German Pioneers," 38–39; Report of Hamilton P. Bee, October 21, 1862, OR, ser. 1, 53:454–55; Robert W. Shook, "The Battle of the Nueces, August 10, 1862," *Southwestern Historical Quarterly* 66 (July 1962): 32; Claude Elliott, "Union Sentiment in Texas, 1861–1865," *Southwestern Historical Quarterly* 50 (April 1947): 455. One German admitted that at the beginning of the war there was a secret plan to capture San Antonio and Austin and hold the cities until Union troops arrived. Some of the more adventurous intended to capture some cannon but were dissuaded from the attempt.

13. Shook, "Battle of the Nueces," 31–32; Wooster, *Texas and Texans*, 13; James Marten, *Texas Divided: Loyalty and Dissent in the Lone Star State, 1856–1874* (Lexington: University Press of Kentucky, 1990), 119. For more on unionism in Fredericksburg, see Biesele, *German Settlements in Texas*, and Andrews, "German Pioneers." On the history of early Fredericksburg, see Robert Penniger, ed., *Fest-Ausgabe zum 50-jährigen Jubiläum der Gründung der Stadt Friedrichsburg* (Fredericksburg, Tex.: Robert Penniger, 1896); and Friedrich Armand Strubberg, *Friedrichsburg, die Colonie des deutschen Fürsten-Vereins in Texas* (Leipzig: Friedrich Fleischer, 1867).

14. Report of Hamilton P. Bee, OR, ser. 1, 53:454–55; Clement A. Evans, ed., *Confederate Military History*, vol. 9, *Texas*, by O. M. Roberts (Atlanta: Confederate Publishing Co., 1899), 68. Confederate troops included the Thirty-second Texas Cavalry. For more see Carl L. Duaine, *The Dead Men Wore Boots: An Account of the 32nd Texas Volunteer Cavalry, C.S.A.* (Austin: San Felipe Press, 1966).

15. Martial Law Decree, June 14, 1862, *New Braunfelser Zeitung*; Entry dated April 25, 1863, in Arthur James Lyon Fremantle, *Three Months in the Southern States, April–June 1863* (1863; reprint, Lincoln: University of Nebraska Press, 1991), 54. The *New Braunfelser Zeitung*, one of the most influential of the German newspapers, had supported secession and was strongly pro-Southern. Located at New Braunfels in Comal County, the German population did not have to worry about the threat of Indian attacks; Jordan, *German Seed in Texas Soil*, 183. See also Hermann Seele, *A Short Sketch of Comal County, Texas* (New Braunfels: Zeitung, 1885).

16. R. H. Williams, *With the Border Ruffians: Memories of the Far West, 1852–1868* (New York: E. P. Dutton, 1907), 236–37. For more on the war on the Mexican border, see James A. Irby, *Backdoor at Badgad: The Civil War on the Rio Grande* (El Paso: Texas Western Press, 1977); and Robert W. Delaney, "Matamoras, Port for Texas during the Civil War," *Southwestern Historical Quarterly* 58 (April 1955): 473–87.

17. Williams, *With the Border Ruffians*, 232.

18. Andrews, "German Pioneers," 36; *San Antonio Herald*, July 19, 1862. See also *Dallas Herald*, June 14, 1862. The Rebel soldier was convinced that Duff's men were responsible for the murder. Entry dated August 5, 1862, "Diary of Desmond Pulaski Hopkins," supplied by G. A. McNaughton to the *San Antonio Express*, January 13, 1918, typescript, Center for American History, University of Texas at Austin.

19. Richard Selcer and William Paul Burrier, "What *Really* Happened on the Nueces River: James Duff, a Good Soldier or 'The Butcher of Fredericksburg?'" *North and South: The Magazine of Civil War Conflict* (January 1998): 56–61.

20. Report of C. D. McRae, August 18, 1862, OR, ser. 1, 9:615. Entry dated August 22, 1862, "Diary of Hopkins"; August Hoffman, "Memoir of August Hoffman," typescript, Center for American History.

21. Reports of the number of Germans killed and wounded (and later murdered) vary. After the battle the Confederates were interred in a common grave, but the Germans were left unburied. The remains were not recovered until August 1865, when they were reburied in Comfort, Tex., under a monument that was inscribed *Treuer der Union*; Shook, "The Battle of the Nueces," 39–41. See also Stanley S. McGowen, "Battle or Massacre? The Incident on the Nueces, August 10, 1862," *Southwestern Historical Quarterly* 104 (July 2000): 64–86; John W. Sansom,

Battle of the Nueces in Kinney County, Texas, Aug. 10th, 1862 (San Antonio: n.p., 1905); Andrews, "German Pioneers," 40; and Lonn, *Foreigners in the Confederacy*, 423–36. For a revisionist version of the events, see Selcer and Burrier, "What *Really* Happened." For the quotes see Williams, *With the Border Ruffians*, 250; Entry dated August 27, 1862, in Thomas C. Smith, *Here's Yer Mule: The Diary of Thomas C. Smith, 3rd Sergeant, Company 'G,' Wood's Regiment, 32nd Texas Cavalry, C.S.A.: March 30, 1862–December 31, 1862* (Waco: Little Texan Press, 1958), 19; Entry dated August 22, 1862, "Diary of Hopkins."

22. Rudolf Coreth to family, August 26, 1862, in *Lone Star and Double Eagle: Civil War Letters of a German-Texas Family*, ed. Minetta Altgelt Goyne (Fort Worth: Texas Christian University Press, 1982), 66.

23. Entry dated August 27, 1862, in Smith, *Here's Yer Mule*, 19.

24. See Richard B. McCaslin, *Tainted Breeze: The Great Hanging at Gainesville, Texas* (Baton Rouge: Louisiana State University Press, 1994), and "Wheat Growers in the Cotton Confederacy: The Suppression of Dissent in Collin County, Texas, During the Civil War," *Southwestern Historical Quarterly* 96 (April 1993): 528–39; Thomas Barrett, *The Great Hanging at Gainesville, Cooke County, Texas, October A.D. 1862* (1885; reprint, Austin: Texas State Historical Association, 1961); Floyd Ewing, "Unionist Sentiment on the Northwest Texas Frontier," *West Texas Historical Association Yearbook* 33 (October 1957): 58–70; Pete A. Y. Gunter, "The Great Gainesville Hanging, October 1862," *Blue and Gray Magazine* 3 (April–May 1986): 48–55; Phillip Rutherford, "The Great Gainesville Hanging," *Civil War Times Illustrated* 17 (April 1978): 12–20; and James Smallwood, "Disaffection in Confederate Texas: The Hanging at Gainesville," *Civil War History* 22 (December 1976); 349–60.

25. E. P. Turner to J. P. Flewellen, December 6, 1862, OR, ser. 1, 15:890. Flewellen was the superintendent of conscripts at Austin.

26. [J. B.] McCown to Tom Green, [January 1863], OR, ser. 1, 15:921; William G. Webb to A. G. Dickinson, January 4, 1863, OR, ser. 1, 15:927–28.

27. Lonn, *Foreigners in the Confederacy*, 434.

28. Marten, *Texas Divided*, 120; "Mathilda Doebbler Gruen Wagner," in *Texas Tears and Texas Sunshine: Voices of Frontier Women*, ed. Jo Ella Powell Exley (College Station: Texas A&M University Press, 1985), 111; Andrews, "German Pioneers," 36.

29. Special Orders, no. 35, January 5, 1863, OR, ser. 1, 15:931; J. Bankhead Magruder to F. R. Lubbock, February 11, 1862, OR, ser. 1, 15:974–75. See also Martin M. Kenney, *An Historical and Descriptive Sketch of Austin County, Texas* (Brenham: Banner Print, 1876); W. A. Trenckmann, *Austin County: Beilage zum Bellville Wochenblatt* (Bellville, Tex.: Wochenblatt, 1899); F. Lotto, *Fayette County: Her History and Her People* (Schulenburg, Tex.: 1902); A. J. Rosenthal, "Fayette County," in *Schütze's Jahrbuch für Texas* (Austin: A. Schütze, 1883);

and Leonie R. Weyand and Houston Wade, *An Early History of Fayette County* (La Grange, Tex.: Journal, 1936).

30. Entry dated April 25, 1863, Fremantle, *Three Months,* 54. See also David P. Smith, "Conscription and Conflict on the Texas Frontier, 1863–1865," *Civil War History* 36 (September 1990): 250–61.

31. Jordan, *German Seed in Texas Soil,* 185.

Select Bibliography on Southern Unionism

GENERAL

Ash, Stephen V. *When the Yankees Came: Conflict and Chaos in the Occupied South, 1861–1865*. Chapel Hill: University of North Carolina Press, 1995.

Beringer, Richard, Herman Hattaway, Archer Jones, and William Still. *Why the South Lost the Civil War.* Athens: University of Georgia Press, 1984.

Clinton, Catherine, ed. *Southern Families at War: Loyalty and Conflict in the Civil War South.* New York: Oxford University Press, 2000.

Crofts, Daniel W. *Reluctant Confederates: Upper South Unionists in the Secession Crisis.* Chapel Hill: University of North Carolina Press, 1989.

Current, Richard Nelson. *Lincoln's Loyalists: Union Soldiers from the Confederacy.* Boston: Northeastern Press, 1992.

Degler, Carl N. *The Other South: Southern Dissenters in the Nineteenth Century.* New York: Harper and Row, 1974.

Grimsley, Mark. *The Hard Hand of War: Union Military Policy toward Southern Civilians, 1861–1865.* New York: Cambridge University Press, 1995.

Harris, William C. *With Charity for All: Lincoln and the Reconstruction of the Union.* Lexington: University Press of Kentucky, 1997.

Klingberg, Frank W. *The Southern Claims Commission.* Berkeley and Los Angeles: University of California Press, 1955.

Lonn, Ella. *Foreigners in the Confederacy.* Gloucester, Mass.: Peter Smith, 1965.

Moore, Albert B. *Conscription and Conflict in the Confederacy.* New York: Macmillan, 1924.

Nagel, Paul C. *One Nation Indivisible: The Union in American Thought, 1776–1861.* New York: Oxford University Press, 1964.

Sutherland, Daniel E., ed. *Guerrillas, Unionists, and Violence on the Confederate Home Front.* Fayetteville: University of Arkansas Press, 1999.

Tatum, Georgia Lee. *Disloyalty in the Confederacy.* Chapel Hill: University of North Carolina Press, 1934. Reprint, with an introduction by David Williams, Lincoln: University of Nebraska Press, Bison Books, 1999.

Wakelyn, Jon L., ed. *Southern Unionist Pamphlets and the Civil War.* Columbia: University of Missouri Press, 1999.

Ash, Stephen V., ed. *Secessionists and Other Scoundrels: Selections from Parson Brownlow's Book*. Baton Rouge: Louisiana State University Press, 1999.

Auman, William Thomas. "Neighbor Against Neighbor: The Inner Civil War in the Central Counties of Confederate North Carolina." Ph.D. dissertation, University of North Carolina at Chapel Hill, 1988.

Buenger, Walter L. *Secession and the Union in Texas*. Austin: University of Texas Press, 1984.

Crawford, Martin. *Ashe County's Civil War: Community and Society in the Mountain South*. Charlottesville: University Press of Virginia, 2001.

Curry, Richard O. *A House Divided: A Study of Statehood Politics and the Copperhead Movement in West Virginia*. Pittsburgh: University of Pittsburgh Press, 1964.

Dunn, Durwood. *Cade's Cove: The Life and Death of a Southern Mountain Community, 1818–1937*. Knoxville: University of Tennessee Press, 1988.

Durrill, Wayne K. *War of Another Kind: A Southern Community in the Great Rebellion* [Washington County, N.C.]. New York: Oxford University Press, 1990.

Dyer, Thomas G. *Secret Yankees: The Unionist Circle in Confederate Atlanta*. Baltimore: Johns Hopkins University Press, 1999.

Fellman, Michael. *Inside War: The Guerrilla Conflict in Missouri during the American Civil War*. New York: Oxford University Press, 1989.

Fisher, Noel C. *War at Every Door: Partisan Politics and Guerrilla Violence in East Tennessee, 1860–1869*. Chapel Hill: University of North Carolina Press, 1997.

Inscoe, John C., and Gordon B. McKinney. *The Heart of Confederate Appalachia: Western North Carolina in the Civil War*. Chapel Hill: University of North Carolina Press, 2000.

Marten, James. *Texas Divided: Loyalty and Dissent in the Lone Star State, 1856–1874*. Lexington: University Press of Kentucky, 1990.

McCaslin, Richard B. *Tainted Breeze: The Great Hanging at Gainesville, Texas, 1862*. Baton Rouge: Louisiana State University, 1994.

McKenzie, Robert Tracy. *One South or Many? Plantation Belt and Upcountry in Civil War–Era Tennessee*. New York: Cambridge University Press, 1994.

McKinney, Gordon B. *Southern Mountain Republicans: Politics and the Appalachian Community, 1865–1900*. Chapel Hill: University of North Carolina Press, 1978. Reprint, with new preface by the author, Knoxville: University of Tennessee Press, Appalachian Echoes Series, 1998.

Noe, Kenneth W., and Shannon H. Wilson, eds. *The Civil War in Appalachia: Collected Essays*. Knoxville: University of Tennessee Press, 1997.

Paludan, Philip Shaw. *Victims: A True Story of the Civil War* [Shelton Laurel, N.C.]. Knoxville: University of Tennessee Press, 1981.

Patton, James Welch. *Unionism and Reconstruction in Tennessee, 1860–1869.* Chapel Hill: University of North Carolina Press, 1934.

Rogers, William Warren, Jr. *Confederate Home Front: Montgomery, Alabama, 1861–1865.* Tuscaloosa: University of Alabama Press, 1999.

Sarris, Jonathan D. "'Hellish Deeds in a Christian Land': Southern Mountain Communities at War" [Fannin and Lumpkin Counties, Ga.]. Ph.D. dissertation, University of Georgia, 1998.

Sumner, Ellen Louise. "Unionism in Georgia, 1860–1861." M.A. thesis, University of Georgia, 1960.

Sutherland, Daniel E. *Seasons of War: The Ordeal of a Confederate Community, 1861–1865* [Culpeper County, Va.]. New York: Simon and Schuster, 1995.

Tripp, Steven. *Yankee Town, Southern City: Race and Class Relations in Civil War Lynchburg* [Va.]. New York: New York University Press, 1997.

Contributors

THE EDITORS

JOHN C. INSCOE is professor of history at the University of Georgia. He is the author of *Mountain Masters: Slavery and the Sectional Crisis in Western North Carolina* (1999), and coauthor, with Gordon B. McKinney, of *The Heart of Confederate Appalachia: Western North Carolina in the Civil War* (2000).

ROBERT C. KENZER is the William Binford Vest Professor of History at the University of Richmond. He is the author of *Kinship and Neighborhood in a Southern Community: Orange County, North Carolina, 1849–1881* (1988) and *Enterprising Southerners: Black Economic Success in North Carolina, 1865–1915* (1997).

THE AUTHORS

ANNE J. BAILEY is professor of history at Georgia College and State University and editor of the *Georgia Historical Quarterly*. She is the author of several books, including *Between the Enemy and Texas: Parsons' Texas Cavalry in the Civil War* (1989) and *Chessboard of War: Sherman and Hood in the Autumn Campaigns of 1864* (2000).

KENNETH C. BARNES is associate professor of history at the University of Central Arkansas and the author of *Who Killed John Clayton? Political Violence and the Emergence of the New South* (1998).

JONATHAN M. BERKEY is a Ph.D. candidate in history at Pennsylvania State University. He is working on a dissertation on the Civil War in the lower Shenandoah Valley.

KEITH S. BOHANNON is a Ph.D. candidate in history at Pennsylvania State University. He is working on a dissertation on the Civil War in the mountains of northeastern Georgia.

THOMAS G. DYER is University Professor of History and Higher Education and vice president and associate provost of instruction at the University of Georgia. His fourth book is *Secret Yankees: The Unionist Circle in Confederate Atlanta* (1999).

ROBERT TRACY MCKENZIE is associate professor of history at the University of Washington. He is the author of *One South or Many? Plantation Belt and Upcountry in Civil War Era Tennessee* (1994), and is currently at work on a book on Knoxville during the Civil War.

GORDON B. MCKINNEY is Goode Professor of Appalachian Studies and director of the Appalachian Center at Berea College. He is the author of *Southern Mountain Republicans, 1865–1900: Politics and the Appalachian Community* (1978) and coauthor, with John C. Inscoe, of *The Heart of Confederate Appalachia: Western North Carolina in the Civil War* (2000).

SCOTT REYNOLDS NELSON is assistant professor of history at the College of William and Mary. He is the author of *Iron Confederacies: Southern Railways, Klan Violence, and Reconstruction* (1999).

WILLIAM WARREN ROGERS JR. is professor of history at Gainesville College in Gainesville, Georgia. He is the author of *Black Belt Scalawag: Charles Hays and Southern Republicans in the Era of Reconstruction* (1993) and *Confederate Home Front: Montgomery during the Civil War* (1999).

CAROLYN J. STEFANCO chairs the history department at California Polytechnic State University in San Luis Obispo and is completing a biography of Nelly Kinzie Gordon.

Index

Dugger, Shepherd, 68
Dunn, Durwood, 63

Eagan, Michael, 58
East Tennessee, 54, 56, 61–63, 173;
    guerrilla warfare in, 57, 66; unionists
    in, 64, 73–90
East Tennessee and Virginia Railroad,
    113
East Tennessee Relief Association, 85
Egan, Michael, 65
Emancipation Proclamation, 8, 86, 148
Espionage. *See* Unionists, as spies
Everett, Edward, 1–2
Executions of unionists. *See* Lynchings

Families. *See* Kinship networks
Faucette, Chesley F., 38–47 passim
Faucette family, 8, 37–48, 48 (n. 2)
Faucette, George, 45
Faucette, William A. Graham, 39
Faucette, Wyatt. *See* Outlaw, Wyatt
Faust, Drew Gilpin, 151, 155
Fayetteville, Ark., 195
Fayetteville, Ga., 124–25
Fellman, Michael, 55, 65–66
Ferguson, Hamilton, 98, 103
Ferguson, Jake, 110–11, 119 (n. 32)
Feuds, 63
Flat Rock, N.C., 57, 64
Florida, 179
Fort Lafayette, N.Y., 136–37
Fort Mason, Tex., 208
Fort Pulaski, Ga., 157
Fort Smith, Ark., 196
Fort Sumter, attack on, 18, 56, 100, 128,
    154, 177, 191
Fort Warren, Mass., 136
Fowler, Edmond, 177, 179, 184
Fowler, Martha, 179
Franklin, Tenn., 189

Frazier, Charles, 64–65
Frederick County, Va., 25
Fredericksburg, Tex., 214–20 passim
Fremantle, Arthur, 215, 221

Gainesville, Ga., 100–101, 113–14
Gainesville Light Infantry, 101
Gainesville, Tex., 6
Gate City Guard (Atlanta), 129
Geer, J. J., 179
Georgia, north, Unionists in, 97–115
German immigration, 209–10
Germans in Texas, 10, 12, 208–21;
    views on slavery, 210
Germans in the Confederacy, 223–24
    (n. 5)
Gettysburg Address, 1
Gettysburg, battle of, 30
Ghormley, Nancy, 62, 67
Gillespie County, Tex., 209, 214,
    215–16
Gilmer, Andy, 98, 101–2
Gilmer, Eliza, 98, 101, 103, 110
Gleason, Rolla, 135, 136
Goldie's Inheritance, 122, 125, 132–33,
    140
Gordon, Anderson, 192
Gordon, Eleanor "Nelly" Kinzie, 8, 9,
    13, 148–63
Gordon, George Arthur, 151
Gordon, Sarah Anderson, 153, 157
Gordon, William Washington, II,
    148–63
Graham, N.C., 45
Graham, William A., 39, 49 (n. 2)
Grand Army of the Republic, 201
Grant, Henry, 58
Grant, Ulysses S., 142
Grayson County, Tex., 219
Greene County, Tenn., 87, 88
Greenville, Tenn., 61, 82, 87

Pierpoint, Francis, 24
Polk County, N.C., 63
Pope, John, 24
Port Hudson, La., 197
Potter, Jack, 61
Price, Sterling, 198
Prison camps, Confederate, 138
Prisoners, escaped, 13, 69 (n. 7), 105;
    Union, 131–32, 177–78, 179, 200, 217

Quitman Rifles, 197

R. G. Dun Mercantile Agency, 89
Rable, George, 151
Ramsey, J. G. M., 77
Rawson, E. E., 125
Raymond, Henry J., 137
Reconstruction: in Alabama, 183–84; in
    Arkansas, 201; in Georgia, 141–42;
    in North Carolina, 44–47
Reconstruction Act, First, 183–84
Red River campaign, 172
Red River, Tex., 209, 219
Red Strings, 38, 40–43. *See also* Heroes
    of America
Refugees, Unionist, 112–13, 195
Republican Party, 142, 202; in North
    Carolina, 44–46
Revolutionary War, 13, 39
Richmond, Va., 134–35, 173, 183
Rio Grande Valley, 213, 215, 217
Roberts, Israel W., 174–76, 183, 184
Robertson, Mary D., 151
Root, Sidney, 125
Ruffin, Edmund, 20

Saffold, Milton J., 177
Salisbury prison, 40, 47, 54
Saltville, Va., 87
San Antonio, Tex., 210, 215, 216, 221
Sandy Basin, Va., 63
Sarris, Jonathan, 63

Savannah, Ga., 9, 142, 148–60 passim;
    bread riot in, 159; surrender to
    Sherman, 160
Scott, Frank, 86
Secession, constitutionality of, 80–81
Secession crisis; in Alabama, 174–75;
    in Arkansas, 190–91; in Atlanta,
    Ga., 127–28; in East Tennessee, 75,
    77–78; in North Carolina, 39; in
    north Georgia, 100–101; in Texas,
    208–9; unionist role in, 2–3, 18–19;
    in Virginia, 18, 21–22
Seelye, Samuel D., 174–83 passim
Seguin, Tex., 210
Seward, William H., 3
Sheats, Charles C., 180
Shelby, Joseph, 198–99
Shelton Laurel massacre, 5, 63
Shenandoah Valley, Va., 9, 21–33 passim
Sheridan, Philip, 24
Sherman, William T., 140, 160–61
Sherman's March, 6, 160
Shiloh, battle of, 177, 191, 197
Sigel, Franz, 24
Slavery: in East Tennessee, 75–76, 80;
    unionist views on, 7–8, 80–82, 90,
    125–27, 152–53, 174–75, 190, 210; in
    Virginia, 21
Slocumb, Abby Days, 155–56
Smith, E. Kirby, 85
Smith, Jack, 214
Smith, William A., 43
Smoky Mountains, 56, 58, 62
Sneed, William H., 77
Sons of Veterans, 202
Southern Claims Commission, 176, 180,
    181, 183
Spanish, in Texas, 209
Sperry, J. Austin, 85, 88
Springfield, Ark., 190, 191
Springfield, Mo., 195
St. Albans, Vt., 124, 130, 135

St. Louis, Mo., 194–95
Starr, Daniel S. E., 182–83
Starr, Sophronia, 182, 184
Steele, Frederick, 194–96
Stephens, Alexander, 4
Steuart, George, 155, 158
Steuart, Maria Kenzie, 148–60 passim, 163 (n.1)
Stiles, Eliza Gordon, 159
Stiles, William Henry, 158
Stobaugh, Frank, 202
Stone, Amherst, 9–10, 13, 121–43
Stone, Charles Birney, 130, 142
Stone, Chester A., 129–30, 142
Stone, Cyrena, 9–10, 121–43
Stow, James P., 174–75, 180–81
Strong, George Templeton, 178
Strother, David Hunter, 7–8, 9, 11, 18–33
Strother, John, 23; capture of, 28–30; death of, 30
Strother, Mary Hunter, 32
Swan, William G., 77, 84

Tatum, Georgia Lee, 4
Temple, Major S., 87
Temple, Oliver, 58, 64, 74–89 passim
Texas, 172; foreign population of, 209–10, 219, 222 (n. 3); map of, 211; unionists in, 10, 208–21
Throckmorton, James W., 208–9, 219
Tourgee, Albion, 51 (n. 33)
Tryon, William, 39
Tug Valley, Ky., 63
Turner, L. C., 136

Uncle Tom's Cabin, 152
Underwood, Augustus, 181
Union Loyal League (Texas), 214, 216, 220
Unionism, categorization of, 3–4, 6–7, 76–79, 104

Unionists: as abolitionists, 7; lynching of, 182–83, 216–18; as newspaper editors, 212; as nonslaveholders, 104; as refugees, 195; as slaveholders, 7–8, 75–76, 125–27, 174, 189–90; as spies, 133–37, 160, 179–80; as spouses, 8–10, 54–68, 97–114, 148–49, 151, 155, 199; strength in South, 1, 4–5; in Union army, 4–5, 11–12, 15 (n.15), 19, 59–60, 68, 189, 192, 214; as Whigs, 7; women, 10, 66–67, 132–33
University of Georgia, 121
U.S. Cavalry, Second, 211, 224 (n. 7)
U.S. Colored Troops (cavalry), 12, 51 (n. 33)

Van Buren County, Ark., 189, 191, 197, 201
Vance, Zebulon B., 4, 40
VanGilder, John S., 86, 89
VanGilder, Thomas, 86–87
Vermont, 122, 125, 130, 142
Vigilante Committee (Montgomery, Ala.), 177, 178, 182

Waller, Altina, 63
War of 1812, 23, 28
Waring, Ella Howard, 156
Watauga County, N.C., 60–61
Webb, William G., 219–20
Weeks, Alfred, 27–28
West Point, Ga., 179
Whig Party, 7, 39, 77–79
White Brotherhood, 45–47
White County, Ga., 99–111 passim
Whitney, Louisa Bailey, 122–23, 133
Wilkes County, N.C., 64
Williams, Catherine, 61–62
Williams, Daniel Webster, 190
Williams family, 8, 12, 188–202
Williams, Henry, 196

Williams, Henry Clay, 190
Williams, Jeff, 11
Williams, John, 83, 189, 194, 196
Williams, Leroy, 189, 192, 192–200
    passim
Williams, Lucy, 62, 67
Williams, Margaret, 199
Williams, Nathan, 195–96, 200
Williams, R. H., 218
Williams' Raiders, 195
Williams, Rebecca, 189
Williams, Riley, 194
Williams, Sarah Jane, 199
Williams, Thomas Jefferson (Jeff),
    188–202; death of, 199, 200
Williams, William Day, 198
Wilson, Isaac, 61, 64
Wilson, James Harrison, 183
Winchester, Va., 28, 66

Wise County, Tex., 216, 219
Wise, Henry A., 20
Witt, Allen R., 197–201
Wofford, Jake, 104, 119 (n. 32)
Women: as Confederates, 151–52,
    155–57; and guerrilla warfare, 58,
    62, 65–67, 108–14 passim; north-
    ern-born, in South, 9–10, 121–42,
    148–49, 155, 164 (n. 4); as refugees,
    112–13, 195; in secession crisis, 22;
    as unionists, 10, 66–67, 132–33
Wool, John, 136
Worth, Jonathan, 4

Yancey, William Lowndes, 173
Yanceyville, N.C., 46
Younce, W. H. (Buck), 12, 58–60, 64

Zollicoffer, Felix, 82–83